'Blades' had that
extra t...

Sheffield Wednesday ... 1

Sheffield United 2

not much luck in th
not much quality, eith

he crowd roaring, but t
per was fortunate not
a penalty kick giv
during a collisi

day had

EDNESDA
ATTEN UN

N HOBY: Sheffield United 0, Sheffield Wednesday 2

te of this thunderous, crashing, all-Sheffield battle
above the jam-packed stands and terraces of Brama
ring leap from centre-half Swan's free-kick, Ell
's lanky centre forward, out-jumped th
ball flashed to right-winger Wilki

It's there! Birchena

e two

URPRISE

Sheffield Football
A History
Volume I   1857–1961

Keith Farnsworth

SHEFFIELD FOOTBALL
A HISTORY
VOLUME I   1857–1961

KEITH FARNSWORTH

The **Hallamshire** Press 1995

Cover: Derek Dooley, Jimmy Hagan. Club pictures of Sheffield FC, Sheffield United and Sheffield Wednesday from the end of the last century.

Text and Design © 1995 Interleaf Productions Limited

Published by The Hallamshire Press
The Hallamshire Press is an imprint of
Interleaf Productions Limited
Exchange Works
Sidney Street
Sheffield S1 3QF
England

Typeset by Interleaf Productions Limited
Printed in Great Britain by
Bookcraft (Bath) Limited, Avon

British Library Cataloguing in Publication Data
  A catalogue record for this book is available from the British Library

  ISBN 1 874718 13 X

Contents

Foreword

I GREW up in Sheffield, went to school in Sheffield, and for the last thirty years I have worked in Sheffield, building up a business in the insulation industry. Throughout this period I have had an abiding interest in Sheffield football, and wherever I have travelled the results of the Sheffield teams have been my first concern in the weekend news.

I saw my first Sheffield Wednesday game 50 years ago and spent many Saturday afternoons selling ice cream at both Hillsborough and Bramall Lane—in an era when the correct response to coins thrown from the crowd was to throw a choc-ice back!

In the early days of Sheffield Insulations our logo was quite deliberately designed so that one word was blue and the other red, on a white background, because I could not afford to alienate either group of supporters in our small team of employees; for the same reason, for several years, we sponsored matches at both Hillsborough and Bramall Lane.

Over the past ten years I have also had an opportunity, in a number of ways, to make some contribution to the regeneration of the city after the economic shocks of the early 80's.

Many of us saw sport and leisure as a centre-piece of plans to compensate for the decline in traditional industries and a spur to create a 'new'Sheffield, and much has been achieved that we can all be pleased

about. As a result of this development, many more people, both in this country and abroad, are now aware of Sheffield as a sporting city because of events at Don Valley Stadium, Ponds Forge and Sheffield Arena.

I am especially delighted to have been invited to say a few words about this excellent new Sheffield football history book. Firstly because I have always had an enthusiasm for both football and local history, and so I enjoyed reading about the early days of the game in Sheffield. I can remember being told about some of the players mentioned in the first part of this book—and I'm old enough to say I watched many of those referred to in the later chapters.

The other reason for pleasure is the coincidence that I have long been familiar with the work of Keith Farnsworth. We first met in his days as editor of the Sheffield Chamber of Commerce Journal, 'Quality', and we became good friends when he subsequently helped my late father, Ernest, pen an autobiography. I shall always be glad that task was completed when it was: it might not have been done without Keith's enthusiastic and professional approach.

Those were the days when we discovered a mutual interest in football and history, and, as it was also a time when, with the closing down of the old 'Quality' magazine, Keith was left with little option but to pursue his career as a freelance, I am delighted that he has survived in the fiercely competitive world of football writing, but not surprised that he has done so by maintaining the high standards evident in this book.

It is often said that people, and football sopporters especially, live very much for the present and have no interest in the past; but I know from friends in the education field that Keith's 1982 Wednesday history was the most requested book in more than one school library. I suspect this volume will also be essential reading for people who love their football.

Norman Adsetts

Norman Adsetts, OBE
Chairman, SIG plc
Sheffield, May 1995

Introduction

OUTSIDE of home and family, the two things that have mattered most to me in my life are writing and football. For more than thirty years it has been my good fortune to enjoy the best of both worlds by pursuing a career as a writer on football. Moreover, I have been able to remain in my home city and follow Sheffield United and Wednesday at close range, thus fulfilling a boyhood ambition.

Back in the old East End in the late '40s, I dreamed of following in the footsteps of Richard A. Sparling, veteran sports editor of the local daily, the *Sheffield Telegraph*, and to this end, I wangled the job of school football reporter at Newhall. However, failing the 11-plus and leaving school with no formal qualifications, I had to wait some ten years before finally breaking into journalism. Once there, on the editorial staff of the *Sheffield* (later *Morning*) *Telegraph*, I did not consciously seek a place in the sports department, but somehow, circumstances not only conspired to push me in that direction but, within a remarkably short time, saw me reach the goal I had set myself as a cheeky kid—sitting in Sparling's sports editor's chair.

I spent ten years in the *Telegraph's* sports department, and they were amongst the most rewarding years of my life. Still being an old romantic at heart, a lot of the pleasure came from being involved with the Sheffield clubs and with past and present players and officials. It added to my enjoyment that, having grown up in Sheffield and been a football-crazy kid, a sense of history was inherent in my approach to the job. Moreover, I loved delving into the more distant past, and nothing was more satisfying than tracking down a player from the '20s or '30s and getting him reminiscing.

I mention all this to explain my enthusiasm for football history and to indicate why I want to share it with old and young supporters, because it is both interesting and relevant to be able to see the modern situation in the context of the past. Some might suggest history is dull, but not if you can create a picture of how things were and show old-time players and officials as real people. The men who have shaped the destiny of Sheffield football and the local heroes of yesteryear deserve to be remembered.

In my anxiety to make the fullest use of the material gathered over the years, I have probably gone into more detail than was originally intended when this project was first mooted. This at least partly explains why it was decided to produce a history of football in Sheffield in two volumes. This first volume spans the period from the mid-1850s to around 1961; and the second volume will cover from the 1960s to the present—and do so in more detail than might have

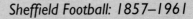

been possible had the entire history been contained in a single volume.

Sheffield has a unique place in the history of football, and the period under review in these pages is filled with intriguing tales of some wonderful characters and the highs and lows in the saga of the rivalry between the Blades and the Owls. I hope the reader will get as much pleasure from reading it as I have had in writing it.

I dedicate this book to the memory of the late Allan and Bessie Lax.

Keith Farnsworth
May 1995

Sheffield's Influence

SHEFFIELD boasts the oldest football club in the world: Sheffield FC, founded in 1857. In the Victorian era, the northern industrial town famed for cutlery and steel enjoyed a reputation as one of the pioneering centres of a winter game which, in the middle years of the nineteenth century, began a period of such dramatic growth in popularity that it soon became an essential part of the sporting fabric of the nation.

Sheffield's influence in that crucial phase when the game and its management were being fashioned was considerable. Within five years of Sheffield FC's birth, there were fifteen clubs registered in 'the home of organised football', and, significantly, when the Football Association was founded in London in 1863, it adopted Sheffield FC's rules with a few amendments. Sheffield formed its own local association in 1867, but when a formal link with the national FA was confirmed in 1871 it was on condition that it stuck to its own rules. This arrangement continued until 1877.

In truth, the conflict between Sheffield and London was seldom more than a disagreement over technicalities, and on the whole there was a mutual respect based on the knowledge that each party knew the other had the interests of the game at heart. The first inter-city match, in 1871, served to show they were close to settling their differences, and,

though the London team came north having agreed with some reluctance to play according to Sheffield rules, the occasion was one of harmony and friendship. Indeed, when London arrived a man short, the Sheffield Association's president, J.C. Shaw, volunteered to fill the gap. The fact that he played in goal and was unable to prevent a Sheffield victory did not dampen spirits at the post-match dinner and sing-song in a local hotel.

London knew the Football Association's hopes of consolidating its position as the game's leading

---

RULES

OF THE

SHEFFIELD

Football 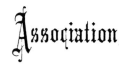 Association,

As re-settled at the General Meeting. held at the Adelphi Hotel, Oct. 10th, 1871.

COMMITTEE ROOMS, ADELPHI HOTEL.

SHEFFIELD:
J. ROBERTSHAW, PRINTER, ANGEL STREET.
1871.

authority could not be fulfilled without Sheffield's support, and in the meantime there was much that was being done in Sheffield that met with their approval.

Sheffield had introduced the corner kick in 1868, four years ahead of the FA; a fixed crossbar on top of the goalposts was common practice in the town from 1867, eight years before the FA outlawed the use of tape; and Sheffield led the way in penalising offences against the rules with, for instance, the award of a free-kick against a player who handled the ball. In on-the-field matters, the differences between the parties seem quite trivial to modern minds, and it is intriguing to note that the last rule to delay final total agreement concerned the offside law.

It was in more practical areas that Sheffield's influence was ultimately beneficial. They pioneered the earliest Players' Accident Scheme, which, in 1874, covered 37 clubs and 560 individuals; promoted the first provincial tournament with the Sheffield Challenge Cup in 1876; and in 1879 broke new ground with a knockout competition specially designed to support local charities, with the trophy donated by the Earl of Wharncliffe. Incidentally, in the late 1860s, two local theatre managers, Tom Youdan and Oliver Cromwell, both ever alert to topical opportunity for publicity, put up trophies bearing their name. Hallam won one, and Wednesday the other.

When, in 1871, the Football Association launched the cup competition that ultimately accelerated nationwide interest in football, the initial arrangement was that officials of clubs paired in the draw should meet to arrange a mutually acceptable venue. Sheffield, however, believed they had devised a much more sensible system, and the FA subsequently agreed that the first club out of the hat should have the choice of ground. Later, when international matches became a regular feature of the football calendar, it was Sheffield who suggested annual North *v* South trials to aid selection of the England team—and, for some years, these matches were held alternately in Sheffield and London.

One could add that Sheffield FC were credited with the idea that led to the creation of the FA Amateur Cup in the early 1890s, and note that it was in Sheffield teams' matches with Nottingham sides that the use of shinguards and a referee's whistle were first recorded. It all serves to highlight the town's place in football history.

At the same time, it does rather prompt the question: why was the first club, from which so much subsequently stemmed, created in Sheffield? In truth, there is no straight answer, for the circumstances are shrouded in mystery, and none of those involved at the outset appears to have placed the details on record. We do know that those young men, mainly former pupils of the local Collegiate School, who were the founding members of Sheffield FC, were far from the first footballers. By the time Nathaniel Creswick, a solicitor, and William Prest, a wine merchant, were formulating plans to launch a club, football was already firmly established in six or seven of the country's leading public schools.

However, it was a game still very much in its infancy, and it bore little resemblance to the one we know today. We can discuss how and why the public schools took up the game later. Here it is sufficient to say that it was still a rough-and-tumble activity, and every school had different rules. But moves were afoot to change all that, and from around 1848 students who progressed to Cambridge University and found the variety of codes confusing had been attempting to promote uniform laws of play which they hoped might be adopted universally. This was an ideal that would come closer following the birth of the Football Association in 1863 and the subsequent split between the dribbling and handling codes which separated soccer and rugby. In truth, it was not until 1882, when the British International Board was established, that it could be said association football was played under the same rules everywhere in the United Kingdom.

Obviously, what was happening in the public schools in the 1850s was evident in inspiring the birth of Sheffield FC, but it is not entirely certain that the influence was direct: that is, we cannot be sure any of the founders had been educated at or brought the game from one of the schools. This has prompted an assumption that some knowledge of the game was passed on by Collegiate masters familiar with the likes of Eton or Harrow; but it is probably more relevant to note that Prest had a brother who was at Eton and Cambridge, while Prest and Creswick, as well as being great sports enthusiasts with country-wide connections, were both involved in the local volunteer movement inspired by the Crimean wars. Each

man held the honorary rank of Major at this time, and their military links with other volunteers and regular army regiments almost certainly included officers with strong public school and university associations.

In any event, football had been played in the schools for some twenty years, long enough for knowledge of it to have spread into other areas; though it does seem significant that, once they began to pursue the idea of taking up the game, the Sheffield men made it their first priority to write to several schools to obtain details of the various rules of play. This suggests that only a vague notion of the game existed in the town, and nobody was over-familiar with it.

You can be sure that neither Creswick nor Prest had any vision of themselves as innovators whose actions would see Sheffield emerge as a leading centre in the development of the game. One suspects that the group in which the pair were involved had been attracted by the novelty of a sport that fitted the bill in terms of offering an enjoyable winter diversion, and it seems likely that Creswick and Prest, because both had a reputation as an organiser, were nominated to investigate the matter.

According to the folklore of Sheffield football, Creswick, then aged 26, and Prest, 23, conceived the idea of a football club while taking a summer stroll one afternoon late in the cricket season. This may be so, but it seems unlikely that the notion suddenly sprang into the mind of one of them without any previous discussion about football as a game. It may well be that the timing of their decision was significant. The cricket season was nearing its end, and it is not hard to imagine that, as members of Sheffield's premier club, they were looking for some activity to interest the players in the winter. This was a pattern that became fairly common in later years: many cricket clubs were to form football sections, and it is surprising how many now-famous soccer clubs have histories rooted in the summer game.

Indeed, this was to be the case with both Sheffield's leading professional clubs, Wednesday and United. The Wednesday Cricket Club started some fifty years before they added a football section; while Bramall Lane came into existence as a cricket ground (run by Sheffield United, a club without a team until 1892) some thirty-five years before the Ground Committee was persuaded to form a football club. Hallam FC, founded within three years of Sheffield FC, had been established as a cricket club since 1805, and at the time they took up football, the membership topped 300.

Sheffield Football Club, however, was always, from the outset, a separate and independent organisation and not formally linked with any other group. A financial crisis in the 1880s prompted amalgamation with Collegiate, and in later years they did operate within the framework of the Sheffield Amateur Sports Club in a long association with Abbeydale Park, but they were always on their own as a club.

Yet the majority of those involved in launching the new football club in 1857 were also connected with the leading local gentlemen's cricket club—indeed, the same club whose members had been prominent in

moves that led to the creation of Bramall Lane a few years earlier. They had grown tired of losing one ground after another to developers as Sheffield began to expand at a dramatic pace in the later years of the first half of the nineteenth century, and had urged their influential friend and fellow cricket fanatic, Michael Ellison, to come to their aid. Ellison, as agent for the Duke of Norfolk's estates, persuaded the Duke to make the land available for the creation of Bramall Lane in 1854. In fact, the new ground's management committee was made up of individuals rather than representatives of the interested local clubs, so no club had any stake in its control; and those who wished to use it did so by hiring a pitch. (William Prest, incidentally, had the distinction of playing in the first cricket match staged at Bramall Lane when it opened in 1855 and he was the first batsman to be dismissed for a duck!)

Prest, like others who had played a part in the creation of Bramall Lane, soon found that his links did not afford him any special treatment when, as a member of the new Sheffield FC, he sought to persuade the Ground Committee to permit football to be played there. In fact, Sheffield FC was to figure in the first football match staged at Bramall Lane in 1862, and they were subsequently allowed to use it for some of their more important games. Their relationship with the Ground Committee was seldom a happy one however, and around 1875 ill-feeling peaked and they vowed they would never play again at Bramall Lane.

In fact they did, but we are digressing from our story.

The People's Game

SOCCER in the final years of the twentieth century might fairly be said to have eclipsed all class barriers and become a game appealing to all parts of society. But it is not so long since 'the people's game' was essentially associated with the working classes. Stemming from the popularity football enjoyed in the industrial regions of the North and Midlands where it inspired the trend towards professionalism from the late 1870s; led to the birth of the Football League in 1888; and evoked an image of thousands of cloth caps on terraces from Accrington to Wolverhampton.

Yet the curious thing is that the roots of the organised game are linked to the upper and middle classes. True, football in its rawest form can be traced to the mob games connected with local festivals, and a more polished version was ultimately given back to the ordinary people. It owed its transformation into a game with form, discipline, organisation and rules to gentlemen rather than artisans. The years when it was first embraced by the public schools and universities constituted a crucial period when it was fashioned into something that began to resemble 'proper' football.

The oldest football club in the world was not created by ordinary working lads but by young gentlemen from privileged backgrounds, all prominent in local industry or the professions. A list of its members

in 1858 shows eleven were manu-facturers and the rest included doctors, surgeons, dentists, solicitors and architects. Not a cloth cap amongst them!

So it was a decidedly exclusive organisation which enjoyed a prestige denied many of the clubs that emerged in the town within a few years. Whilst they did play some games with local rivals (and Hallam were the keenest of these), after one or two experiences that they plainly failed to enjoy, Sheffield FC members had a spell of some twenty years up to the 1880s when they were very selective in their choice of opponents.

Later, however, attitudes changed, a necessity as the growth of the game and the rise of professionalism diminished the influence of the likes of Sheffield FC. The Football Association continued to be dominated by amateurs, and many felt that the welfare of the game was better in the hands of those who were in it for love rather than profit. But, at grass-roots level, finance was the key to survival, and adjustments had to be made with increasing regularity as the times and circum-stances continued to change and affect even the more exclusive organisations.

It is perhaps not without irony, that some 140 years after it all began, the oldest club of them all is fighting a constant battle just to stay in business in a very different world from that in which the founders made history. There is a certain inevitability about this, and in a sense only the name remains and one might question what real connection the present club has with that of 1857. In the summer of 1994, the present Sheffield FC, having played at the new Don Valley Stadium and found it costing more than they could afford, re-located to Owlerton Stadium.

In modern times people are more likely than ever to suggest that tradition counts for nothing, and few people now will be familiar with or even care about Sheffield FC's beginnings, believing they have little relevance to present circumstances. Yet while it is true that you cannot live in the past, what happened in 1857 was conditioned by the pattern of history in the same way that today's situation stems from a similar but more recent chain of events. At the same time, the steps taken and the people involved in the 1994 attempt to keep Sheffield FC going, are less likely to be assured of a place in the records and history books than those at the very beginning. But it is good that someone cares enough to ensure the old club keeps surviving.

IT IS generally accepted that football, in one form or another, has existed almost as long as man has populated the planet, though the earliest recorded examples date from the fourth and fifth centuries in Japan. It has been suggested that kicking a leather ball at a target formed part of the military training arranged for ancient Chinese soldiers—intended, perhaps, more as a co-ordinating

exercise for individuals than as a basis for a team game; though it is not difficult to imagine the young men occasionally using the ball in groups enjoying a spontaneous kick-about.

In England, football has been known since at least the twelfth century, but it seems to have been largely confined to the mob matches which, despite frequent attempts to outlaw them, survived as annual events linked to certain festivals. The best known of these were the traditional Shrove Tuesday games such as the ones synonymous with Ashbourne in Derbyshire— (incidentally, the county in which the term 'derby' originated to denote a fixture between local rivals).

These mob matches were a particular feature in many towns from about the sixteenth century. They usually lasted two or three days and were played with the goals three miles or more apart; they were invariably wild and furious affairs involving hordes of young men who charged through the narrow streets in pursuit of a ball while risking life and limb and leaving a trail of destruction in their wake. It is little wonder that the authorities were far from impressed and tried to ban these events, viewing them as mere excuses for physical excesses and riotous behaviour—as no doubt they were.

In Sheffield one of these 'great' football matches was staged not in the town's streets but out at Bents Green in 1793, involving teams from Norton and Sheffield. It was not the first such event, but is remembered because it was reported in the following words by Bernard Bird in,

The Perambulations of Barney the Irishman:

> There were selected six young men of Norton, dressed in green; and six young men of Sheffield, dressed in red. The play continued for three consecutive days. At the arch which was erected at each end of the place selected, there was a hole in the goal, and those on the Sheffield side would prevent the ball from passing through the hole. Then those on the Norton side (not being so numerous as those of Sheffield) sent messengers to the Peak and other places in the county of Derby; in consequence thereof, a great number of men appeared on the ground from Derbyshire.
>
> Then those of Sheffield sent fife and drum through the streets of the town, to collect recruits and sufficient force against Derbyshire men. The fashion then was for all responsible gentlemen, tradesmen and artisans of Sheffield to wear long tails. Hence, at the conclusion of the third day, a general row or struggle took place between the contending parties, insomuch that the men of Derbyshire cut and pulled nearly all the tails from the heads of the gentlemen of Sheffield.
>
> I understand there were many slightly wounded, but none were killed; thus ended the celebrated football match which aroused the bad passions of humanity for many years afterwards, insomuch so that the inhabitants of Norton felt a dread in coming to Sheffield, even about their necessary business.

As late as 1876, a fixture was arranged between Ecclesfield and Pitsmoor, two villages where football (at least of the more conventional kind) was to enjoy great popularity; the match was played on or around the main Sheffield-to-Barnsley road. In this instance the game was probably an exercise in nostalgia, as it marked the end of an era. 'Proper' football had arrived, and it was much more acceptable to the community, far more entertaining for the spectators, and more enjoyable (though sometimes only marginally less dangerous!) for the players!

Of course, the mob football bore little relation to the real game, and in some ways it is difficult to credit those events as the true forerunners of modern soccer. Yet apparently it was the basic concept within this raw and violent activity that was seized upon by the public schools, on whose playing fields it was fashioned into a game with rules and some semblance of order.

It was a development that was as much social as sporting, in that it stemmed from the 1880s reforms in higher education. The public schools, seeking to bring discipline to the playing fields as well as the class and lecture rooms, looked for a manly winter game that they could mould to suit their own ideals and culture and use to foster the ethics of team performance and spirit. Football looked a fair candidate, though in truth, despite all attempts at refine-ment, it remained a fearsome, ugly and often brutal business for many years. Even as late as the 1890s, in the professional game that eventually emerged, it was not uncommon to hear players from 'good' backgrounds referring to matches as 'akin to going into a bear pit'.

Yet in testing a young man's courage it served to form an important part of his education and development, and it is evident that

Sheffield and Glasgow teams pictured before an early inter-city association game in Glasgow.

many students maintained an enthusiasm for the game after their schooldays ended. In some schools it appears the activity developed into a form of rugby, in others it emerged as more a combination of soccer and rugby (though nobody could have described it thus at the time), but there were those who eliminated the hacking and, though handling persisted for some time, the gradual tendency towards an emphasis on the use of the feet created the basis of genuine association football.

It was a game ripe for expansion beyond the playing fields of the public schools. Though initially it was former students who were most likely to promote it in the outside world, the rise of an industrial society created ideal circumstances for football to attract the masses. That, of course, was a development still a few years hence, but when Messrs Creswick and Prest received details of the rules in the schools and reported to their friends, the decision to call a meeting to form Sheffield FC was, so to speak, the long-awaited signal for the kick-off in a whole new ball game destined to change the face of popular sport.

Almost 47 years after their formation, Sheffield Club won the FA Amateur Cup.
The players are: Bolsover, Chambers, Milnes, Green, Potts, Frost, Sylvester, Bedford, G. Hoyland,
J.E. Hoyland, Forsdyke.

The Oldest Football Club in the World

Colonel Nathaniel Creswick

NATHANIEL Creswick and William Prest are all but forgotten today, but they were prominent figures in the town in the mid-nineteenth century and are much deserving of a place in Sheffield's sporting hall of fame as many more 'famous' people whose contribution to the cause has been much less significant. They were an ideal pair for the task of launching Sheffield FC, for not only were they outstanding all-round sportsmen but natural leaders with a flair for getting things done; their success in creating the Hallamshire Volunteer Rifles was typical of their drive and enthusiasm for everything they tackled.

Creswick came from an ancient Sheffield family with local roots going back to the fourteenth century. The Creswicks were in silver plate manufacture, the firm having premises in Pepper Alley, off Fargate, but Nathaniel chose to become a solicitor. However, it was in the volunteer movement that he made his name, serving the cause for forty years, rising to the rank of Colonel and becoming a Companion of the Most Honourable Order of the Bath. Prest was a product of York who came to Sheffield as a young man to join his brother in a wines and spirits business; but his claim to fame was his sporting achievements, notably cricket, for he captained Yorkshire and played for the All-England XI.

That Creswick and Prest, representative of a younger generation full of new ideas, were popular within an influential circle in the town, is evident from the group that joined them to form Sheffield FC when the inaugural meeting was held on the 24th October 1857 at the Parkfield House, Highfields, home of

Creswick's solicitor friend, Harry Waters Chambers. Chambers' name did not appear on the original committee, which is curious considering the major part he was to play in the club's story. He later took on the role of secretary, a job he filled for 22 years, and in his time he emerged as a leading figure on a wider front. He was the club's representative at the meeting in London at which the Football Association was formed in 1863, and he was involved in all the debates about rules and other developments that concerned the national body in the following years.

The Chambers family had a unique link with Sheffield FC which lasted until 1950. One of Harry's sons, Ernest, was in the team that won the FA Amateur Cup in 1904; while his other boys, Harry Jnr and Geoffrey, both served as club president. Only the Willey family (and notably H.B. Willey, who was secretary for 35 years after long service as a player) could boast anything like a comparable record.

At that inaugural meeting, Prest, because of other commitments, was content simply to join the committee, but Creswick, anxious to have a leading role at the outset, took on the duties of secretary and treasurer. The first president, Frederick Ward, was probably best known as the son of Thomas Asline Ward, one of the most famous local figures of his day—a past Master Cutler and a man who had been a close friend of three of Sheffield's greatest men: Chantrey the sculptor, Montgomery the poet, and Hunter the historian. The old man was already 76 at the time of Sheffield FC's birth, and Frederick was running the family firm, Eyre Ward & Co.

Frederick Ward provided the club

with its first headquarters—a greenhouse in the gardens of the family home in East Bank Road! One suspects that the greenhouse was not often used for committee meetings, but it was probably popular as a dressing room when the footballers staged the annual athletics meetings which were a feature of the club's calendar for many years.

The club's first vice-presidents, T.A. Sorby and Joseph Ellison, were, like Ward, prominent manufacturers, while the committee also included Tom Vickers, a famous figure in local steelmaking. Vickers was the grandson of the founder of Naylor Vickers, a firm that began at Millsands and later established the River Don Works. Though only 23, he was already in sole charge of the firm's technical affairs; and it is worthy of note that while, like Creswick and Prest, he devoted much of his spare time to the Hallamshire Volunteers, he was such a great football enthusiast that subsequently, along with another Sheffield FC member, J.C. Shaw, he helped form the Hallam Football Club. Other members of the committee were William Baker, a lead specialist, John Kent Turner, an ironmaster, and Thomas Pierson, a solicitor.

As far as the original members of the club were concerned, to play was the thing—and, initially, it did not matter that because they belonged to the only football club then in existence they had to play amongst themselves! Even doing that, they felt they could get value for their 2s 6d (12½p) annual subscription.

It was agreed that the playing season would begin on the first day of November and end on Easter eve, with Saturday designated as 'play day', when matches would kick off at 2pm and continue until dark. The very first games saw members whose surnames began with a letter from the first half of the alphabet form a team to face a side made up from the rest. This pitted Creswick and Prest against each other, but Prest soon discovered that most of the natural footballers were in the A–M team. A compromise was agreed, and various permutations were tried, with one favourite being a clash between the professional men and the merchants and manufacturers.

The first playing rules made no reference to kit other than that each member had to equip himself with both a red and blue flannel cap—the headgear that was then the only way the teams were identified. This use of the cap explains why, even today, we talk of international players being 'capped'.

One of the earliest decisions of the committee was that the club's season would always end on a festive note, and for this purpose they introduced an annual sports meeting at which everyone who had been a member for two months was expected to perform.

Thus in April 1858 was organised the first major amateur athletics event ever staged in the town. Held in the field adjoining Frederick Ward's home, it proved a great social as well as sporting occasion, and the idea subsequently caught on when the Hallam and Wednesday clubs were formed. Sheffield FC and Wednesday were to stage most of their sports days at Bramall Lane; while Hallam, of course, used Sandygate, and their enthusiasm for athletics prompted the creation of the now-famous Hallam Chase, a ten-mile race which was first staged in 1862.

Sheffield FC's 1858 event was notable in that it apparently attracted 4,000 people, including all the town's leading figures and their wives; policeman were stationed at the gate to ensure that only invited guests were allowed in. It was probably no surprise to those who knew him that William Prest dominated the prize list, winning eleven events, including the 100-yard dash, five jumping contests, throwing the hammer, heavyweight wrestling and even the sack race and backward sprint.

Harry Waters Chambers

The Battle of Bramall Lane

SHEFFIELD FC's earliest attempts to find 'outside' opposition saw them organise fixtures with the soldiers from the local barracks (with whom of course, Creswick and Prest had close links). But Hallam FC came into existence in 1860, and within two years these clubs had the distinction of playing in the first football match staged at Bramall Lane.

This was a more significant milestone than modern enthusiasts might appreciate, for the Bramall Lane committee was at that time strongly opposed to the use of the ground for anything but cricket, and viewed football with a distaste they found difficult to disguise. This was in spite of the fact that, after barely seven years in business, the place was already losing money and the committee desperately needed to find ways of generating income because it was obvious they could not survive on cricket alone.

The truth was that, even in the summer, the fees received from cricketers hiring the pitches were insufficient to finance maintenance and developments. This was one reason why the committee, and Michael Ellison especially, sought to put Yorkshire cricket on a formal basis with the formation of a county club. Yet, when this was achieved in 1863, it did not really solve the problem, and they still had the challenge of exploiting the place in the period from September to April.

It was a situation that would not improve until they accepted that football was here to stay and necessary as a means of subsidising the cricket. (Goodness knows what those early committee men would have said if they had only known the contempt with which certain members of the Sheffield United club, and notably chairman Dick Wragg, would treat cricket in the 1970s!)

Sheffield FC, having started at East Bank Road, subsequently had a spell at Newhall in the town's East End, this was probably because the Bramall Lane authorities refused to discuss the possibility of allowing the ground to be used even for occasional special fixtures. In fact, when the breakthrough came, in late 1862, it was due to circumstances that made it difficult for the Ground Committee to say no—they insisted it was a one-off arrangement they did not intend to repeat.

The situation that left them without much choice but to permit a football match on their treasured turf, came about because of the American Civil War. This had such a severe effect on the cotton trade in Lancashire that a great wave of sympathy swept across the country, and a distress fund was launched. There was a particularly emotional response in Sheffield, a town familiar with the consequences of trade slumps. When fund raising was discussed, one suggestion was a football match between Sheffield and Hallam at Bramall Lane.

The clubs were keen. Since Hallam's formation they had met three times, and indeed in December 1861 had played in the town's first charity football match, a fourteen-a-side game that had attracted 600 spectators to Hyde Park and was in aid of the new public hospital and dispensary in West Street (later the Royal Hospital).

Hallam FC, as noted earlier, was the brainchild of two prominent Sheffield FC members, steelmaster Tom Vickers and John C. Shaw who worked in the legal profession and became an attorney's clerk. In sporting terms, Shaw was perhaps the more interesting figure, for, like his old Collegiate schoolpal Creswick, he is largely forgotten now and yet made a notable contribution to Sheffield football. As a player, he was something of a Peter Pan: he did not hang up his boots until he was 56, and was one of the town's most respected referees. A measure of his prowess as an athlete was that he not only organised the first ten-mile Hallam Chase but finished second in the inaugural race despite an ankle injury—and won it with ease a year later.

However, like Charles Clegg, he made his mark as an administrator. At Hallam he was captain, secretary and treasurer, becoming a vice-president of the Sheffield FA when it was founded in 1867, and later being president from 1869 to 1885—an eventful phase during which Sheffield's influence on the national scene was probably at its peak. He organised the first inter-association games with London, Glasgow and others in the early 1870s (indeed,

when London arrived in Sheffield for the first match in 1871, a man short, Shaw played in goal for them); and it was during his time in office that he had to cope with the emergence of a rival group with the creation of the Sheffield New (later Hallamshire) Association. His talents as a leader and negotiator led him into extensive involvement in politics as a local Conservative agent, and, ultimately, the man who refereed the first Sheffield Challenge Cup final landed a plum job as secretary of the Conservative Party for the Midlands region and left the town to settle in Birmingham.

In fact, Shaw had more cause than most to remember that famous Bramall Lane match of 29th December 1862, and he did not do so with much pleasure because it was an occasion blighted with so much ill-feeling that he was prompted to resign from the Hallam committee until good relations were re-established with Sheffield FC. The match, which lasted three hours but failed to produce a goal, confirmed all the Lane committee's worst fears about football. The term 'hooliganism' was not used in contemporary accounts, but it was probably appropriate for a game that passed into local sporting folklore as 'the day the waistcoats came off and the fighting began'.

A leading Sheffield player of the period, William Chesterman (a son of the founder of one of Sheffield's top tool firms and destined to become Master Cutler in 1880), said that matches with Hallam were invariably 'bull strength' affairs in which the football was incidental. 'I have often seen the ball lying on the pitch totally ignored, while half-a-dozen players have been pre-occupied with butting each other,' he once said. 'Men on both sides were more interested in having a go at an opponent than getting the ball.'

The irony was that a central figure in the incident that sparked all the trouble on this occasion was Nathaniel Creswick, though there were conflicting accounts about the part he played in provoking what turned into a free-for-all in which almost every player on the pitch was fighting. One report suggested that Creswick, being held by Hallam's William Waterfall, accidentally hit his opponent, but the Hallam players later wrote to the local press to claim that he had done so deliberately.

'Earlier in the game,' they said, 'Waterfall charged the Major, who threatened to strike him if he did so again. Later, when play stopped to await a decision from the umpires,

Creswick, very unfairly, took the ball from the hands of one of our players and commenced kicking it towards the goal. He was met by Waterfall, who charged him, and the Major struck Waterfall in the face, which Waterfall immediately returned.' According to another report, Waterfall threw off his waistcoat, raised his fists, and hit Creswick several times. Creswick apparently declined to return the blows, but the two men were immediately surrounded by all the other players, plus scores of spectators, everyone joining in a general fight which held up the game for several minutes.

Waterfall, noted one report, escaped dismissal from the field, and indeed was regarded as a hero by some Hallam supporters who 'seemed to rejoice that the Major had been hit'. Unfortunately, the teams in this game were not recorded in the local press, but they were probably

An early Sheffield FC team

not too different from the sides that lined up in the Hyde Park match:

Hallam: *Shaw, Snape, Vickers, G.H. Waterfall, Warburton, W. Waterfall, B. Elliott, A. Waterfall, G. Elliott, Hobson, Pearson, Pye-Smith, Moore, Vickers*

Sheffield: *Creswick, Prest, Baker, Appleton, Chambers, Dixon, Favell, Gould, Hall, Moore, Wightman, Wild, Turton, Sellars*

Sheffield FC played their first out-of-town game in 1865, when they faced eighteen of Nottingham in another three-hour marathon and were so delighted at winning 1–0 that, when they arrived home on the train, they put a ball down in the Wicker (where the Midland Station then was) and kicked it all the way up the town! In March 1866 they accepted an invitation to play London in Battersea Park in what might be described as the game's first representative match. In wet conditions that threatened to mar a very special occasion, London won by two goals to four touches down, and the highlight of the trip was a post-match dinner at the Albion Hotel in Covent Garden.

Chesterman, Harry Chambers and J.C. Shaw were Sheffield's best-known players, and it is worthy of note that the London team included two of the most famous figures in early football history: Lord Kinnaird and C.W. Alcock. Kinnaird, who served the FA for 55 years and was president from 1890 to 1923, played with The Wanderers and the Old Etonians. He made quite an impression with his red beard, long white flannelled trousers and blue and white cap, and his talents were such that he was in no fewer than five FA Cup-winning sides between 1873 and 1882. Alcock, who

was FA secretary for 25 years, was in The Wanderers side who were the first winners of the FA Cup in 1872, but his greatest claim to fame was as the man behind the creation of the national knockout competition that did so much to stimulate the popularity of football.

Sheffield FC entered the FA Cup for the first time in 1873–74. After two draws with Shropshire Wanderers, they went through on the toss of a coin, beat the London Pilgrims in the second round but then lost to Clapham Rovers on a neutral ground at Peterborough. Later in the 1870s they were knocked out by the Royal Engineers and twice fell to the mighty Wanderers in the quarter-final. But they had their moments, and one victory, at Darwen in 1877–78, earned them a novel place in FA Cup history because the entire Sheffield team took one look at the muddy pitch and insisted on playing in white kid gloves to protect their hands! (Or so the story goes.)

That Sheffield FC boasted some outstanding players in those years is evident when you consider that not only the Clegg brothers, Charles and William (of whom more will be said later), but William H. Carr (1875), John R.B. Owen (1874) and Thomas H. Sorby (1879) played for England; while their ranks also included the Rev. Arnold Kirke Smith (of the Barnes Hall, Ecclesfield family) and the Rev. Francis William Pawson (he was vicar of Ecclesfield from 1903 to 1921), who were both capped while at Oxford and Cambridge University respectively.

However, things did not always go as well as Sheffield might have wished, and, coinciding with outside developments which were to gradually diminish the club's influence and station within the game, came economic problems. In 1885 there was an amusing incident which illustrated the tightness of club funds. After they had struggled to buy a wooden stand that they had erected at their Attercliffe ground, they arrived for a match to find the structure had blown down in a gale. The timber merchant had charged them £35 and was still owed the bulk of the money. Now the club, lacking funds to rebuild the stand, asked him if he would accept the return of the timber in part payment.

The Sheffield members noted with interest that, in 1886, the Hallam club was dissolved and then quickly re-established, and, with financial problems growing, they wondered about their own future. In the event, they solved the problem in 1887 by amalgamating with the Collegiate Cricket Club, who had formed a football section some time before.

Sheffield FC survived, and indeed was to prosper and enjoy many good years. For instance, in 1904 they peaked with a triumph in the Amateur Cup competition which they had been responsible for persuading the FA to organise. But the fact that the amalgamation with Collegiate came within two years of the legalisation of professionalism, in the same year that the Wednesday Club relinquished its amateur status, and just a couple of years ahead of Sheffield United's formation, all served to confirm the role of the world's oldest football club would never again be the same.

Wednesday, formed ten years after Sheffield FC, had never dreamed that the trend towards professionalism would affect them, and indeed they resisted it for as long as they could, but finally discovered they had no choice but to embrace it if they wanted to go with the tide which was sweeping the game into a new and challenging era.

This Pauline Shearstone drawing recalls the famous Adelphi Hotel where Wednesday FC was founded 13 years after the decision to build Bramall Lane was taken at the same place.

Birth of
The Wednesday

SHEFFIELD Wednesday Football Club came into being in an upstairs room of Harry Sampson's Adelphi Hotel in Arundel Street on the evening of 4th September 1867 when members of The Wednesday Cricket Club held a meeting to discuss the best means of keeping everyone together through the winter.

The cricket club had existed since 1820. Until now there had been little worry about out-of-season activities, but more and more members were wintering with clubs who played football. The new game was catching on in a big way, and no doubt it made sense to organise a team, if only to ensure players remained Wednesday men all the year round! (They did not, at that stage, envisage that football would prove so popular that the income it generated would support the cricket, and, ironically, eventually lead to the two sections going their separate ways.)

Sampson's hotel (which stood where the Crucible Theatre now is) was an appropriate venue: the landlord was a famous Wednesday cricketer, and his pub was assured of a niche in local sporting folklore as the birthplace of the Yorkshire County Cricket Club. Here, too, the meeting had been held at which the decision was taken to build the Bramall Lane ground. Brewery traveller John Pashley, a notable cricketer, had the honour of formally proposing 'that a football club be formed in connection with the cricket club', and William Littlehales, an engraver, seconded the motion.

Ben Chatterton, a financial agent, was elected president, F.S. Chambers vice-president, and John Marsh secretary and captain; the committee comprised Pashley, Littlehales, John Rodgers, John White, Charles Stokes. Bill Fry, W.F. Pilch, T.J. Anderson and a Mr Knowles. Henry Hawksley, who was to begin a seventeen-year spell as president in 1870, and Littlehales, the club's second secretary, merit special mention because they gave notable service in the club's amateur phase. They both died prematurely and suddenly, and the death of Littlehales in particular was a blow that precipitated the problems leading to the crisis that finally forced the adoption of professionalism on the club. That, however, was twenty years in the future.

It was often suggested that Wednesday did not play their first game until the end of December 1867 when they visited the newly-formed Dronfield FC, but recent research by John Brodie has revealed a match at Norfolk Park on Saturday 19th October when John Marsh led his men to victory over Mechanics, the success being by the margin of three goals and four rouges to a single rouge from the opposition.

To explain what 'rouges' were, you need to know that the goals in those days were twelve feet wide and nine feet high, but you could only score a goal by putting the ball through the middle part, separated by 'inner' posts, and if it went between the 'outer' posts on either side it counted as a rouge. One goal was worth any number of rouges. Thankfully, before the Wednesday FC was a year old, rouges had been abolished by the Sheffield FA on the proposition of the Pitsmoor club, and the width of the goal became eight yards.

Wednesday, whose initial ground was at High Field, near the library, enjoyed a promising first season, in February 1868 collecting their first trophy, donated by the Theatre Royal's manager, Oliver Cromwell. He got the idea from the legendary Tom Youdan, flamboyant manager of the Surrey Music Hall on West Bar, whose Youdan Cup had been won by Hallam after defeating Norfolk in the previous year. Cromwell confined his tourney to teams less than two years old, which meant only Wednesday, Garrick, Exchange and Wellington

qualified—and it emerged that Cromwell, a patron of the Garrick in Sycamore Street, had anticipated they would win the trophy.

However, after Wednesday beat Exchange 4–0 on the Mackenzie ground, and Garrick, with the aid of seven 'guests' from Heeley, defeated Wellington, a crowd of some 400 saw Wednesday scramble victory with a fortuitous deflection in extra time in the final at Bramall Lane. Cromwell presented his cup to John Marsh on the stage of the Theatre Royal a few weeks later. Ironically, had the one-off competition gone as Cromwell wanted, he and his trophy would probably be forgotten now—whereas the cup still has a safe home at Hillsborough, and at least his surname is mentioned every time it is brought out for someone to look at it.

Marsh, incidentally, had the distinction of captaining the Sheffield team in the first inter-association games with both London (1871) and Glasgow (1874), but soon after the latter fixture he appears to have returned to his native Thurlstone, a village just beyond Penistone. There he soon organised a local team, but in 1880 suffered a bad fall, and, largely as a consequence of poor treatment when a broken arm was set, he caught an infection from which he died—still a young man, and leaving a wife and four small children.

After their Cromwell Cup success, Wednesday had to wait until the mid-1870s to embark on their first run of local cup successes, being the first winners of both the Sheffield Challenge Cup, introduced in 1876–77, and the Wharncliffe Charity Cup, donated by the Earl of Wharncliffe in 1879. Wednesday won

The Cromwell Cup — the first trophy Wednesday won.

one trophy or the other eleven times between 1877 and 1888, doing the 'double' in 1883.

In 1876 the Sheffield FA, through the local School of Art, offered a £5 prize for the best original design for a trophy, and the new Challenge Cup, valued at £50, was completed in the workshops of Martin Hall & Co. (makers of the original FA Cup five years earlier) just before the start of an inaugural tournament in which Wednesday and their great rivals Heeley reached the final. This match, a twelve-a-side game played at Bramall Lane on Saturday 10th March 1877, produced an abundance of goals and excitement for a crowd of around 8,000.

Heeley at that time was probably the best-supported club in the district. Their team included Peter Andrews, who was the first Scottish international to play in English football. He had been in the Glasgow side that met Sheffield and, when his job brought him to Yorkshire, Heeley were quick to recruit him. Almost immediately he was chosen to play for the Sheffield Association.

By coincidence, Wednesday's team included James J. 'Reddie' Lang, who was also a Scottish international and said to be the game's first professional in that, unlike his friend Andrews, he had come to Sheffield specifically to play football. In view of Wednesday's subsequent staunch opposition to professionalism, Lang's story is not without irony, but it probably serves to show how keen the club was to succeed.

Wednesday's first sight of Lang had been on the day Glasgow beat Sheffield at Bramall Lane in February 1876. A month later he collected his

first Scottish cap against Wales, and then, in April, played for Clydesdale against Wednesday. He made such an impression that he was invited to Sheffield, making his debut for the club in October and helping in the run to that first Challenge Cup final.

Officially, Lang was not a professional, for it had not then been legalised by the FA, but Walter Fearnehough, a member of the Wednesday committee, gave him a job in his knife-making works in Garden Street, where he did not have any formal duties and spent most of his time reading newspapers. Remarkably, many years later Lang revealed that, following an accident in 1869 at the John Brown Clydebank shipyard, he had lost the sight in his left eye, and thus passed the peak years of his playing career officially listed by the Government as blind!

Lang was not singled out for special mention in that 1877 final, and, in the first half, as Heeley established a 3–0 lead, Wednesday hardly got a look-in. However, they recovered after the interval. The brothers Tom and Frank Butler each notched a goal, William Clegg hit an equaliser which took the game into extra time, and Skinner snatched the winner just before the end. The occasion was rounded off with a celebration dinner at the Imperial Hotel in Castle Street. The teams were:

Wednesday: F. Stacey, W.H. Stacey, E. Buttery, W.E. Clegg, T. Butler, H. Muscroft, J. Bingley, F.M. Butler, T. Bishop, W.E. Skinner, J.J. Lang, J.C. Clegg

Heeley: W. Beard, T.A. Tomlinson, P. Andrews, J. Deans, R. Martin, J. Tomlinson, F. Brownhill, T. Leslie, J. Hunter, J. Thorpe, H.M. Barrington, J. Lindley

A Wednesday team from around 1878, the year they won the Sheffield Challenge Cup for the second time, beating Attercliffe 2–0, goals by Butler and Bishop.

Wednesday won the Challenge Cup six times in the next eleven years. In 1878 they beat Attercliffe, another notable club of that period, 2–0 in the final; and they achieved notable victories over Lockwood Brothers and Sheffield Collegiate in 1883 and 1887. Their biggest triumph was in the 1881 final when they crushed Ecclesfield 8–1, with Bob Gregory scoring five after Jack Hulley had given the outsiders the lead. Hulley, by the way, came from the same family as the present Wednesday director of the same name.

In 1879 the Wharncliffe Charity Cup was launched, but the fact that the first game in the competition was arranged only two days after the trophy had been handed to the Sheffield FA, caused some dismay. The fixture involved Wednesday and Attercliffe, but, on the appointed day, Attercliffe could not raise a team. They felt aggrieved when they were told they had forfeited the tie, and Wednesday were accused of 'having friends at court'.

The first final of the new competition brought another Wednesday–Heeley clash; again it was at Bramall Lane, and once more was a triumph for a Wednesday side captained by local headmaster William H. Stacey. Hero of the day was Woodcock with a hat-trick in a 3–1 victory.

Wednesday won the Charity Cup four times in the next nine seasons; but the most significant development at the start of the 1880s was their impressive debut and early progress in the FA Cup.

It is an oft-forgotten fact that Wednesday were scheduled to make their debut in the English Cup in Scotland, for, in that 1880–81 season, they were paired in the first round with the mighty Queen's Park of Glasgow. However, for some reason

Wednesday in 1880–81, the year they crushed Ecclesfield 8–1 in the Sheffield Challenge Cup final. The players pictured (not in order) include W.H. Stacey, E. Buttery, A. Malpass, C.L. Stratford, S. Charles, Jack Hudson, R. Gregory, Billy Mosforth, H. Newbould, J.J. Lang and J. Bingley.

which was never explained, the Scots withdrew, and Wednesday were given a walkover. They weren't exactly disappointed about that, for, only a few weeks earlier, Queen's Park, hailed as 'the champions of Great Britain' and regarded as practically invincible, had been to Sheffield and thrashed Wednesday 5–0 with a memorable display of football skills.

The second round took them to Blackburn Rovers and, while the Lancashire side were not yet the power they were to become within a few years, it was nevertheless a splendid achievement by Wednesday to emerge with a 4–0 victory. On an icy pitch, they literally skated to success, with Bob Gregory notching a hat-trick and Harry Winterbottom getting the other, all the goals coming

in the second half. A star of this triumph was Jack Hunter; indeed, his display so impressed Rovers' neighbours, Blackburn Olympic, that it was not long before they lured him across the Pennines and he became one of the earliest professionals.

Wednesday returned to Lancashire in each of the next two rounds, but after winning at Turton they crashed to a 5–0 defeat at Darwen, where, so it was said, goalkeeper William Stacey was blinded by snowflakes. In view of the fact that the schoolmaster had played so magnificently in the triumph over Blackburn, his excuse was accepted with good grace!

Wednesday's second FA Cup campaign (1881–82) was the most notable of their amateur phase, for they reached the semi-final, where they lost in a replay; but they so nearly denied Blackburn Rovers the honour of being the first northern club to reach the final and challenge the dominance of the southern gentlemen.

There were plenty of talking points worthy of recollection raised by that 1882 cup run. In the first round, against the local Providence on Quibell's Field, near Hyde Park, Wednesday won 2–0 but only one of the goals was achieved with the ball crossing the line. The other, credited to Anthony, was awarded by referee William Clegg instead of a penalty when the Wednesday man's goal-bound shot was stopped by a defender's hand. This was the only season in which the FA allowed match officials to use their discretion in such matters.

Then in the second round, Rhodes became the first Wednesday man to claim four goals in the FA Cup when Staveley were beaten 5–2 after two drawn games. After another triumph over local opposition with a defeat of Heeley, Cawley finished with a hat-trick in a 6–0 crushing of Upton Park (London) in the fourth round.

This was the season in which, thanks to the efforts of Walter Fearnehough and William Stacey, Wednesday recruited the legendary Billy Mosforth, who might fairly be described as Sheffield's first great football idol, a player who enjoyed astonishing local popularity. He had mostly been associated with Sheffield Albion, though in truth he tended to play wherever it was most profitable to do so, for he was well aware of the value of his talents. He may well have been an amateur, but he knew how to make a bob or two, and, after all, this

was an era when a man could play for several clubs and regard himself as a free agent.

Two stories epitomise Mosforth. One recalls how he was once stripped ready to play for Hallam in a local cup tie *against* Wednesday, but, when a supporter called 'Ten bob and free drinks all week, Billy, if you'll change your shirt', he returned to the dressing room and re-emerged in Wednesday's colours. George Waller, a Wednesday colleague, recalled a game in which he broke through and had only the goalkeeper to beat when he heard Mosforth cry: 'Give us the ball, George.' He did so, Mosforth duly scored, promptly dashed away to the dressing room, and returned to the field with a golden sovereign. 'Here, George, and thanks,' he said, 'I'd got myself on a five-to-one bet to score today!'

Mosforth, who stood less than 5ft 4ins and normally played at outside-left, was known as 'The Little Wonder'. He had terrific speed and ball control. It is said there wasn't a finer dribbler in the game, and contemporary reports abounded with accounts of solo runs the length of the field concluded with memorable goals. Yet he made many goals for his team-mates with his penchant for the perfectly-timed cross.

He made his Sheffield Association debut at 18 and was barely 19 when he won the first of his nine caps, against Scotland at The Oval in March 1877 as the only non-university or public schoolboy in the England team. Typically, he refused to be overawed by the occasion and, indeed, criticised the Hon. Alfred Lyttleton for selfishly running with the ball and failing to pass to unmarked colleagues.

Apparently Lyttleton said: 'I am playing purely for my own pleasure, sir!'; and Mosforth replied: 'Aye, and the pleasure of playing for England is not summat tha'll enjoy very often, Mister!' Sure enough, it was the Old Etonian's only cap.

There were three recorded cases of Billy being carried off on the shoulders of spectators after match-winning displays: once when he helped England beat Scotland in 1879; again at the end of a Sheffield–Glasgow match; and finally after contributing to the victory that put Wednesday into their first semi-final in 1882. It was a tie that went to a replay, and Mosforth played in both games, as well as two international matches, all in the space of ten days.

There was a novel footnote to the first semi-final game with Blackburn, for it was staged at Huddersfield, a rugby stronghold where the FA aspired to encourage an interest in soccer. As no equipment was available, Wednesday were asked to take some goalposts with them! The match ended with a 0–0 scoreline, though in fact Wednesday did put the ball into the Rovers goal, and, according to the referee, Major Marindin, it should have counted. The fact that it didn't seems to have been due to a misunderstanding, and the unexpected failure of Bob Gregory, Wednesday's captain, to complain. When the teams went to Whaley Bridge, Manchester, for the replay, Marindin, according to Mosforth, said: 'Well, Mosforth, you shouldn't be here today, because you won at Huddersfield. That was a perfectly good goal you scored.'

It is difficult more than a century later to appreciate why the referee

Willie Mosforth

should admit this and yet, when Gregory scored and Blackburn appealed to their umpire for offside, he should disallow the goal. However, apparently it was the custom then for referees to accept appeals and only use his own judgement if the umpires disagreed. Wednesday's mistake was in not appealing to their umpire. All this was of little consolation to Wednesday, and it simply added insult to injury when they crashed to a 5–1 defeat in the replay after an Arthur Malpass corner had been deflected past the Rovers goalkeeper to give them an early lead.

Malpass, incidentally, was a focal figure in the following season when, after Wednesday had beaten Spilsby 12–2 and Lockwood Brothers 6–0 to reach the third round, their opponents Nottingham Forest lodged a protest ahead of the fixture that Malpass had been paid thirty shillings (£1.50) to assist Sheffield Wanderers in a match at Bolton.

Malpass was suspended, but Wednesday went to Nottingham and drew 2–2 after losing a two-goal lead. Before the replay, Wednesday were staggered to discover that Sam Widdowson, the Forest captain, was in town seeking further protest evidence. He went so far as to demand to see the club's books to satisfy his doubts about the bona-fide membership of certain players. When documents revealed nothing,

Widdowson arranged for placards to be displayed in Sheffield offering a £20 reward for evidence that might lead to Wednesday's disqualification.

When Forest lost the replay 3–2, they lodged a further protest which the FA rejected. Ironically, Wednesday's next opponents were Notts County, and, when they telegraphed 24 hours before the scheduled date of the next round to say they would not play because they could not raise a team, the view in Sheffield was 'here we go again'. However, when the match was finally completed—incidentally in appalling weather conditions of heavy rain and high winds—County won, but the circumstances left Wednesday's followers with unpleasant opinions of Nottingham football.

When, later that season, Bramall Lane staged its first international, and the England team to face Scotland included three Notts County men but not a single player from Sheffield, many felt that it added insult to injury. In fact, it was to be four years before another Sheffield player was capped, and when that happened, in 1887, it coincided with a traumatic season that marked the end of Wednesday's amateur era. Moreover, the man who was the club's newest international that year was also one of the leading advocates of professionalism.

The Early Professionals

AS THE popularity of football increased, notably in the industrial districts of the North and Midlands, the trend towards professionalism was inevitable. While the FA Cup was only one of several key influences, the success of this competition was probably the factor that did most to hasten the development.

When the FA Cup was launched in 1871, it was initially dominated by the likes of The Wanderers, Oxford University, The Royal Engineers and the Old Etonians. But by the early 1880s the clubs taking over were a very different breed, led by the Blackburn teams, Rovers and Olympic, whose clubs sought to attain success and boost local pride with the aid of players imported from Scotland and any place where talent was available for hire.

The years from 1878, when professionals were first reported in Lancashire, to 1888, when the new era was confirmed with the creation of the Football League, were as eventful off the field as on it. It was a remarkable and intriguing phase in soccer history. The Football Association grappled with the implications of professionalism before and after they had finally succumbed to pressure from the powerful Lancashire clubs, who threatened to form a breakaway organisation if the practice was not legalised.

Sheffield, in the front line in the resistance to professionalism,

responded with bitterness to the FA's 1885 defeat. Indeed, Charles Clegg insisted the decision would not materially affect football in the town. Wednesday felt the same way until circumstances forced them to capitulate under pressure from some senior players and they agreed to embrace professionalism in 1887.

The real drive towards professionalism was generated by the Lancashire clubs, who imported Scottish players in such large numbers that nobody really believed so many had migrated simply to work in the local mills. The truth, of course, was that the jobs many were given did not exist, and they were only expected to exert themselves on the football field.

Sheffield's fierce opposition was curious considering the cases of Peter Andrews and James Lang, whom everyone considered the earliest professionals when they arrived in the town in 1876; but it was the local FA's continued resistence after 1885 that was really surprising. The influence of Clegg was evident; and though W. Pierce-Dix gave up the job as secretary of the Sheffield FA in 1882, he remained one of Clegg's most loyal supporters—as befitted someone who had married into the Clegg family!

At the height of the debate, Clegg, who was just beginning a link with the FA Council that would span fifty years, said: 'If professionalism is allowed it will only place greater power in the hands of the betting men and, if ever the gamblers get control of the game, I wouldn't give tuppence for it.' Shortly before the FA finally bowed to the tide of history, Pierce-Dix was still telling the Council: 'Professionalism is an evil which must be repressed!'

W.F. Beardshaw (Sheffield Club) viewed the Lancashire professionals as 'wicked' and insisted the legalisation of payments would 'tend to lower the game of football', yet some years later he supported Sheffield United's formation as a professional outfit. The local Lockwood Brothers, having at the height of the troubles refused to meet the Lancashire clubs, had clearly had a change of heart by the time they happily hired (and paid!) Wednesday's professional rebels for their famous FA Cup run of 1887.

Local problems with professionalism dated back to the formation of the Sheffield 'Zulus', a band of well-known footballers, who played a series of novelty matches and were successful and popular between 1879 and 1882. At the outset they enjoyed the favour of the authorities (their first game in Sheffield was in aid of the Mayor's fund) because, with the Zulu War at its height, the idea of devoting the proceeds of matches to the widows and orphans of soldiers was applauded. However, travelling around the North and Midlands attracting big crowds as they played in painted faces and Zulu dress, they developed a system of charging fees, and though it was debatable whether they made large profits, allegations emerged that the bulk of the money was going into the pockets of the players. In short, they were accused

of professionalism, and the Sheffield FA promptly called a halt to their activities.

The situation took a dramatic turn early in 1881 when, having defied the ban, eleven 'Zulu' players were suspended by the Sheffield FA shortly before the Wharncliffe Charity Cup semi-final between Heeley—deprived of Jack Hunter, their captain, and W. Moss—and Wednesday, who lost Arthur Malpass. (Exchange, who were awaiting the winners in the final, had no fewer than seven players on the blacklist issued by Pierce-Dix!)

Hunter, one of the best and most popular players of the period, was doubly unfortunate, for he was forced to miss playing for the North in the international trial two days before the Wharncliffe game. The local papers carried several letters expressing astonishment at his omission from the match with the South. Local supporters were not impressed when Pierce-Dix, replying, agreed that Hunter was one of the best half-backs in the North and the absence of such a brilliant player was regrettable, but the selectors had simply supported the Sheffield Association's necessary stance.

In the event, the international trial was postponed owing to bad weather, but the cup game went ahead—by coincidence two days after Heeley's formal protest at the suspension of their players had been delivered to Pierce-Dix, who just happened to be refereeing the tie with Wednesday. Perhaps it was no surprise that Heeley's supporters vented their anger on the official all through the match. Wednesday emerged winners 7–2, and, at the end of the game, spectators invaded the pitch.

The Sheffield team that beat Glasgow 3–1 at Bramall Lane in the inter-association match of February 1882.
Back row: J.C. Shaw (president), J. Harvey (hon sec), N. Wilkinson, William Clegg, J. Stevens, Charles Clegg, E. Buttery, W.P. Ducref.
Middle row: Jack Hudson, W. Harrison, Jack Hunter, (capt), T.E. Cawley, Billy Mosforth.
Front row: Harry Winterbottom, A. Mallinson, H.P. Marples.

According to Charles Clegg, their target was Pierce-Dix, who was hooted, hustled and kicked. He was so upset by his ordeal that he promptly resigned as Shefield FA secretary, but, in fact, returned to the job and continued his duties for another year.

The following week all the suspended players submitted apologies for having defied the Zulu ban and these were accepted, while Heeley's protest at being denied the services of Hunter and Moss induced the Association to re-instate them. But if Clegg and his colleagues thought that

was the end of the problem, they were mistaken.

The committee decided that Heeley should now meet Exchange and the winners would face Wednesday in the final, but, of course, as Exchange had already reached the final, they refused to co-operate and were ruled out of the competition. When Wednesday declined to meet Heeley again, the red-faced Sheffield FA had no choice but to withdraw the trophy for that season.

The only positive thing to come out of the whole affair was that Hunter did, after all, play for the North

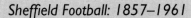

against the South in February, when the fixture was re-scheduled. Bramall Lane patrons got two games for the price of one as a match between Sheffield FC and Notts County preceded the international trial. Perhaps it was as well that there was a double bill though. The South's players were so anxious to catch an early train back to London that the duration of their match was reduced by half an hour!

It is perhaps worthy of note that Pierce-Dix looked back on 1881 with mixed feelings, for after his ordeal in the Wharncliffe Cup semi-final he was severely criticised for his handling of the Lancashire Cup final . . . being taken to task for officiating while carrying an umbrella! The explanation he gave in a letter to the *Blackburn Standard* is worth recording.

> . . . a considerable grievance to some gentlemen appears to be that I put up my umbrella. I quite admit that this is not the most convenient thing to do on a football field, and had I known that the weather would have turned out so unfavourably I should have prepared myself for it in a more effective manner, but seeing I had only a very light overcoat to protect me from the drenching rain, and that I had to travel back to Sheffield the same night without any opportunity of changing my clothes, it does appear unreasonable to object to my taking to the friendly protection of my umbrella.
>
> As to the position on the field which I took up, this is a matter upon which I am certainly entitled to use my own judgement, although it is quite contrary to fact to say I did not follow the play.
>
> Of course, as I have stated, when the heavy rain came on, I did not expose myself to it more than I

could help, but for my own satisfaction I always kept such a position as would enable me to see the play, and as the ground was small and the play slow, and as I am fortunately possessed of good sight, this was not a matter of much difficulty for me.

> I do not find it needful, in order to follow the play, to be, as I have seen some umpires and referees, constantly in the way of the players, although on this particular day, much as it was said I kept out of the way, I think I got accidentally charged twice.

Pierce-Dix concluded the season on a happier note when he became Sheffield's first FA Cup final referee, taking charge of the game between the Old Carthusians and the Old Etonians. A year later, when he ended his spell as the Sheffield Association's secretary, he was given a splendid send-off at a dinner at the Imperial Hotel in Castle Street, and was presented with a massive, magnificently-carved drawing room cabinet and an illuminated address. Coincidentally, a few days earlier, Jack Hunter, having raised his tally of England caps to seven, played for Heeley against Blackburn Olympic and, soon afterwards, was persuaded to cross the Pennines to become a publican in the Lancashire town.

Olympic's punishment for recruiting Hunter and another Heeley man, George Wilson, was suspension from the Lancashire Cup in the following season. At least that left them free to concentrate on the FA Cup, and they became the first Northern club to win it—with Hunter, in a role that can only be described as player-manager, the key influence. One touch of irony Hunter appreciated, as the Old Etonians were beaten in the final was that one of the umpires was Pierce-Dix, who had done so much to make him want to leave Sheffield!

In the meantime, the increasing number of complaints about professionalism continued to trouble the Football Association, and in October 1882, Sheffield's W.F. Beardshaw urged the FA Council to launch an investigation. This was in fact, the first of several attempts to get to the heart of the problem but, while everyone admitted it existed, few were ready to produce documentary evidence.

Then, in January 1884, came a turning point, when, after a drawn FA Cup tie with Preston North End, Upton Park protested that their opponents had used professionals. Remarkably, when Preston's representative, Major William Suddell, went before the FA, he admitted the charge was true—but claimed the practice was commonplace and his club had only followed the trend as a means of self-defence. He offered to produce proof that professionalism was rife and the trend unstoppable.

Suddell's military title related to his role in the local volunteers, and his occupation was that of a cotton mill manager. Spurred by the example of the Blackburn clubs, he was determined to see Preston enjoy similar success, which was why, in 1883, he had recruited a number of Scottish players. His ambition knew no bounds, and he earned a place in history as a key figure in prompting the legalisation of professional football. When this led to the creation of the Football League, his beloved Preston kicked off the new era with the first League and Cup double (and,

incidentally, on the way to achieving it, helped influence the pattern of Sheffield football history when they played in the first FA Cup semi-final staged at Bramall Lane). There was an intriguing footnote to the Suddell story in 1895 when he was sent to prison after being found guilty of misusing his firm's funds, these having been diverted for the purpose of supporting Preston's cause.

In 1884, Suddell's frankness set in motion a train of events which, within eighteen months, would see the FA finally relent. They did so only after a succession of debates in which Sheffield and Birmingham persisted with their aggressive opposition, while R.P. Gregson of the Lancashire FA emerged the chief crusader for professionalism, and Charles Alcock, the FA's secretary, remained the model of common sense.

When a Birmingham delegate told the FA Council he felt it was degrading for respectable men to play with professionals, Alcock's response typified a moderate approach which was evident if not always voiced among many others in the meeting. 'I cannot be called a supporter of professionalism,' he said, 'but until it is legalised the deadlock which now exists will continue. I consider that veiled professionalism is the evil to be repressed, and I am sure it now exists in nearly every football district, "pure" Birmingham not excepted. Professionals are a necessity to the growth of the game and I object to the idea that they are the utter outcasts some people represent them to be. Furthermore, I object to the argument that it is immoral to work for a living, and I cannot see why men should not, with that object, labour at football as at cricket.'

How Charles Clegg, Beardshaw, Pierce-Dix and others reacted to Alcock's comments is not known, though it is not difficult to imagine; for the Sheffield FA's top brass did not take kindly to having lost the fight to stop the professionals, and Clegg refused to believe that the situation would change in the town. As late as February 1886 an incident occurred that not only showed how reluctant the local football authorities were to accept that things would never be the same again, but certainly did much to further antagonise the Sheffield players who supported the professional cause.

Wednesday men Tom Cawley, Teddy Brayshaw, Harry Winterbottom and Billy Mosforth were invited to play for Sheffield against a joint Oxford and Cambridge Universities side, but someone reported that the quartet had tried to dissuade others from going unless some payment was forthcoming.

The upshot was that they were banned. The decision angered the Wednesday club, and as a consequence of their complaints Cawley was exonerated. Then, after appearing before the Sheffield FA's committee, Brayshaw and Mosforth had their bans lifted; but poor Winterbottom, who claimed he had been too busy working at his trade to attend the meeting, was suspended from football until the end of the season. The injustice in Winterbottom's case was all the greater considering that, long after the situation changed, he was one of the players who actually insisted on remaining an amateur, and everything points to the local FA having punished the one totally innocent man in the group.

In fact, the period between January 1886 and April 1887 was to prove one of the most significant in local football history, as circumstances conspired to sweep Wednesday into a new era, with the decision to embrace professionalism, concluding a traumatic phase and setting them on course to become one of the country's leading football clubs.

The End of Wednesday's Amateur Era

THERE WAS never much doubt that The Wednesday Football Club considered progress their goal, and the break with the cricket club in 1883 hinted at a sense of reality that would point them towards a new phase in their history. They went for independence because the cricket club was content to play only friendly games, while the footballers wanted to win things; and anyway it seemed unfair that the footballers should be generating the bulk of the income but the cricketers were spending it!

Yet Wednesday FC's ambitions did not include embracing profes-sionalism, even after it was legalised by the Football Association in 1885. When they finally did so, in April 1887, it was only with great reluc-tance. They were pushed into taking the step by a group of their leading players, who went so far as to form a rival professional club to stress that if Wednesday did not move with the times, they would lose their best men and risk falling into decline and obscurity.

If there was one misfortune that precipitated the chain of events shaping Wednesday's destiny, it was the death of secretary William Littlehales in January 1886—just when the Sheffield Association's treatment of Brayshaw, Cawley, Mosforth and Winterbottom (who were banned over allegations of pressing for payments) was stirring up anger amongst players. They could

not understand the local FA's continued anti-professional stance (which was being maintained with such fervour) when set against what was happening elsewhere in the country.

The majority of Wednesday's committee supported the Clegg line in this matter. They could not conceive that the Football Asso-ciation's change of policy need affect Sheffield, and had Littlehales not died when he did, one wonders how different the pattern of subsequent events might have been at the club. For it was only when the club's administration fell into unexpected disarray without the loyal and efficient secretary, that the situation got out of control—to the detriment of those who felt Wednesday should remain an amateur organisation.

Jack Hudson, a popular member and an outstanding player, was charged with the task of sorting out the confusion, but unfortunately, the stand-in secretary discovered that Wednesday's application to enter the FA Cup in 1886–87 had been submitted too late. In normal circum-stances, it was an oversight that might not have been more than a minor embarrassment, but in fact it sparked a crisis that eventually brought the whole question of the club's future to a head.

Five Wednesday men—Jack Hudson, Teddy Brayshaw, Tom Cawley, Billy Mosforth and Harry

Winterbottom—were persuaded to help another local side, Lockwood Brothers, in the FA Cup. This was not unexpected, for players then often turned out for more than one club. It was slightly different this time in that the works team (connected to a well-known cutlery firm) went all the way to the last 16 in the national competition. They caused quite a stir as they knocked out Nottingham Forest and only fell to West Bromwich Albion (who reached the final) after a replayed game at Derby.

Wednesday, without their 'stars' more often than they had anticipated, suffered some embarrassing setbacks, notably a 16–0 defeat at Halliwell. The men returned to help them win the Sheffield Challenge Cup (ironically they beat Lockwood Brothers in the semi-final) for the first time since 1883; but there was a feeling that the players had decided they would only be available to help the Wednesday cause when it suited them.

Lockwoods, captained by Billy Betts, a player Wednesday coveted, had become one of Sheffield's strongest clubs. Having recruited the likes of Tom Buttery, Jack Houseley and Fred West, all highly-rated local players, they had claimed a cup double in 1884. The arrival of goalkeeper Brookes and Ned Stringer from Ecclesfield, plus the Wednesday men, had meant remarkable success for them in the year the firm's boss, George Lockwood, became Master Cutler.

Whether that 1886–87 Lockwood Brothers team received financial reward was never confirmed, but significantly perhaps, their success and Wednesday's continued refusal to discuss turning professional, prompted the players to take matters into their own hands. With the support of three other Wednesday men—Fred Thompson, T.E.B. Wilson and Jim Clarke—and Sam Hetherington, a prominent local publican, they formed a club called Sheffield Rovers. The idea was that this should be a professional outfit and the new club played a match with Eckington Works in order to qualify for the FA Cup. When the FA confirmed that its application had been accepted, the writing was on the wall for Wednesday.

It is important to appreciate that whilst the Wednesday men involved in provoking this development could be described as 'rebels', they were all respected figures in local sporting circles and every one was a leading player. Mosforth, as noted earlier, was not just a brilliant footballer but perhaps the most popular one in the town; Teddy Brayshaw had just gained his first England cap; and Jack Hudson and Harry Winterbottom were regarded as two of the steadiest lads you were ever likely to meet— and genuine Wednesday men, too. (Incidentally, Winterbottom, though he had been punished over allegations of professionalism, always remained an amateur, and when his displays for Lockwoods prompted an offer from West Brom he turned it down and said he was happy to continue working as a bone cutter.)

Tom Cawley, who was about 27 at the time of these events, was probably even more popular within the Wednesday club than Mosforth, for, though the nearest the Neepsend product had got to an England cap was an international trial, he was regarded as the most complete footballer in the town. Since joining

Wednesday in 1876 he had played in every position in the team and had become a fixture in the Sheffield Association side. Moreover, he was invariably described as the least impetuous of men; not the kind given to getting into trouble on or off the field.

Cawley, Mosforth and Winterbottom were all members of the Wednesday club's committee, yet despite being able to argue their case from within, they still came to the conclusion that the only solution to the problem was to create Sheffield Rovers. Cawley and Winterbottom never really wanted or expected to make a living from football, but they felt they should have the same right as footballers elsewhere in the country to seek and accept rewards for their talents and services.

Cawley, perhaps more than most, had been hurt by the Sheffield Association's stance. He had seen how Jack Hunter had been treated and felt an outstanding player had been virtually driven from his home town and forced to make a new life in Lancashire, and he resented the sneers of amateurs who regarded professionals as inferior beings. In fact, the majority of the men seeking to persuade Wednesday to adopt professionalism were skilled craftsmen able to earn very good wages; and of this group, only Teddy Brayshaw would end his life in poverty—and his case was excep-tional in that he was plagued by illness, misfortune and domestic problems which conspired to lead him into the workhouse in his later years.

Cawley was a model of moderation and a modest man torn by the circumstances that forced him to make a choice between his club and his principles. He argued that if Wednesday continued to insist on remaining amateur they would diminish in importance, and all the time he was seeking to organise the new Sheffield Rovers he was hoping the old club would have a change of heart. Thus when members of the new Rovers attended a meeting at Sam Hetherington's Brunswick Hotel in the Haymarket, one evening in the early spring of 1887, with the intention of formally adopting professionalism, Cawley made the speech that, in retrospect, was the saving of Sheffield Wednesday. He begged his colleagues to recognise that the step they were taking could signal the end of Wednesday as a footballing force in the town, and urged them to give the old club one final chance to change its mind on the question of paying players.

All the Wednesday men at that Rovers' meeting signed a requisition calling for a special meeting of the old club, and when this was held, in an upstairs room at the Garrick Hotel in Sycamore Street, the 'rebels' soon recognised that the tide was finally turning in their favour. Wednesday had got the message at last.

The meeting was adjourned to give the committee time to discuss a formula, and when it was reconvened on the 22nd April 1887 the motion to adopt professionalism was passed unanimously. This was the moment when the likes of big John Holmes, as president and Arthur Dickinson, installed as financial secretary, emerged as major figures in plotting a new Wednesday era. Meanwhile, Sheffield Rovers played one more

Arthur Dickinson: a major figure in the first 40 years of Wednesday's professional era.

task of finding a ground. Meanwhile, they decided that match fees should be five shillings (25p) at home and seven shillings and sixpence (37½p) away. Considering that West Brom had been paying ten shillings (50p) in 1885 and Blackburn twelve shillings (60p), Wednesday's initial payments were hardly generous, though one is tempted to suggest the figures are treated with caution, for if documentary evidence had survived, it might show they were intended as minimum fees.

It is worthy of note that some surviving minutes from January 1888 give a more accurate picture. The committee then agreed to give each player 25 shillings (£1.25) for training expenses for a cup-tie, plus fifteen shillings (75p) for the match, and the trainer was paid £1. Even in that first season, a donation of £1 made to a player for loss of time from his work mocks the suggestion that the five-shilling fee was realistic.

If Wednesday did begin the new professional era with a hint of financial caution, it was because they knew their ability to pay whatever fees or wages they agreed would depend on what it cost to acquire and equip a new ground—and whether they could achieve success. In the event, the Olive Grove years were to bring more triumph than trauma.

game, then folded—a club all but forgotten now made worthy of a place in local sporting folklore because of its contribution to the moves which ensured that Wednesday survived.

The new Wednesday committee had plenty on its plate, not least the

The World of the Clegg Brothers

THE Clegg brothers, John Charles (1850–1937) and William Edwin (1852–1932), were two of the most remarkable figures in local sporting and political history. They were solicitors who were typical of their time and place, notably in a philosophy moulded by a background in Methodism and temperance. The power and influence each wielded in his chosen field at the height of their fame made them a unique pair.

Charles, top man in the Football Association for 47 years and head of the local FA for even longer, was dubbed the Napolean of Football. William, whose 40 years on the Town (later City) Council as a Liberal included 24 years as its leader, was called the Uncrowned King of Sheffield before his party was sensationally defeated, as Labour swept to power in the 1926 municipal elections. The brothers were both knighted: William in 1906, Charles in 1927.

They were the sons of a remarkable father. William Johnson Clegg (1826–1895) served three terms as Mayor in the late 1880s and was so respected that, when the decision was taken to build a new Town Hall to mark Sheffield's elevation from town to city, he was singled out to lay the foundation stone. Old Clegg's story was a model of Victorian self-help, for he was well into his thirties and already the father of six when he chose to change his career, he finally qualified as a solicitor at the age of 42.

His boys were great sports enthusiasts from an early age, with Charles capturing dozens of athletics prizes at every distance from 100 yards to the quarter-mile. They played football for Broomhill, Perseverance FC and Sheffield Albion long before becoming synonymous with the Wednesday club, which they joined in 1870, at the start of a decade that made them household names on the local soccer scene.

In the 1870s, both played for England against Scotland, Charles in the very first international in 1872, William in the second a year later; and they figured in Sheffield's first inter-association match with London in 1871, and the first game with the Royal Engineers (the pioneers of 'combination football') in 1873. They also played in Sheffield FC's first FA Cup tie the same year, and in 1877 starred in the first Sheffield Challenge Cup final, in which Wednesday came from 3–0 down to beat Heeley 4–3 in extra time. They were also rival captains in the famous floodlit match at Bramall Lane in 1878. Incidentally, when William gained his second England cap, against Wales in 1879, he did so whilst taking a weekend break from defending the notorious Sheffield murderer Charlie Peace!

Any football event of note in the town invariably featured one or both of the Cleggs, initially as players and later as referees or umpires. Indeed, as he began to establish himself in the management of the game, in 1882 Charles took charge of both the FA Cup final and the England–Scotland game. The only surprise was that his brother-in-law, W. Pierce-Dix, had a year earlier pipped him to the honour of being the first Sheffield man to referee the English Cup final.

Of the two, William was the one more given to reminiscing about their early football days, recalling what it was like to have to change behind hedges and then play in matches in which the emphasis was more on physical strength than skill. Even when they graduated to inter-city

William Clegg

fixtures, brute force was an accepted part of the game, and, looking back in 1932, he admitted that even such subsequently distinguished men as Lord Kinnaird and C.W. Alcock practised tactics in London games with Sheffield that were far from gentlemanly, but within the rules that then existed.

'People used to think it was only good football when they knocked a man down and hurt him, and the ball was an incidental,' said William, whose playing days were ended in 1880 when, falling during a Wednesday game with Vale of Leven, his arm was trampled on by an opponent and he ended up with a dislocated elbow. 'My arm was stiff for months, and the reason I stopped playing was not due to the discomfort but because I objected to carrying on under sufference, for you see, opponents began to show a certain tenderness towards me: they would get out of my way sooner than charge me, and while I appreciated their thoughtfulness, I couldn't bear being afforded treatment out of character with the spirit of the game as it then was.'

He added: 'If you couldn't take the knocks, you didn't play, and the man who was given the hottest time in terms of physical ill-treatment was the goalkeeper. Those were the days when there were two outer goals, in which rouges were scored, as well as an inner goal, and, if it wasn't enough to have to defend this large area, a goalkeeper was constantly shadowed by an opposing forward. It was this forward's sole task to wait until the ball was kicked towards the goal and then knock the poor goalkeeper about as much as possible.'

Charles seldom spoke of his own playing days, but once reflected that he did not enjoy the experience of playing for England against the Scots at Partick in 1872. Ironically, his captain on this historic occasion was Arnold Kirke Smith, whose family home was at Barnes Hall, Ecclesfield, but, according to Clegg, his colleagues were 'snobs from the south who had no use for a lawyer from Sheffield'. He claimed that they never passed the ball to him during the game, and afterwards nobody spoke to him. He decided he didn't want their company anyway, and the lesson was one he remembered in his later years of fame.

As the elder brother, Charles initially concentrated on the family practice, though there was a spell when both he and William served on the Town Council. However, while he did become a magistrate and succeeded his father as Official Receiver, Charles was happy to leave the political field to his brother. William went on to complete a family double on the aldermanic bench and in 1899 emulated his father by becoming Sheffield's leading citizen, Charles was encouraged to pursue his work in the cause of football.

He had already emerged as the kingpin of local football administration when, in the mid-1880s, he was elected to the Football Association Council, and by the end of the decade he had become FA Chairman (a position he would hold until his death in 1937 and, from 1923, supplement with the role of president following the death of Lord Kinnaird). Charles arrived on the national scene at a time when those responsible for running football were

Charles Clegg

struggling to halt the rise of illegal professionalism and fighting to keep the game 'pure', and the FA had no greater advocate than the quietly-spoken solicitor from Sheffield. Clegg's background and training made the concept of anyone playing football for financial gain abhorrent, and he feared that if the game moved in that direction it would lead to its ruin. He often told his colleagues on the FA Council that they were the guardians of the game and men who must always do their duty without fear or favour. In his view, that meant protecting football from people who might care more for their own interests than that of the game, and he wanted to avoid creating any circumstances in which control might fall into the wrong hands.

When the FA's struggle failed and professionalism was legalised, he accepted it with great reluctance and insisted that the only way forward was to keep it under the tightest possible control and when, within a few years, the Football League was formed he turned his attention and energy to the task of resisting the increasing influence of the new organisation in matters relating to the handling of professionals in the areas of wages and transfers.

It was perhaps no surprise that, when Clegg returned to Sheffield after the Football Association's historic decision, he told the local FA that the change need not affect the game in his home town. At the time, he was more concerned about the circumstances that had left Sheffield football with two governing bodies, for it was a situation that was damaging the town's status within the national Association. Significantly, Clegg's elevation to FA chairman did not happen until the separate Sheffield groups were united.

The problem dated back to around 1877 when the Sheffield FA, overwhelmed by the growth of interest in the game and anxious to control the increase in the number of local clubs, insisted that it could only accept as members those organisations that had been in business for at least two years. The upshot was the creation of the Sheffield New Association (subsequently known as the Hallamshire FA), which, thanks largely to the work

of secretary David Haigh, quickly grew in strength and influence and was never denied equal status with the older organisation in the eyes of the national FA.

Ironically, just when Clegg, thanks to groundwork by his friend Charles Stokes, had set in motion the amalgamation that in October 1887 would create the Sheffield & Hallamshire FA, his illusions about Sheffield's immunity from the threat of professionalism were shattered. Wednesday, under pressure from some of their leading players, finally succumbed, joined the trend and launched a new era in local football history.

Perhaps it said much for Clegg that, by 1889, he had sufficiently adjusted to circumstances to back Stokes when the man who had helped found Wednesday conceived the notion of forming Shefield United FC—though it should be noted that when this idea was initially mooted the plan was to have a team boasting the best local amateurs! As will be explained in more detail later, Stokes came up with his idea immediately after Clegg had refereed the first FA Cup semi-final staged at Bramall Lane in March 1889 . . . an occasion remembered in the Clegg family because old W.J., the father of Charles and William, had at the age of 63 and in his third term as Mayor thrown himself into the midst of the spectators and helped restore order when there was a pitch invasion!

Charles Clegg was an autocrat and a man of iron will and rigid principle, but the image of him as lacking wit or a sense of humour was wide of the mark. He was proud of having been the first boy to have signed the pledge when the Band of Hope was formed in Sheffield, and he firmly believed that 'nobody gets lost on a straight road'; but he was far more broad-minded than many expected. In his later years he was a dignified old man who was invariably treated with great respect and many were in awe of him; but, as he showed while chairing a local FA disciplinary meeting, he could still surprise a few people.

A young player who had been sent off for making ungentlemanly remarks to the referee was asked by Clegg: 'What exactly did you say to him, my boy?'

The youngster blushed: 'I don't like saying, sir'; but, when pressed by Clegg, added, 'Well, I said I've shit better referees.'

'I see,' said Clegg. 'All right, I'll tell you what I'll do. I'll give you a week to prove you can do just that. But if you can't, I'm afraid you'll have to pay a £1 fine.'

If Clegg had been the staunchest opponent of professionalism, he was not slow to fight those all-amateur county associations who, in early 1907, refused to accept an instruction from the FA that they should forth-with admit to membership all professional clubs in their areas. This was an issue that eventually led to the creation of the independent Amateur Football Association, but, long before that happened, there were some fierce debates on various aspects of the subject in Council.

At one stage a motion that Clegg had supported when it was passed two years earlier was rescinded by the FA Council behind his back, and, without hesitation, when the Sheffield man learned what had happened he resigned as FA

chairman. 'This is a change of view and practice with which I am not in accord,' he wrote. 'If I am correct in this opinion, I think the Council is entitled to have a chairman who is in sympathy with its changed view, and I therefore tender my resignation.' But his colleagues would not let him resign, and a requisition signed by 49 members of the Council was wired to Sheffield assuring him of their support and urging him to reconsider his decision. He stayed, his position strengthened by his stance.

Another of his famous battles came when the threat of a players' strike was averted just before the start of the 1909–10 season. The trouble arose when the Players' Union, formed a couple of years earlier and accepted by the FA, lost the favour of the game's governing body when it affiliated itself with the General Federation of Trade Unions.

Clegg was under fire from all angles at the height of the trouble: the FA was accused of being anti-unionist, the clubs were described as 'the enemies of the players' and the PU urged all trade unionists to boycott any Football League matches which went ahead using amateurs in place of striking professionals.

William Clegg sprang to the def-ence of his brother. It was not true, he argued, that Charles was opposed to professional footballers or anyone else combining legitimately for the purpose of securing their proper rights, but the management of football had to remain in the hands of a supreme authority—and what was resented was the interference of a body that knew nothing about football or its management, and which had 'set itself up as quasi-dictators as to what should be done or left undone in the management of the sport'. When a truce was called, it was largely on Clegg's terms, and there was to be no similar confrontation again between the players and the FA during Clegg's lifetime.

It was said that Clegg's influence cast a shadow for many years after his death and inhibited Sheffield football —in the sense that Wednesday and United, the clubs with which he was synonymous, long continued to adhere to his principles of straight dealing and never remotely risking the accusation of not doing things strictly by the book.

This was perhaps an over-simplification, but some felt this was the reason that the Sheffield clubs lost out in competing with rivals who were prepared to bend the rules. Some believed the 'Clegg code', instead of merely ensuring the Sheffield clubs did not act improperly, coloured their judgement and induced them to err on the side of caution when others were at least ready to look for every means of exploiting a situation without breaking the law.

A minor example probably serves to illustrate the point. Some twenty years after Clegg's death, one Sheffield club was seeking to sign a prominent local boy who had excelled in schools football, and all was set for the formalities to be completed when the lad's mother quite innocently scuppered the deal. The family was living in poor accommodation, and the mother simply asked whether the club might be able to help them find a nice house. She had not the slightest notion that her request might be interpreted as a bid for an illegal inducement, all she had in mind was that the club might be able to influence a landlord to rent them a house. But the club's official, horrified at the possibility that the mother was seeking an illegal inducement, quickly concluded the interview . . . and the boy was not signed.

In fact, he later joined the other Sheffield club, where he enjoyed considerable success and was eventually able to help his mother buy a little house; she did not ask the same question when he got a second chance to become a football apprentice!

Today, in the mid-1990s, it is hard to appreciate fully the way things were in the Clegg era. There have been so many changes in the last thirty years that it is not easy to recreate the circumstances in which Clegg's immediate inheritors operated. Football, as ever, simply mirrored the current moment, and in that context, the Wednesday club was simply responding to the climate as it existed when embarking upon a new beginning as a professional outfit in the spring of 1887.

Early Years at Olive Grove

WEDNESDAY'S first priority after turning professional was to find a permanent home, for clearly they could no longer afford to continue hiring Bramall Lane where the authorities insisted on taking a hefty slice of the gate receipts from matches. In fact, the committee at the old ground was dismayed by Wednesday's decision, for it meant the loss of substantial income, and ironically, it was their efforts to make up for this shortfall that, within a couple of years, prompted them to create the rival Sheffield United FC.

John Holmes, the Wednesday president, and financial secretary Arthur Dickinson did not take long topersuade the Duke of Norfolk to grant a seven-year lease on a site just off Queen's Road and adjacent to the Midland railway line. The Olive Grove Ground Committee was formed to manage an operation that involved converting a swampy field (which had a stream and a public footpath

The Earl of Arundel and Surrey pub which provided the first dressing rooms in the Olive Grove era.

running across it!) into a level, well-drained and professional-looking enclosure in time for the start of the 1887–88 season.

The club spent around £5,000 on improvements and when funds were exhausted before dressing rooms had been built, they made arrangements for changing facilities to be available in the nearby Earl of Arundel and Surrey public house. For the players it meant a long walk which took in a railway footbridge. Meanwhile, W. Russell, who had already agreed to undertake the task of fetching the ball whenever it was kicked on to the railway line, was named as doorman at the pub on match days. His all-in fee was 1s 6d (7½p)!

Olive Grove was to be Wednesday's home for twelve eventful years during which they had their trials and triumphs, but overall enjoyed more success than failure. They had a splendid FA Cup record at the ground, for they lost only four of the 23 ties they played there. They also reached two finals—winning the second, in 1896, to bring the game's most-coveted trophy to the city for the first time (though, in fact, the 'pot' had been made in Sheffield by the firm of Martin Hall & Co.).

Wednesday had hoped to persuade Preston North End or Aston Villa to play in the match to mark the formal opening of the new ground, but in the end it was Blackburn Rovers, FA Cup winners in 1884, 1885 and 1886, who accepted the invitation—though they demanded a £12 guarantee and half the gross receipts if the takings topped £24. Those figures seem paltry by today's standards, yet when the appointed day (Monday 12th September 1887) arrived, half an hour before the kick-off there were fears there would be insufficient spectators to cover the guarantee.

In the end, a late rush at the gates saw just under 2,000 watch a game in which Blackburn, whose side included former Sheffield hero Jack Hunter, were held to a 4–4 draw after leading 4–1, while a home man, Billy Mosforth, had the distinction of scoring the first goal at the new ground. The teams lined up as follows:

Wednesday: Smith; Thompson, Brayshaw; Hudson, Betts, Beckett; Winterbottom, Waller, Wilson, Cawley, Mosforth

Blackburn: H. Arthur; A. Chadwick, J. Beverley; J. Haynes, J. Hunter, J.H. Forrest; J. Douglas, N. Walton, J. Berrisford, R. Rushton, L.H. Heyes

In their first season as a professional outfit, Wednesday won 32 and lost only seven of their 45 matches, scoring 158 goals. They clinched a Sheffield Challenge and Wharncliffe Charity cup double and reached the last eight of the national knockout competition before falling to the mighty Preston in the first FA Cup tie staged at Olive Grove.

In reaching the last eight, Wednesday had some memorable moments on their travels. When they won at Long Eaton Rangers, they collected their cut of the gate money and found the £4.15s (£4.75) had been paid in pennies—1,140 of them! Their share of the receipts at Leyton, where they beat Crusaders, was 8s 4d (about 42p)—paid by a cheque that took months to cash because the banks refused to accept that the signature on it was legitimate.

Preston, already a power in the game, remarkably tried to avoid travelling to Sheffield because, having heard there had been a smallpox epidemic in the town, claimed the lives of their players would be at risk. In the end, the FA threatened to expel them from the competition if they did not fulfil the fixture.

Wednesday's second term at Olive Grove was equally successful. This was the season when the Football League was formed but the Sheffield club was not invited to join the twelve founding members: so there was some satisfaction when Wednesday's 35 wins in 52 fixtures included defeats of Preston and Burnley in friendly matches. (Preston were on their way to clinching the very first League and Cup double, and their Cup run, in bringing them to Sheffield at the semi-final stage, would have an important influence on local football history—as we shall see from the next chapter.)

Skipper Billy Betts, who got his only England cap during that 1888–89 campaign, was perhaps the first great idol of Olive Grove. That the crowd appreciated his pluck was shown in the Christmas match with Lincoln when he was carried off with a bad injury but insisted on returning though he was obviously in great pain. In the end, he had to go off again, and, with another defender, Hazlewood, injured, Wednesday finished with nine men but still won 5–0. Spectators took a collection for Betts and raised £2.15s (£2.75), which he insisted on sharing with Hazlewood. The injury sidelined Betts for a few weeks, but he returned to help Wednesday add another trophy to their collection: the Gainsborough News Cup.

Incidentally, it was in an earlier game with Lincoln, when Wednesday

won 6–1, that Tom Cawley, the most gentlemanly of players, scored a hat-trick but was then sent off in a blatant case of mistaken identity. He had just reached the edge of the field when the referee, having accepted his error, called him back; but Cawley was so upset at having been considered the villain of the piece that he refused to return!

In the spring of 1889, Wednesday were not exactly thrilled by news of the formation of Sheffield United FC and hoped to confirm their superior status by joining the Football League. However, despite a stirring speech by John Holmes at the annual meeting in Manchester, they failed to generate any support. Of course, they were not alone, and twelve of the unsuccessful applicants returned to Manchester a week later, when, with Holmes in the chair, they formed a rival league, the Football Alliance.

Wednesday were determined to make an impact in that 1889–90 season, and they succeeded, for they won the initial Football Alliance title and also reached the FA Cup final for the first time. Incidentally, just in case anyone had any doubts about who played at Olive Grove (or, perhaps, to ensure people did not confuse them with the new club at Bramall Lane), they had the main stand repainted in blue and white, with 'Sheffield Wednesday Football Ground' emblazoned on the roof in letters you could see for miles!

Kicking off the Alliance era with a home victory over Bootle, Wednesday won 15 and lost only 5 of their 22 league games, and of the 90 goals they scored in league and cup, 70 were shared by Cawley, Billy Ingram, Albert Mumford and newcomer

Olive Grove, Wednesday's home from 1887 to 1899: the site is now a Sheffield Corporation depot, and a heritage plaque unveiled in 1995 is the only reminder of the area's links with the start of the professional era in the town.

Mickey Bennett—Bennett notching 16 even though he did not begin the season until November. Like his brother Walter, who was to enjoy great success with Sheffield United Mickey Bennett was an outstanding forward whose services were in heavy demand, the authorities suspended him for eight weeks when it was alleged he had joined Wednesday after already signing for Rotherham.

Wednesday's Alliance record included 9–1 defeats of Long Eaton and Small Heath, but real excitement came in the FA Cup, with the run to the final starting with an impressive 6–1 victory over star-studded London Swifts and the following 2–1 triumph against Accrington Stanley. Three games were then required to dispose of another Football League club, Notts County, in the quarter-final, for after Wednesday had romped to a 5–0 success the visitors complained that the Olive Grove quagmire had been unfit. When County won the replayed game 3–2, it was Wednesday's turn to protest—this time about the ineligibility of two members of the

Notts team. The third game, staged at the neutral Racecourse Ground in Derby, saw Wednesday win 2–1.

In fact, Notts lodged a further protest, and the FA did not finally reject this until 24 hours before the semi-final, in which Wednesday met Bolton at Birmingham. The Lancashire side had thumped Sheffield United 13–0 and beaten holders Preston in earlier rounds, so they presented a daunting challenge. The game was played in rain and hail, and Bolton were the first to score, but Winterbottom equalised and Mumford sealed a famous victory.

The final, at Kennington Oval on 29th March 1890, pitted Wednesday against their old foes and perhaps the most famous Cup fighters of that era, Blackburn Rovers, and it proved a chastening experience for the Sheffield team as they crashed to a 6–1 defeat. The difference was not only in terms of ability on the day but a matter of confidence, for Wednesday were apparently quite overwhelmed by the occasion of their first final appearance while Rovers, having been there four times before, took everything in their stride.

Ahead of the game, Wednesday certainly did not feel victory was beyond them, for the week before they had clinched the Alliance title with a notable triumph at Grimsby, and felt that, at their best, they could match anybody. However, they had come out of that bruising battle against Grimsby with several key men injured. In the event, only skipper Harry Winterbottom, whose swollen ankle failed to respond to treatment, was missing, but two or three others later admitted they had not been fully fit but had played down their knocks during the special training at Matlock.

It was when the team reached the Oval that nervous tension began to affect them. According to R. Gregson of the Lancashire FA, while the Rovers players were laughing and singing in the dressing room, the Sheffield men were 'sitting quiet as mice'; and afterwards, someone in the Rovers camp said they knew they were going to win because, when the traditional souvenir autograph book was passed into the Lancashire team's dressing room, they noted how shaky were the signatures of the Wednesday players.

Rovers were a goal up after five minutes, led 4–0 at half-time, and the 20,000 crowd saw Bill Townley, one of nine internationals in the Blackburn team, complete what was then a unique Cup final hat-trick after the interval. Mickey Bennett scored for Wednesday, but, despite the humiliation, the Sheffield supporters remained in good heart and at the end insisted on carrying acting skipper Haydn Morley shoulder-high from the field. The 1890 final teams were:

Wednesday: *Jim Smith; Haydn Morley, Teddy Brayshaw; Jack Dungworth, Billy Betts, George Waller; Billy Ingram, 'Toddles' Woolhouse, 'Clinks' Mumford, Tom Cawley, Mickey Bennett*

Blackburn: *Horne; Forbes, James Southworth; Barker, Dewar, Forrest; Lofthouse, Campbell, John Southworth, Walton, Townley*

The season ended on a sour note when Wednesday concluded their Alliance programme at Newton Heath in late April, for the home side had a man sent off and spectators attacked the Wednesday players at half-time and at the end. Billy Ingram, who was pushed over a hoarding, and Teddy Brayshaw, who was prodded in the face with a stick, were injured. Winterbottom, still not fit to play but acting as the team's umpire, was grateful to emerge unscathed, except for the loss of his cap, when chased by the crowd amid astonishing scenes after the match.

Similar crowd disturbances occurred at Olive Grove in the following season when Wednesday supporters endured the frustration of seeing their favourites defend their Alliance crown so badly that they finished at the foot of the table with only four victories. True, they crushed Halliwell 12–0 in an FA Cup tie in which Woolhouse scored five goals, and things did improve late in the season when the arrival of Duncan Gemmill, Ferguson, Gibson, McConachie, Richardson and a trio of Brandon cousins, signalling a sudden burst of transfer activity in Scotland; but overall it was a disappointing season. In all, they won 19 of their 56 games, losing 27.

The first crowd incident occurred at an Alliance match with Crewe in October 1890 when Wednesday, still seeking their first win of the season after ten games, lost 6–4 to Crewe, and the target for spectator abuse was, ironically, the home umpire, William Robert Wake, who, according to contemporary reports, seems to have brought the trouble upon himself. He took on the job against the wishes of the home team, and then, throughout the match, seemed disinclined to fulfil an umpire's duties in that he consistently refused to appeal on Wednesday's behalf.

This was, in fact, the last season that the system of each club providing an umpire was practised prior to the introduction of linesmen, but the problems on this occasion stemmed from Wake's attitude. The crowd's anger peaked when, after Wednesday, 5–2 down, had pulled back to 5–4, Crewe scored a sixth goal from a blatant offside position and Wake ignored the home team's calls for him to raise his flag and appeal.

One wonders why Wake, a local solicitor and a member of a well-known Sheffield family, had taken on the job when it was clearly an act of provocation. He was a former player, having helped Thursday Wanderers win the Sheffield Challenge Cup in 1879, and was always described as a big Wednesday supporter; though his chief claim to fame was as a former Yorkshire cricketer whose great enthusiasm was the Pitsmoor club.

When the Crewe game ended, hundreds of Wednesday fans surrounded Wake, who only reached the safety of the club's committee room with difficulty. Then, instead of disappearing inside, he chose to stand in the doorway and argue with the nearest supporters until John Holmes, the Wednesday president, intervened.

A cab was called to take Wake home, but when it arrived he refused to climb into it and instead called to the crowd: 'What do you want to do to me?' When, with exaggerated nonchalance, he affected to light his pipe, some spectators suddenly surged forward, and Wake was only rescued from the mob by the intervention of two constables. Subsequently, the police ordered Wake to get into the cab and go home, and Wednesday spent the next few weeks fearing that Wake's actions might cause the Football Association to inflict heavy punishment on the club.

In the following January, it was the referee, L.G. Wright of Derby, who was attacked by the crowd after Wednesday (at that stage they had only two Alliance wins to their name all season) lost 2–1 at home to Newton Heath. The trouble was inspired by Mr Wright's refusal to disallow the visitors' first goal, which allegedly was offside. At the final whistle, some spectators made a rush for the official, besplattering him with mud and jostling him until he was rescued by Wednesday officials.

It is relevant to note that, a year later in January 1892, Wednesday were involved in a third Olive Grove incident, and this time it led to the ground being closed by the Football Association for two weeks. However, on this occasion—an FA Cup tie with Small Heath—the trouble stemmed from rough play which led to both Richardson and Duncan Gemmill being sent off. A nine-man Wednesday side still won 2–0 and as the ground closure coincided with a fortnight during which no home game was scheduled it was hardly a painful punishment.

Despite finishing bottom of the Alliance in 1891, Wednesday had hopes of joining the Football League, though by this time the Alliance clubs had decided they would stick together and neither apply for nor accept election except as a group. Holmes and the others were trying to persuade the League to accept the notion of trebling their membership, and they thought they might be moving in the right direction when, in April 1891, they managed to fix up a representative match between the League and the Alliance—and it was a feather in Wednesday's cap when the game was staged at Olive Grove.

However, though officials from the rival camps dined together in Sheffield's Maunch Hotel afterwards, the Football League people soon made it plain that they would not accept the Alliance plan. As it happened, Wednesday ensured they got some consolation from the fixture, for they persuaded Blackburn's Tom Brandon, who had played for the League XI, to sign for them. This had not been difficult in view of there being three Brandons at Olive Grove already, but it provoked an angry reaction from the Blackburn club. They induced the League clubs to refuse to play Wednesday in the 1891–92 season.

The presence of Tom Brandon and another astute signing, Fred Spiksley from Gainsborough, helped ensure that Wednesday recovered from the temporary slump of the previous season, they lost only once at home and finished fourth in what was to prove their last campaign in the Alliance, before, in May 1892, they were finally admitted to the Football League.

In their first five terms as a professional outfit, Wednesday had played 256 games winning 148 and suffering 76 defeats. They had averaged over 150 goals a season. It might not be so easy to succeed with such consistency at a higher level, but they were ready for the challenge; all the more so considering Sheffield United had also attained a place among the élite after a mere three years in business. More eventful times were just around the corner!

This 1887 picture of the Ecclesfield team which enjoyed a remarkable run in the FA Cup includes several players later synonymous with Sheffield United, notably Arthur Watson, Rab Howell and Ned Stringer; and the presence of a Hemmingfield and a Woolhouse confirms the village also supplied some Wednesday men. The player on the left of the front row is Tom Hulley, a relative of 1990s Owls director, Geoff Hulley.

Bramall Lane and the Birth of United

THE STORY of Bramall Lane dates back to 1854 when, at the same Adelphi Hotel in Arundel Street where the Yorkshire County Cricket Club (1863) and the Wednesday Football Club (1867) were sub-sequently founded, the Sheffield United Cricket Club was created. Its purpose was not (at least initially) to run a team, but to organise the erection and management of a new cricket ground built on a site 'free from the smoke of the town' leased from the Duke of Norfolk at the instigation of his agent Michael Ellison.

Ellison, who was very much the autocrat, dreamed not only of making a first-class cricket ground but one that would consolidate Sheffield's position as the home of Yorkshire cricket. There had been a county club of sorts operating from the early 1830s, but this was not formalised until 1863. Had Bramall Lane not existed, the Yorkshire club might not have been created when it was, with Sheffield the headquarters for its first forty years.

The first disappointment Ellison suffered came when the new ground, despite its popularity with clubs who hired pitches in the summer, failed to pay its way. He believed the birth of the Yorkshire club would solve that problem, but it didn't, and he ended up paying the Duke's rent out of his own pocket more often than not. The Lane was something of a financial millstone to the Ground Committee.

The problem, of course, was that cricket alone could never generate sufficient income to meet the costs of maintaining and developing the ground, but, for many years, the men responsible for its management stubbornly refused to allow other sports to be played on the treasured turf. In truth, they were horrified when the first football match, between Sheffield FC and Hallam, was staged in 1862; and, had the fixture not been in aid of the Lancashire Distress Fund, which had civic backing, they would never have agreed to host the game.

Only two more football matches of note—the finals of the Youdan and Cromwell cup competitions—were played at the Lane in the 1860s. There was however a dramatic increase in football activity in the 1870s, when it was the venue for Sheffield's first inter-association games with London (1871) and Glasgow (1874), and the visit of the famous Royal Engineers (1873) who introduced the merits of the passing (or combination) game to the town. The Sheffield Challenge Cup (1877) and Wharncliffe Charity Cup (1879) finals served to confirm football's astonishing rise in popularity.

The Ground Committee took a long time to come to terms with the new winter game, and many members continued to view it with utter disdain, but secretary Joseph

Wostinholm, though steeped in cricket, knew the ground could not be developed and maintained, indeed would not survive, without embracing other sports. Thus he even encouraged novelty events to aid his bid to wipe out heavy losses, and in 1874 teams from Boston and Philadelphia played two American baseball matches. In the same year, Sheffield raised a team to face Glasgow at lacrosse. Then, in October 1878, the committee agreed to let the ground be used for a unique football match, the purpose of which was solely to promote a new invention called the electric light.

The game, between teams captained by the Clegg brothers and featuring the town's leading players, has passed into folklore as the first floodlit match in football history. It attracted 12,000 sixpenny patrons, plus around 2,000 ticket holders (called proprietors) but, such was public response to the novelty, it was estimated that at least 6,000 spectators scaled the walls and got in free. According to the *Sheffield Telegraph*:

> There was an overwhelming interest in the experiment, and excursionists arrived in large numbers from distant towns. Between six and seven o'clock, it seemed as if all Sheffield was heading for Bramall Lane. The streets were thronged from all directions. At the game curiosity conquered customary courtesy, and the few who were really interested in the play were obliged to give way to the many who had eyes only for the new lights. Many of the ladies, once within the rays, shot up umbrellas as they would parasols to shield them from the sun at mid-day!

Two engines, one behind each goal, were used to drive Siemen dynamo apparatus which threw belts of electric light across the playing area from four lamps atop of thirty-foot high staging at each corner of the ground. According to reports, the game (in which William Clegg's team won 2–0) was followed with ease.

John Tasker, the local pioneer of electricity and a member of the Wednesday Cricket Club, simply aimed to sell the concept to shops and firms, and he succeeded in persuading Hovey's store and Davy's works to experiment with the first commercial use of electricity in Sheffield. Meanwhile, £300 match receipts delighted Wostinholm.

In the 1880s, football at Bramall Lane entered a new era, with the ground staging its first England–Scotland game in March 1883, followed by an England–Ireland match in 1887. By the time Wostinholm bowed from the scene soon after the turn of the century, he had seen the Sheffield stadium, complete with new pavilion and a new football stand, recognised as one of the North's top sports venues. An international double was completed in 1902 with a cricket Test between England and Australia. Shortly after the old secretary's death, a rugby league representative game (1911) and an FA Cup final (1912) were added to the list.

However, in the late 1880s there were still serious financial problems. When, in 1887, Wednesday, seceding from the local FA and adopting professionalism, elected to go it alone and find their own ground, the loss of substantial revenue from a club that had staged all its important fixtures at

Bramall Lane was a big blow to the Ground Committee. Wostinholm, all the more determined to seek alternative ways of plugging the gap, was pleased when Charles Clegg, already a major figure within the Football Association, asked if the Sheffield ground might be used to stage the 1889 FA Cup semi-final between Preston North End and West Bromwich Albion at short notice. When the committee agreed to take on this fixture, they did not realise it would mark a milestone in the history of football in the town.

That 1888–89 campaign was the first season of the new Football League, and Preston, as well as lifting the championship without losing a match, were destined to win the FA Cup without conceding a goal. Albion, their opponents, had won the Cup the previous year, but had conceded eight goals without reply in their two League games against a Preston side already dubbed 'The Invincibles'.

It was no surprise when Preston, with a first-half goal from Russell, won the tie. On a fine sunny day a crowd officially given as 22,688—at the time the biggest ever seen at a match in Sheffield—paid around £700, with special trains arriving from all over the country as well as Lancashire and the Midlands.

The *Sheffield Telegraph* reported:

> The great throng in the streets around the ground prompted officials to open the gates at 1.15pm, earlier than planned, for the 3.30 kick-off. Every nook and corner, every wall and roof and rail was occupied in a bid to get the ideal vantage point. The householders directly round the ground took the occasion by the forelock and let their top rooms to those who cared to use them at a very fair rental, and these positions of advantage were rapidly procured by those who believed that distance lent enchantment to the view.

Some of the West Brom supporters had brought pigeons in order to send details of the game home and, long before half-time, they may well have dispatched messages suggesting the game was in danger of not being finished. After the kick-off was delayed ten minutes, because the crowd at the Shoreham Street end had encroached onto the pitch, the game was halted after fifteen minutes and held up for a quarter of an hour when hundreds of spectators suddenly swarmed across the pitch towards the Bramall Lane shed.

The 24 policemen on duty, aided by referee Charles Clegg and his veteran father, W.J. Clegg the Mayor, tackled the crowd. Said the *Telegraph* man: 'The Mayor was angry when the crowd broke onto the pitch, and he bundled several youths neck and crop from the playing part. One of the men in blue looked on in amazement and admiration!'

When the chaos was at its height, the captains suggested the tie should be abandoned and a friendly played once order was restored, but Charles Clegg insisted that the semi-final would be completed on schedule. He promised there would be no more trouble with the crowd once the police had cleared the pitch—and there wasn't. Subsequently, however, West Brom protested that the disorder, largely generated by Preston supporters, had affected their players, and claimed the game should be replayed.

The Football Association rejected the plea. Meanwhile, although the Bramall Lane Ground Committee admitted lessons had been learned, the view in Sheffield was that the occasion had been a big success. One committee man, Charles Stokes, said things had gone surprisingly smoothly considering the event had been planned at such short notice.

Stokes told his colleagues that the real lesson to be learned from the occasion was that the time had come for Bramall Lane to have its own football club. What better way was there to ensure regular income at the ground in the winter months? Charles Clegg agreed it was a good idea, and while he felt his position as head of the local FA precluded him from being formally involved in planning the venture, he promised to give it his full support.

Stokes, then aged 41 and nearly three years older than Clegg, has often been described as a junior member of the Ground Committee, but in fact his status was the equal of any of his colleagues. Indeed, he was one of the most respected figures in local sporting circles. As a young man he had played for Heeley and Wednesday at both cricket and football, being one of the founders of Wednesday FC and a member of the team that won the Cromwell Cup in 1868. He had become president of both Heeley CC and the Norton & District Cricket League as well as serving on the Yorkshire CCC committee alongside the likes of other football-loving cricketers such as David Haigh and Joe Tomlinson—two men just as keen to see United have a football club.

His strength was his reputation as a man of culture and common sense.

Nobody revelled in the rivalry of sport with more enthusiasm, but he never lost his sense of fair play, and was regarded as a wise head—a good man to have around in a crisis. One of his notable successes was in the role of peacemaker in healing the rift between the Sheffield FA and the Sheffield New Association with the 1887 creation of the Sheffield & Hallamshire FA.

In over a decade on the Yorkshire CCC committee, Stokes, who was a dentist by profession, had confirmed his support for the cause with a contribution that won him much praise. If his allegiance to cricket was never in doubt, nobody did more to persuade the Lane Ground Committee that the key to financial stability was learning to live with football. Even people such as Ellison (who insisted he hated the winter game) were ready to listen to Stokes. Indeed, it was a source of irony that Stokes had persuaded Ellison to come to Wednesday's rescue and offer Olive Grove when they had wanted a ground two years earlier.

Six days after the 1889 semi-final, a meeting was held in the Norfolk Row office where Joseph Wostinholm conducted business as a partner in a firm of stockbrokers and estate agents. It was resolved to form a football section to be operated jointly with the Sheffield United Cricket Club.

Wostinholm and his assistant Harry Stones (a former Sheffield Albion and Wednesday player) took on the administrative duties, while, in addition to the Ground Committee, key figures who lent their weight on the original executive were a trio of leading local football men: W.F. Beardshaw, David Haigh and Joe Tomlinson.

Joe Wostinholm, the key administrator at the start of Sheffield United FC.

Beardshaw, as noted earlier, was a prominent member of Sheffield FC. He had helped launch the Corinthians, serving on that famous amateur club's first committee in 1882, and his abilities as a player had taken him close to a place in the England team. The only puzzle about Beardshaw's involvement with the new United club (and few were more enthusiastic supporters than he and his father, Josh) was that he had always been one of the fiercest opponents of professionalism.

Haigh, a colliery agent, had come to prominence as secretary of the Sheffield New Association, where his leadership and election to the national FA Council alongside Charles Clegg had enhanced his reputation.

He was the natural choice to administer the amalgamated local associations. A deformed foot had prevented him from playing football but not from making a mark in the game. His service to Sheffield United over the next 27 years was to include a five-year spell on the Football League's management committee.

Tomlinson had given long service to the Heeley club as a cricketer and footballer. In more recent years, serving on the local FA, he had emerged as a notable referee. He was by nature a man who spoke his mind, and it was said he had already fought many a verbal battle with Michael Ellison during the long debate about football at Bramall Lane.

It is probable that nobody who sat in at that historic meeting on Friday 22nd March 1889 was more delighted at the formation of Sheffield United FC than Tomlinson, who threw himself into United's cause with a dedication that made him an outstanding figure in the club's early history, and he remained in the forefront right up to his death at the age of 70 in 1925.

The following advertisement appeared in the local newspapers on the morning after the meeting:

SHEFFIELD UNITED CRICKET CLUB

**The Committee have decided to form a
FOOTBALL CLUB**
for next season for Bramall Lane Ground.
**Professionals may send testimonials
and particulars on or before March
30th to**

**Mr J.B. Wostinholm,
10 Norfolk Row.**

There was a suggestion that support might be forthcoming from some of the other local clubs, but only Sheffield FC responded to their circular and, in the end, they kept their distance. In the following August, however, they did participate in a joint practice match (an event that received no advance publicity and was supposed to be secret) at the Sandygate ground of the Hallam club.

Wednesday, of course, were not pleased by United's decision, and some of the older club's members saw the rival organisation as a threat to their existence. There were many who did not believe there was room for two professional clubs in the town, and some claimed United had acted in spite because Wednesday had chosen to go it alone. Noting that United's leaders included several people prominent in the local FA, some even suggested United's formation was some kind of organised reprisal aimed at forcing Wednesday back into the fold.

Stokes and Tomlinson remained connected with the Heeley club, who, like Owlerton, had formally declined to risk losing their identities by linking with United; but it was evident that these smaller clubs would soon lose the status they had enjoyed for many years. Significantly, the likes of Heeley and Sheffield Albion, two of the most famous early names in the sport, have long since disappeared without trace.

At Bramall Lane, the initial plan was to run a team combining the best local amateurs and some leading professionals, but it didn't work out like that. In fact the response to their first advertisement was surprisingly poor. In May, after the search had been widened, they were able to

announce that the players already recruited included: Walter Hobson (Owlerton), Bill Madin (Staveley), S. Humberstone (Sheffield), Charles Howlett (Gainsborough), A. Jackson (Heeley), W. Robertson (Dundee), Dug Galbraith (Dundee), A. Deakin (Edinburgh), H.C. Scotter (Norwich), J. Arnott (Glasgow Clyde) and N. Ross (Glasgow Clyde). Later they recruited the Wednesday veterans Jack Hudson (United's first captain) and Billy Mosforth, Scots Bob Gordon and Donald Fraser, Ecclesfielder Ned Stringer, and S. Mack from Gainsborough.

When United played their first official match, against Notts Rangers of the Midland League at Meadow Lane, Nottingham, on Saturday 7th September 1889, the team was: Howlett; Gordon, Stringer; Mack, Fraser, Hudson; Madin, Galbraith, Robertson, Duncan, Mosforth. Unfortunately, they arrived late and never really got going, losing 4–1. Robertson, who had the honour of scoring United's first goal, subsequently raised his tally to 20, including two hat-tricks, as United won 25 of the 56 games they played in their first season. He also had the dubious privilege of being the first United man to be sent off.

United played their first game in Sheffield with a 2–1 defeat of Heeley at Sheaf House a week after the Nottingham trip, but their first appearance at Bramall Lane in late September saw them beaten 4–0 by Birmingham St George's. However, they enjoyed a splendid start to their FA Cup history, with a 6–1 victory at Scarborough, and, dismissing Heeley, Sheffield FC and Rotherham Town, they reached the first round proper, in which they beat Burnley of the Football League. Inevitably, perhaps, Robertson got one of the goals, but United had fortune on their side when Galbraith, as he admitted later, handled a shot from a Burnley forward on the line—escaping with a free-kick which was cleared. In those days there was no such thing as a penalty kick!

After that game, Charlie Howlett, the goalkeeper who played in spectacles, was carried shoulder-high from the field by delighted Unitedites, but he had a less rewarding experience at the next stage. United accepted £40 to switch the second-round tie to Bolton, where, in the muddy goalmouth, poor old Howlett

lost his glasses as his team crashed to a 13–0 defeat.

They also suffered heavy setbacks at home to Everton (1–10) and at Staveley, Newton Heath and Grimsby, but reached the final of the Sheffield Challenge Cup (losing to Rotherham Town in a replay) and the semi-final of the Wharncliffe Charity Cup (knocked out by a Staveley side in which the star was a certain Ernest Needham).

In that first season, with Wednesday reaching the FA Cup final and lifting the championship of the new Alliance, United were often cast in the role of the outsiders, but they were determined to make an impact in the town. The local paper was amused when the club 'tried two men from

This 1887 picture of the Ecclesfield team which enjoyed a remarkable run in the FA Cup includes several players later synonymous with Sheffield United, notably Arthur Watson, Rab Howell and Ned Stringer; and the presence of a Hemmingfield and a Woolhouse confirms the village also supplied some Wednesday men. The player on the left of the front row is Tom Hulley, a relative of 1990s Owls director, Geoff Hulley.

north of the border who rejoiced in the *noms de plume* of "Jones" and "Smith" . . . just imagine two Scotsmen with such names!'; but they were impressed when United signed three Ecclesfield-based players (Rab Howell, Arthur Watson and Mick Whitham) all destined to become big favourites.

All that was missing from the Sheffield football calendar was a United–Wednesday fixture. Officials denied this was due to ill-feeling, but it was evident in little niggles, such as

when United, learning that season tickets in 1890–91 at Olive Grove were being priced at 7s 6d, said theirs would cost five shillings—and promised to charge only 3d admission at matches that clashed with Wednesday's home games where the cost was 6d.

However, they agreed to meet in 1890 in the week before Christmas, and that first Sheffield derby was the town's most eagerly-awaited football match yet.

The strong links between Ecclesfield and Sheffield United were never better illustrated than by the Johnson family. W.H. 'Old Harry' Johnson (centre) served the Blades for over 40 years as player and assistant trainer from the 1890s; his elder son Harry (right) was the club's record scorer in the 1920s, and younger son Tom (left) captained the team in the late 1930s.

The First Sheffield Derbies

WEDNESDAY insisted that the first Sheffield derby should be played at Olive Grove. Finally, in 1890, United agreed and the game was fixed for Monday 15th December, at the start of what was known in the town as 'bull week' because it was when local workers put in as many hours as possible to ensure a bumper pay packet to carry them through the Christmas holiday.

'Saint' Monday was not just a customary 'rest' day in Sheffield's working week, but one synonymous with merriment and a boozy time for the cutlers in their favourite pubs. On this occasion the prospect of a long-awaited clash between the town's premier clubs added to the fun. Around 10,000 enthusiasts converged on the Wednesday ground, and long before the start of the match old Billy Whitham the scorecard seller, already a legendary figure on Yorkshire cricket grounds, was busy disposing of team sheets and exchanging banter with the crowd.

Wednesday's supporters no doubt felt their favourites could have chosen a better time to face their greatest rivals. The team stood bottom of the Alliance, where they had won just once in ten games; and their overall record showed only 4 wins in 24 matches during which they had already conceded 75 goals. United, meanwhile, boasted 13 wins and 7 defeats in 23 fixtures. One local newspaper noted:

The atmosphere was raw and slightly laden with fog and smoke. The light was bad and the outlook altogether far from agreeable. Yet everybody was in good spirits and probably not a single gloomy individual could be found among the throng. It was an interesting sight that was presented from the stand. Around the ground was a

Billy Whitham, the legendary scorecard printer, always on duty at big football matches in Sheffield in the 1890s.

black mass of fidgety humanity, relief of colour only being afforded by the partisan cards worn by many in their hats and the occasional striking of matches. At the back of the picture came the greenhouses of the Queen's Road amateur gardeners, in the rear of them being the long rows of red-brick cottages.

Wednesday included six of the men who had played in the FA Cup final, plus Fred Thompson, recovered from illness, and Harry Winterbottom now fit again. Having recruited a new centre-forward, Bob Brandon from Glasgow Clyde in October, they had managed to sign his cousin, Harry Brandon, from the same club in time for him to make his debut on this momentous afternoon. Harry was destined to remain with the club for eight years, early evidence of his talents came when he was the only Wednesday man chosen to play in the Alliance XI that faced the Football League at Olive Grove in 1891.

United's side boasted the Ecclesfield lads Mick Whitham, Rab Howell and Arthur Watson, plus newcomers W.L. Bridgewater, Bernard L. Shaw and Harry Lilley. Shaw was connected with Hallam and son of the famous John C. Shaw; Lilley, who came from Staveley, was already showing the form which,

Mick Whitham, the Ecclesfield product who, along with Harry Lilley, was United's first England international in March 1892.

within less than two years, would see him become the Lane club's first international.

Wednesday attacked the town end in a first half in which United's prettier football gave them the edge, with Robertson putting them in front after twenty minutes. Reports indicated it grew so dark in the second half that it was difficult for spectators to follow the ball; but Wednesday's sudden improvement ensured a bright finale for their followers as 'Toddles' Woolhouse headed an equaliser and then, with five minutes remaining, Winterbottom snatched the winner.

In noting the teams, it is relevant to explain that, for some reason, the Wednesday goalkeeper used the psuedonym 'Jim Smith', when his real name was Jim Clarke, his full-time occupation being a foreman in the crucible department at John Brown's Atlas Works. Incidentally, he was involved in establishing the firm's Atlas & Norfolk sports club, one of the most famous works organisations of its kind which was immensely popular for many years.

Wednesday: Smith; Thompson, Brayshaw; H. Brandon, Betts, Cawley; Winterbottom, Mumford, R. Brandon, Woolhouse, Hodder

United: *Howlett; Lilley, Whitham; Cross, Howell, Groves; Calder, Watson, Robertson, Bridgewater, Shaw*

Referee: *J.C. Clegg*

Umpires: *W.E. Clegg, W. Liddell*

The return game, played at Bramall Lane (the pitch was on the pavilion side of the ground) on Monday 12th January 1891, attracted a 14,000 crowd who saw United win 3–2 after Billy Ingram and Bob Brandon had given Wednesday a 2–0 lead before the game had been in progress 25 minutes. Watson pulled one back, and Howell equalised with a long shot before, a few minutes from the end, Calder grabbed the winner from a position that the *Sheffield Telegraph* reporter described as 'a barefaced infringement of the off-side rule'!

A few days after this game, the Sheffield clubs were involved in home FA Cup matches, but while Wednesday crushed Halliwell 12–0, United slumped to a 9–1 defeat against Notts County. United's consolation was they had the bigger crowd—which may have been partly due to the fact that they had cut their match-day admission charges to half of Wednesday's rates. A price war was being fought between the clubs that season, for while Wednesday's season tickets were priced at 7s 6d (37½p) United reduced theirs to five shillings (25p).

However, the real lesson that United took to heart from that heavy FA Cup defeat was the need to continue to strengthen the team. Later that same season, they obtained from Preston a trio of players—Bill Hendry, Jack Drummond and Sammy Dobson—their arrival served to emphasise how seriously Bramall Lane's top brass were taking their bid to match and better their local rivals.

Billy Hendry — a major influence as United's captain in the early 1890s, and a key figure in Needham's early progress at Bramall Lane.

The Preston deal came about after Charles Stokes, on holiday and staying in a Southport hotel, overheard a remark made by North End's famous boss, Major William Suddell, who indicated that certain players might be available for transfer. When Stokes approached Suddell, the Preston man denied the story, but later sent for United's football chairman, who opened negotiations and hurried back to Sheffield to get the approval of his colleagues. Hendry and Drummond proved outstanding captures, though Dobson's hopes of sustained success were hampered by injury problems.

United had finished fifth in the Midland League in that same 1890–91 campaign in which Wednesday never got off the bottom rung of the Alliance. However, when they applied to join their neighbours in the higher grade they received a firm rejection—Stokes and his colleagues were not entirely convinced by Wednesday's denial that they had influenced the decision.

Snubbed by the Alliance, United instead joined the Northern League in 1891–92 and finished a very creditable third, seven points behind champions Middlesbrough Ironopolis. In addition to the trio from Preston, their team now included three other men who made a big impact: defender Bob Cain and centre-forward Harry Hammond, two ex-Evertonians, and the third perhaps the most famous player in the club's early history, Ernest Needham, a teenager who had already built a notable reputation at Staveley. The bustling Hammond was leading marksman in his first term.

The rivalry between the Sheffield clubs was illustrated when they both reached the final of the Wharncliffe Charity Cup in 1892. These games had always been played at Bramall Lane, but of course, with United in the final, the ground could not be considered a neutral venue. When Wednesday refused to play them there, the local FA decided the only solution was to cancel the tie.

Wednesday may have been influenced by the fact that, in the previous October, they had gone to Bramall Lane and been crushed 5–0 by United, for whom Hammond and Dobson both scored doubles after Tom Brandon, the recruit from Blackburn Rovers, had headed into his own net. This was the occasion when United's triumph prompted the following 'funeral card' to circulate in the town:

> In Loving Remembrance of
> the
> **SHEFFIELD WEDNESDAY FOOTBALL TEAM**
> who were safely put to rest on Monday October 26th
> at Bramall Lane
> Poor old Wednesday were fairly done,
> When United beat them five to none;
> Although they lost, they did their best,
> So let them quietly take their rest.
> (Friends of the above club kindly accept this
> intimation).

It is said that this defeat so stunned Wednesday officials that they promptly called an emergency meeting, and forthwith all professionals were instructed to attend regular training sessions—the first to be organised on a formal basis in the club's history. The extra work paid off, for when the return derby was played at Olive Grove some three weeks later Wednesday won 4–1, with Woolhouse and a new Wednesday idol, Fred Spiksley, each scoring twice.

Naturally, Wednesdayites were keen to respond with their own 'funeral cards' and the following lines were soon being broadcast throughout the town:

> In pitiful remembrance of
> Our idols, the
> **SHEFFIELD UNITED FOOTBALL TEAM**
> who departed their football life,
> Struggling to the end,
> At Olive Grove on Monday November 16th 1891.
> When United died, they struggled hard
> Enough to live a brighter and longer life;
> Do as they would, they could not ward
> Neat kicks by Wednesday, and thus the strife
> Ended, thus closed famous United's reign;
> Sheffield now mourns their death the more,
> Dying as they did—ne'er to rise again
> And kick for fame at Wednesday's door.
> Yes, United have lost four to one.

The teams in the November game were:

Wednesday: *Smith; Darroch, Mumford; Hill, Betts (capt.), McConachie; Gemmill, R.N. Brown, Thompson, Woolhouse, Spiksley*

United: *Howlett; Lilley, Cain; Whitham, Hendry (capt.), Howell; Drummond, Watson, Hammond, Dobson, Needham*

Wednesday finished fourth in the Alliance that year, and perhaps it was no surprise that they considered they had a stronger case for admission to the Football League than their neighbours. Previous applications had failed, but there were hints that they might succeed this time, for Blackburn's anger at the alleged poaching of Tom Brandon had abated and they had withdrawn their request that no League club should have anything to do with the Sheffielders. In the early spring of 1892 Wednesday, determined to be as well prepared as possible, announced plans for extensive improvements at Olive Grove.

They intended to level the playing area, which meant raising the pitch (which was being increased to maximum dimensions) by as much as six feet on the railway side. New drainage was envisaged, and the centrepiece of the redevelopment was an impressive new stand which would contain dressing rooms, baths and, at the rear, a refreshment saloon.

United, of course, believed they were candidates with as much chance of success as their rivals, and, in the early days of May 1892, all the talk among sportsmen in the town was of the forthcoming Football League meeting and the Sheffield clubs' hopes of finally joining the élite.

Ernest Needham — a 'Prince of Half-backs' and a great captain in United's Victorian heyday.

Ernest Needham:The Making of a Lane Legend

ERNEST Needham arrived at Bramall Lane at the age of 18 in the summer of 1891. He was hailed as one of the most exciting young players in the Sheffield and North Derbyshire region, having already spent two years in Staveley's Midland League side and gained his first representative honour with the Sheffield Association team at the age of 16 after only a handful of senior appearances.

Off the field, he did not look anything special: slightly-built, modest and so quiet and reserved, yet so obviously an athlete with that lithe figure, natural balance and eyes that hinted at awareness, alertness and intelligence beyond his years. There was, too, a strong hint of physical toughness borne of experience in a tough school in which he had done so well that Staveley made him their youngest-ever captain.

Needham, who was destined to become Sheffield's most-capped player in his era and a local folk hero with a national reputation as 'The Prince of Half-Backs', had always excelled against United, but the club's officials did not expect to get him as easily as they did. In this they were fortunate that Harry Lilley, the former Staveley defender, knew the youngster and was respected by him. He did not take too much persuading to move to Bramall Lane on a winter-only wage of thirty shillings (£1.50) a week.

Needham did not want to leave home, and in seeking a club where he might get the chance to develop he could not have chosen a better moment to join United. They had confirmed their ambition with the recruitment of several men who brought a thoroughly professional touch to the dressing room—and who would foster the teenager's talent. One player in particular, Bill Hendry, was destined to prove a major influence and happily slipped into the role of Needham's mentor.

In fact, Hendry was less than four years older than Needham, but the difference in experience was vast. The Scot, who had begun with Dundee Wanderers, had served such a tough apprenticeship with West Brom and Stoke that he had hurried back north of the border and might have been lost to the English game but for the persistence of Major Suddell in persuading him to try again at Preston, where he had matured into a highly-respected defender.

Hendry was promptly installed as captain when he joined United six or seven months ahead of Needham, and by the time the youngster arrived was almost filling the role of player-manager. Needham quickly responded to his influence, and the pair were practically inseparable for the next five years. The present skipper not only groomed his successor at club level but instilled the wisdom and knowhow that earned the Staveley product such respect that he was to captain England—a rare honour for a professional in those days.

The other major influence on Needham was George Waller, the Pitsmoor player who had helped Wednesday win the Alliance and reach the FA Cup final in 1890. He had subsequently thrown his lot in at Bramall Lane because he was offered professional terms as both a cricketer and footballer following the formation of a United Cricket Club. He began as a player, but it was his appointment as trainer in 1893 that proved a turning point for him—and the club.

In those days the management of the team was left to the trainer and the captain, with perhaps some support from a director who had the ability to mix with the players. Tom Bott was the director who fitted the bill, but the key figure was Waller. His friendly disposition, quiet manner and deep wealth of experience and wisdom instilled confidence and camaraderie into a dressing room where such as Arthur Watson, Mick Whitham, and perhaps Bob Cain, supplemented the efforts of Hendry and Waller to complete the football education of Ernest Needham.

Needham was to make some 550 senior appearances for United and help them to a League Championship and two FA Cup final triumphs, his strength was not so much any tactical awareness as an ability to lead by example. His name was synonymous with one of the smallest half-back lines United ever had (Howell–Morren–Needham, all under 5ft 6ins tall), but he filled almost every position on the field. His adaptability often proved crucial to the team's

success; all the more so in that he invariably excelled in whatever role he filled.

He earned the nickname 'Nudger' because, despite his lack of inches and pounds, he seldom failed to win the ball in a challenge, even against much bigger and stronger men; and his speed in possession and his perceptive passing marked him out as a man with a rare combination of talents. Someone once said he never seemed to actually look at the ball, yet never lost control and always knew exactly when and where to put it to give a colleague the initiative. Indeed, he had that capacity to bring out the best in team-mates and could help a player exploit his strengths.

Because of his reputation, he tended to get more than a fair share of rough treatment, but somehow he could never be provoked into retaliation. In his later years, however (and he played until he was nearly 40), he did admit to occasionally feeling dismay that youngsters did not always show respect for his advancing years. In truth, he knew he would have done exactly the same when he was a lad!

He was fond of what today we would call the long-ball game, especially in cup-ties, and he would often say: 'It's no use fiddling with the ball in the middle of the field, you've got to take the quickest route to goal and have a pot!' He admired skill but was impatient with 'fancy dans' whose abilities were seldom matched by achievement. He believed that everybody in a team had to pull his weight.

His favourite cry in his heyday was 'Leave it to me!' as if he believed it was his sole responsibility to take control, and it was when the chips were down and the outlook at its bleakest that he so often produced the kind of run that would turn a game. There was one semi-final during that memorable series of cup successes when United looked set for defeat, and Needham, abandoning the defensive formation which was the basis of the team's achievement, ordered everyone to throw everything into attack. 'We have nothing to lose: if they score again, we'll be no worse off, but one last effort might save the day,' he said. The philosophy paid a dividend and United pulled level and then went on to win the replay.

It was in 1893, towards the end of United's first term in the Football League and when they were pushing for promotion from the Second Division, that Needham gained the first of his ten Football League caps, and a year later came the first of his sixteen England appearances: two milestones that no doubt gave Hendry particular satisfaction.

It was Hendry's misfortune that, when Needham succeeded him as skipper, it was because injury had curtailed the Scot's Bramall Lane career. Though he went on to play at Bury, Brighton and Shrewsbury,

Hendry did not again enjoy the success he had known in Sheffield, and, sadly, he died in May 1901 when he was only 32.

Needham, who played on in the First Division until 1910, had two benefits in his time with United, but he did not do as well out of them as might have been expected. However, when receipts from his benefit match with the Corinthians in 1898 were barely £90, it was arranged for him also to receive one-fifth of the proceeds from the match with Aston Villa a month later. In 1907 the Stoke fixture chosen for the beneficiary was hit by bad weather and only 9,053 turned up, but in this instance there was no suggestion of him getting another bonus.

The old hero was grateful simply to be still part of the scene, and he did not formally hang up his boots until around 1912 after a couple of years in the reserves—a period, incidentally, during which he brought a certain Billy Gillespie to the attention of the directors. He remained connected with United, performing scouting duties, right up to his death in 1936— two years after the First Division status he had helped to clinch was surrendered ending a remarkable run of forty continuous years at the top.

Fred Spiksley — as immaculate in his dress off the field as he was on it

Fred Spiksley: A Wednesday Wizard

SHEFFIELD football in the 1890s abounded with players of outstanding ability and there was no shortage of genuine characters on the local scene. In terms of talent and popularity however, few outshone Fred Spiksley, a slightly-built winger who, in thirteen years with Wednesday, scored around 130 goals in some 350 games. So often a match-winner, he was one of the great favourites of his day, and seven caps did not reflect the consistent high standards he achieved in his peak years.

Spiksley's secret was not so much his ball control, pace or lethal finishing as the knack of combining all three qualities. His ability to run with the ball at speed made many goals for others, and a flair for anticipating forward passes and timing his runs into the opposition's penalty area brought many goals. He would have recorded a lot more except that his quickness over short distances often deceived referees into believing he had to have been offside when the ball was played into his path.

A classic example of his speed and awareness came the first time he faced Scotland, at Richmond in April 1893. Two weeks before, he had marked his England debut with a double in the 6–0 defeat of Wales: now, all in the space of ten minutes, he scored twice and set up a third goal, the Scots protested he was offside. But the referee happened to be Charles Clegg, and nobody was more familiar with Spiksley's pace and perception. Alas, a year later, the Wednesday man had not one but two efforts disallowed in an FA Cup semi-final because the match official did not know his man.

Spiksley was a natural who complemented his instinctive skills with a tactical awareness that invariably put him one step ahead of the play. Yet, while he made a great study of the game, he remained to the end a reluctant professional, and there was always a sense in which he felt uncomfortable in the role. Not that he didn't appreciate making a few bob: when his benefit match raised £195 and the club failed to make it up to a round £200, he was not slow to express his dismay.

His son once told me that the Wednesday wizard, while he was a good mixer and indeed, acted as the team's pianist on social occasions and away trips, was seldom enthusiastic about starting out for the ground on match days. He viewed these trips as 'a descent into the bear pit' because he knew he could expect some rough treatment from opposing defenders and did not find the environment to his liking.

Spiksley never allowed his kit to be washed with that of the other players, always taking it home to be laundered; and he kept two shirts and two pairs of shorts with him on match days, so that he could change into clean gear at half-time. Moreover, the image of a man apart was highlighted by the fact that, except for his first year at the club, he never lived in Sheffield but resided in his native Gainsborough, invariably training alone other than when the team gathered for the traditional pre-season workouts and specially arranged preparations for cup-ties.

That he was allowed to go his own way highlights the esteem in which Wednesday officials regarded his unique talents, though the irony was that many recognised that football was always second on Spiksley's list of priorities. His first love was horse-racing, and the reason he quickly tired of living in Sheffield was that it did not afford him easy access to the courses on which he wished to spend his spare time.

Spiksley's earliest ambition was to be a jockey, but his father, a farmer turned engineer, paid £50 to apprentice him to a printer instead. He had only been in the job six months when he walked out after his boss refused him half a day's leave to

Wednesday 1891–92 at the start of the Spiksley era.
Back row: Bill Muscroft (trainer), H. Vessey (committee), Tom Brandon, Jim Smith, Jock Darroch, John Holmes (President).
Middle row: Harry Brandon, Arthur 'Clinks' Mumford, George Thompson, Tom Cawley, Fred Spiksley.
Front row: Duncan Gemmell, Billy Betts, Richardson. Note: Smith was the goalkeeper's pseudonynm, his real name was Clarke.

attend Lincoln races. It took some months to negotiate a new apprenticeship at the *Gainsborough News*, and perhaps the chance to play football with the local Trinity, a Midland League side, helped him recognise the wisdom of fulfilling the terms of his indentures before going absent without leave again.

He had just finished serving his time when he joined Wednesday, his arrival at Olive Grove in the spring of 1891 coming about by sheer chance. Having helped Gainsborough Trinity win the Midland League title, his displays had prompted Accrington to offer him terms. It was after a visit to the Lancashire town to discuss the move that he found himself stranded in Sheffield when he missed his rail connection to Retford. He booked into the Maunch Hotel for the night, and popped down to the Bull and Mouth pub in Waingate for a drink.

Fred Thompson, the Wednesday player, happened to be in the bar, and when he learned that Spiksley was set to accept Accrington's offer of £2.10s (£2.50) a week he persuaded him to meet John Holmes and Arthur Dickinson the following morning. The upshot was that Wednesday came up with a deal that gave the winger £3 a week plus a berth in the *Sheffield Telegraph* composing room.

Spiksley was to be engaged by the newspaper in the close-season but, as that was quickly found to conflict with his race-going (which he invariably turned to profit anyway), he soon gave up the position, and after a successful first season with Wednesday he managed to persuade the club to let him live in Gainsborough—even agreeing to pay his own travelling expenses to away matches. It was suggested that, following a health scare which had the directors worried, Spiksley argued the wide-open spaces of the Lincolnshire countryside would be more beneficial than the smoke of Sheffield!

He kept fit with running and swimming, and though Wednesday were not keen he even managed to pursue an enthusiasm for ice-skating—once bringing to Olive Grove a trophy he had won in a championship in Lincoln. He ensured the arrangement worked, and as he invariably turned on the style on the field, the club had no complaints.

Of course, there were times when travelling proved irksome, but it produced a few humorous episodes too. There was one occasion when the team was delayed on the journey from an away game and Spiksley, having managed to get from Sheffield to Retford, discovered the last train to Gainsborough had gone. Rather than spend the night in the waiting room, he chose to walk the ten miles or so home—and decided the quickest route was along the railway track. Everything went well until he reached a tunnel. Halfway through it, he heard a train approaching and dived into an inlet just in the nick of time. He arrived at the family house as dawn was breaking, hammered on the door, and heard his father open an upstairs window and peer out. 'Hey up, mother,' the old man called into the bedroom, 'Have you ordered a chimney sweep? There's a bloke down here who's covered in soot from head to toe!'

The highlight of Spiksley's Wednesday career was undoubtedly the part he played in the FA Cup triumph of 1896, especially the brilliant double which sealed victory in the final; but many of the 100 goals he scored in the Olive Grove era were memorable. A classic example came in the 1894 FA Cup quarter-final with Aston Villa when he turned certain defeat into a famous victory, scoring a superb 88th-minute equaliser and then setting up Woolhouse's extra-time winner after a dazzling solo run. In 1893 he scored twice in the last two minutes after Wednesday trailed 2–0 to Derby, and then went on to hit the winner in extra-time. There was another famous occasion when a Wednesday supporter was so thrilled with a Spiksley treble that he went out and bought his hero a bowler hat!

A Spiksley characteristic was his pluck. He once played with two broken ribs (and scored the winner!) in a cup game with Burnley. Despite a run of injuries in the later stages of his career, his form on his last great comeback in 1902–1903 brought a final representative honour, his first for five years; he celebrated with a treble in the Football League's defeat of the Scottish League in Glasgow. More significantly, just before bowing out from the first team he helped Wednesday clinch their first League Championship—and the medal that he had feared was destined to elude him.

Spiksley was 33 when he quit the top grade, concluding his playing days at Glossop and Southend. It was no surprise that his stay with Glossop was brief, for he refused to live there because it was inconvenient for his racing. When he joined Southend, they were happy to let him live in London, and it was while resident in the south that his 'outside interests' cost him the chance of becoming manager of Watford.

He answered an advertisement in the *Athletic News*, and Watford, impressed by the ex-Wednesday man at the interview, asked the Sheffield club's secretary, Arthur Dickinson, about Spiksley. 'I can't imagine a better judge of a footballer,' said Dickinson, 'and if you can get him to give up racing you'll have an excellent manager.' Told of this comment and asked for his thoughts, Spiksley said: 'I'd like this position, but what I do in my private life is no business of my employers. I'm not prepared to forfeit my racing, and if you wish me to do so I'll say goodbye right now gentlemen!'

Spiksley guested briefly in Fred Karno's Football Sketch, which toured the music halls. He was already known to the famous comedian when he learned of Karno's search for professionals to appear in the show, he suggested that the old Aston Villa stars, James Crabtree and Charlie Athersmith, should be recruited. The trio proved successful and Spiksley, who earned £7.10s (£7.50) a week, found the theatrical experience illuminating. All the same, he was dismayed that time passed and no club seemed interested in engaging him as a manager or coach.

Thus he broke new ground in becoming one of the first English footballers to coach abroad, and over the next twenty years he worked in Sweden, Germany, Mexico, Switzerland and Spain, with a brief spell at Fulham his only link with the game at home. He had the misfortune to be in Germany when the Great War broke out in 1914, but managed to escape and, after a short stay in America, returned to Sheffield to work in munitions. He resumed his foreign coaching in Mexico, where, because of his knowledge of languages, he was able to supplement his income with a spell in charge of the mailing department in the Canadian Bank of Montreal in Mexico City!

When he finally quit football at the age of 58 in 1928, he returned to England and, in the last twenty years of his life, devoted himself to the sport that had always given him the most pleasure. He remained remarkably fit and active, so much so that, at turned 70, he won several professional sprints as 'Fred Hayward'; but nothing compared with a day at the races, and appropriately

perhaps, his death in July 1948 occurred while he was attending the big meeting at Goodwood. He had just placed a bet on Aurelia and when he rejoined his friends said 'I do feel bad.' He sat down . . . and died, never knowing that he had backed the winner of the Goodwood Stakes.

When news of his death reached Sheffield, there were only a few people still around who could claim to have seen him in his heyday, but as the local newspapers noted, there was plenty of evidence in the record books that Fred Spiksley had a special place in Sheffield football history: an entertainer who had helped Wednesday win both the League and the Cup . . . and always been first past the post in the affections of Olive Grove regulars.

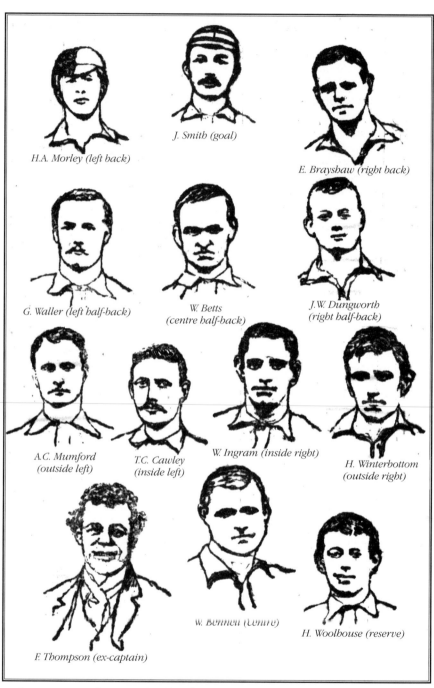

H.A. Morley (left back)

J. Smith (goal)

E. Brayshaw (right back)

G. Waller (left half-back)

W. Betts
(centre half-back)

J.W. Dungworth
(right half-back)

A.C. Mumford
(outside left)

T.C. Cawley
(inside left)

W. Ingram (inside right)

H. Winterbottom
(outside right)

F. Thompson (ex-captain)

W. Bonnen (centre)

H. Woolhouse (reserve)

Contemporary drawing of Wednesday's 1890 team.

Into the Football League 1892–1893

FRIDAY the 13th of May 1892 ranks among the major dates in Sheffield soccer history. It was the day Wednesday and United finally gained election to the Football League. When the news reached the town from the League's annual meeting in Sunderland, there were impromptu celebrations in local sporting circles; though, in truth, United's delight was tempered by the disappointment that they were only in the new Second Division while Wednesday had gone straight into the enlarged First Division.

The Football League, having been increased from twelve to fourteen clubs in 1891, now doubled in size and absorbed the majority of the members of the Football Alliance. Wednesday (ten votes) topped the poll at the election (which in part reflected the efforts and influence of John Holmes, the club president) and, with Nottingham Forest and Newton Heath (later Manchester United), went into the upper grade. United's five votes left them in a group that included the likes of Northwich Victoria, Burton Swifts, Bootle and Darwen, as well as Ardwick (later Manchester City), Small Heath (later Birmingham City), Port Vale, Grimsby, Lincoln, Crewe and Walsall Town Swifts.

United felt they had been condemned as the poor relations, and at Bramall Lane they consoled themselves by insisting they would be up with their Olive Grove rivals within a year—a prediction they fulfilled by clinching promotion at their first attempt after finishing second in the table and winning their Test match.

In the first six years after the creation of two divisions, the League used end-of-season Test matches to decide promotion and relegation, with the bottom three clubs in the higher grade pitted against the top trio in the lower section. As we have discovered in modern times with the play-offs, the system is not entirely just, and luck in the pairings invariably influences the outcome. But at least these days the club finishing top gains automatic promotion. In 1892–93, Small Heath pipped United to the Second Division title, but then fell to Newton Heath in a replay of their Test match (ironically at Bramall Lane), while the Sheffielders defeated Accrington at Nottingham. (Incidentally, it is often forgotten now that, had Wednesday not won their final game of the season, they too would have been involved in a Test match. That fate instead befell Notts County, who were subsequently condemned to relegation.)

Sheffield's first Football League campaign was always going to be special, but, as it unfolded and Wednesday and United began to experience sharply-contrasting fortunes, notably in the second half of the season, it made for an even more exciting and intriguing phase than anyone had anticipated.

The season began on a bright note, with Wednesday winning 1 0 at Notts County and United defeating Lincoln City 4–2 at Bramall Lane. Remarkably, both matches kicked off late: problems with a 13,000 crowd at Nottingham (including 2,000 from Sheffield) delayed the start for twenty minutes, but the 4,000 spectators at United's game were kept waiting thirty-five minutes simply because Lincoln could not be bothered to take the trouble to get to the ground on time.

Wednesday's line-up on that first Saturday in September included two new forwards, Alec Brady and Harry Davis, who were to make a big impact throughout what remained of the Olive Grove era. A significant change from the team that had started the previous campaign was in goal, where Jim Smith had been succeeded by Bill Allan, who was to be a fixture in the side until the mid-1890s.

Brady, regarded as one of the cleverest inside-forwards of the period, had helped Everton lift the League title in 1891 and had been in Celtic's 1892 Scottish Cup-winning side. The success of his partnership with Spiksley made him a big favourite at Olive Grove—all the more so in that, in his first season, he helped the winger top Wednesday's scoring charts with eighteen goals and gain the first of his England caps.

An amusing tale is told about Brady's arrival. He was recruited by Arthur Dickinson on one of the Wednesday secretary's frequent scouting missions in Scotland, and at the same time Jack 'The Rooter'

Madden, an outstanding centre-forward, was also persuaded to try his luck in Sheffield. Celtic were so upset at the prospect of losing the pair that they sent a Roman Catholic priest south to 'spirit' them home, and Wednesday, hearing of this, sent the players into hiding. Alas, the holy man found Madden, who was to figure in two more Scottish Cup finals before he again tried English football—at Tottenham.

At least Brady remained. As well as his successful link-up with Spiksley, in that first term he helped Arthur Rowan (who scored twelve goals) and Davis make an early impact. Davis, incidentally, might never have joined Wednesday if his club, Birmingham St George's, had not been in deep financial distress. They had almost failed to fulfil a fixture at Olive Grove at the end of the previous season, and Wednesday had to wire them their travelling expenses in advance. When they arrived and explained their problems, it was suggested these might be eased by the sale of Davis!

Allan was the character of the team, known as 'William the Silent' because he so seldom had anything to say. He was signed in December 1891 after Smith was injured, and, on the eve of his debut, it had been discovered the club had no boots big enough to fit him. Dickinson, ever resourceful, located a local cobbler prepared to stay up all night to make a special pair thus enabling a notable career to be launched!

On paper, Wednesday looked to have a team capable of doing better than they did. They started well enough, and their prospects looked especially good in late October when they claimed their finest victory of the season with a 3–2 defeat of Sunderland after twice being behind. This was the time of Sunderland's famous 'team of all talents': they had won the League in the previous season and were on their way to repeating the feat. Indeed, they arrived in Sheffield having dropped only one point in their first eight games, and had scored 38 goals while conceding only 8. Their visit attracted a record 20,000 crowd to Olive Grove.

Over the Christmas period, Wednesday won 5–1 at Newton Heath and crushed West Brom 6–0 at home. They then suffered an astonishing slump, losing seven games on the trot and collecting just one point from ten matches. This left them facing their last game, at home to Notts County, needing a win to avoid having to play in the Test matches. In the event, despite falling behind, they won 3–2, and their hero was skipper Tom Brandon—coincidentally the man who had begun the season by scoring the club's first League goal (and who was now about to return to Blackburn Rovers).

Wednesday's decline in the second half of the season may have been partly due to FA Cup exploits which took them to the quarter-finals and involved a succession of the kind of protests that were threatening to turn the competition into a farce. In fact, it was one of the cases involving the Sheffield club that prompted the Football Association to revise their approach to the whole unsavoury business.

In the first-round tie at Olive Grove in January 1893, Wednesday looked doomed when, with barely three minutes left, they trailed 2–0 to Derby County. As glum-faced supporters streamed from the ground, Spiksley suddenly produced two moments of magic to take the game into extra-time. Then, seven minutes from the end, the wing-wizard completed his hat-trick and Wednesday were through . . . or so they thought.

Derby promptly protested that Brady was ineligible, and the FA ordered a replay at Derby, where the home side won 1–0. Now Wednesday lodged a protest (on the grounds that a young County man called Steve Bloomer had played in an unauthorised competition) which was upheld. When Wednesday won the third duel 4–2 at Olive Grove, Derby's attempts to succeed with yet another protest met with failure.

Those were the days when it sometimes seemed as if the actual ties were incidental to the the detective work done in advance in the hope of getting the opposition disqualified by producing evidence of ineligibility or illegal practices. When Wednesday reached the second round, Burnley, their opponents, lodged a protest which thankfully was dismissed, and no doubt the club's officials felt that justice was done when the visitors from Lancashire were defeated 1–0 thanks to another brilliant piece of finishing by Spiksley.

In fact, this was a game in which Fred's pluck as much as his skill was highlighted. Early on, the winger was involved in a terrific collision with a Burnley defender and he was carried off. He lay in the dressing room in great pain and it seemed unlikely he would be fit to return, but John Holmes, the Wednesday president, asked him to give the team five or ten minutes. He trudged back, scored a goal, and immediately retired. When he got home to Gainsborough, he visited a hospital and was told his discomfort was hardly surprising: 'Mr Spiksley,' said the doctor, 'You've got two broken ribs!'

United had their heroes, too: notably Bill Hendry (who played on against Burton despite a dislocated elbow); Ernest Needham (chaired off after scoring a stunning winner against Ardwick); and those prolific marksmen, Harry Hammond and Jack Drummond.

At Bramall Lane they felt they had built a side capable of matching the best, and a team that had strength and talent in every department was expected to fare reasonably well in the 'inferior' Second Division. They did not lose a game at home and the defeats they suffered on their travels all came in their first three away games—the last being at Darwen, where, after goalkeeper Lilley was injured, Mick Whitham deputised in goal.

Sheffield United circa 1894, but members of the triumphant promotion side of 1892–93 were still around, including prolific marksman Harry Hammond.
Back row: George Waller (trainer), Mick Whitham, Bill Foulke, Docherty, Bob Cain.
Middle row: Yates, Harry Hammond, Ernest Needham, Hill, Arthur Watson.
Front row: Harry Thickett, Rab Howell.

It was after the Darwen setback that, rattled by critics who claimed they were not good enough to reach the top, United embarked on a fifteen-match unbeaten run in which they dropped only two points and made qualification for a Test match place a formality. The sequence started on 26th November with an 8–3 defeat of Bootle in which Hammond, who had scored a hat-trick in the opening-day victory over Lincoln, bagged five. Two weeks later, on 10th December, more history was made as United romped to their first away win of the season—a 10–0 crushing of Burslem Port Vale on a snowy day in the Potteries.

This remains the biggest away victory in League history. Hammond scored four, Watson and Davies each notched a double, and Drummond and Wallace were the other marksmen. Snow was still falling at the start of a first half in which, despite facing a strong wind, United established a 5–0 lead after hitting three in the first six minutes. At 7–0 an old Vale player, plainly the worse for a prolonged spell in a local alehouse, ran onto the pitch to show the home men how to play. He had to be ejected three times (on the third occasion United skipper Hendry picked him up and dumped him on a pile of snow!) before he stopped interrupting the game.

Hammond, late of Everton, had an outstanding season and claimed 32 goals, 19 of which came in the Football League. At 5ft 6½ins he was on the small side, but, thick-set and as tough as they come, he was the scourge of goalkeepers, against whom he never hesitated to use every ounce of his 11st 9lb. His only honour was a

place in the Football League XI against the Irish League in 1894, but a record of 57 goals in 107 League games (in all senior matches for United he scored some 140 goals between 1891 and 1896) sealed his popularity with Bramall Lane regulars.

He was not, however, a favourite on away grounds. There was a famous occasion towards the end of the 1892–93 season when, during a 4–0 victory at Crewe, he was sent off for kicking an opponent and the crowd invaded the pitch determined not to allow play to resume until they had dealt with the United forward. Hammond, however, made a dash for it, scaled a wall at one end of the ground and disappeared. He was not seen again until he turned up on Crewe railway station, where he greeted the United party still wearing his football kit—and was most concerned that his colleagues had remembered to rescue his street clothes!

United and Small Heath both finished the season with nine successive victories, but United were not entirely dismayed when the Birmingham side pipped them into top place by a point, because they fancied that the pairing with Accrington in the Test match offered them a better chance of success than a date with Newton Heath.

Saturday the 22nd of April was fine and sunny, and there was some disappointment that the attendance at Nottingham was barely 6,000. The truth was that Accrington did not boast a big following, and their followers were heavily outnumbered by Sheffield supporters. In fact, United were probably fortunate still to be on level terms at half-time, for

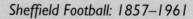

the Lancastrians missed a number of good chances. However, eight minutes after the interval, the game was settled in one moment of sheer drama and brilliance when Jack Drummond, seizing on Hodge's hesitancy, gained possession and embarked on a dazzling forty-yard run in which he waltzed past two defenders before shooting with power and precision beyond the reach of Mason, the Accrington goalkeeper. It was Drummond's fourteenth goal of the season, and Ernest Needham always said it was the best he ever saw scored in his entire career. It was certainly the most important of the 36 the former Preston man claimed in his three years at Bramall Lane.

Defeat in this match had unfortunate implications for Accrington, for they decided they could not generate sufficient income to survive as a Second Division club, and so

resigned from the Football League and moved into the Lancashire League. This club eventually folded and was ultimately superseded by Accrington Stanley, who did not make their way into the Football League until 1921 and survived only until 1962.

United supporters no doubt sympathised with Accrington and, indeed, with Small Heath when they missed the promotion boat. In truth, though, they were more concerned for their own club; and their next goals were to finish above Wednesday in the First Division and, if possible, beat them to the League Championship!

1892–1893
It will be of interest to compare the records of the Shefield clubs (Wednesday in Division One, United in Division Two) in their first season in the Football League (see opposite).

Wednesday

Sep	3	Notts C. (a)	1–0
	10	Accrington (h)	5–2
	12	Preston (a)	1–4
	17	Bolton (a)	0–1
	24	Accrington (a)	2–4
	26		
Oct	1	Burnley (h)	2–0
	3	Forest (h)	2–2
	15	Blackburn (a)	2–0
	22	Newton H. (h)	1–0
	29	Sunderland (h)	3–2
Nov	5	Bolton (h)	4–2
	19	Blackburn (h)	0–3
	26	Everton (a)	5–3
Dec	1	Forest (a)	0–2
	3	Aston V. (h)	5–3
	10	Derby (h)	3–3
	17	Stoke (a)	0–2
	24	Newton H. (a)	5–1
Jan	2	West Brom (h)	6–0
	7	Aston V. (a)	1–5
	14	Preston (h)	0–5
	23		
	28	Sunderland (a)	2–4
Feb	6		
	11	Wolves (a)	0–2
	13	Everton (h)	0–2
	18		
Mar	4		
	11	Wolves (h)	0–1
	18	West Brom (a)	0–3
	25	Derby (a)	2–2
	31	Burnley (a)	0–4
Apr	1	Stoke (h)	0–1
	3	Notts C. (h)	3–2
	12		
	15		

United

Lincoln (h)	4–2
Bootle (a)	0–2
Small H. (h)	2–0
Grimsby (h)	2–0
Lincoln (a)	0–1
Darwen (h)	2–0
Darwen (a)	1–3
Bootle (h)	8–3
Small H. (a)	1–1
P. Vale (a)	10–0
P. Vale (h)	4–0
Walsall (h)	3–0
Northwich (h)	1–1
Burton S. (h)	3–1
Northwich (a)	3–1
Ardwick (a)	3–2
Crewe (h)	4–0
Ardwick (h)	2–1
Grimsby (a)	1–0
Burton S. (a)	3–0
Crewe (a)	4–0
Walsall (a)	1–0

	P	W	D	L	F	A		P	W	D	L	F	A
Home	15	8	2	5	34	28	Home	11	10	1	0	35	8
Away	15	4	1	10	21	37	Away	11	6	2	3	27	11
	30	12	3	15	55	65		22	16	3	3	62	19

Ambrose Langley—A hero of Wednesday's 1896 cup triumph who later became a manager with Hull and Huddersfield.

The Cup Comes to Yorkshire: Wednesday 1896

THE twelve years spent at Olive Grove saw Wednesday establish a reputation as famous FA Cup fighters. In nine successive seasons between 1888 and 1896 they reached the quarter-finals or beyond, though it was not a phase without trauma and disappointment (not least in the humiliating defeat in the 1890 final). After failing in the semi-finals of 1894 and 1895, they finally captured football's most coveted prize and brought it to Yorkshire for the first time in 1896.

In their initial years in the Football League it sometimes seemed their preoccupation with the quest for cup glory affected their First Division form. Overall, after narrowly escaping the Test matches in 1893, there was some gradual improvement in their League record, but there was a stage in 1893–94 when they were faring so badly that John Holmes, desperate to avert the very serious threat of relegation, offered the players an extra £50 to share if they won five of their last six League games. They achieved this and finished well clear of the danger zone. Moreover, their dramatic improvement inspired another cup run, this time taking them to a semi-final in which the circumstances of their defeat no doubt contributed to the added resolve they showed in the knockout games in the following two years.

The 1893–94 season saw the arrival of the first of several men who figured prominently in what was to prove one of the most memorable phases in the history of Wednesday and indeed, football in Sheffield. Jack Earp, lately with Nottingham Forest and Everton, and Ambrose Langley, signed from Middlesbrough Ironopolis, formed an outstanding back partnership, and both made their mark as men with notable leadership qualities.

Earp was a model skipper, an amateur of the old school: tough, fearless and uncompromising, but a man of strong principle (he refused to play on Christmas Day) with a strict code of conduct on and off the field. Langley was similar in many ways, but, at times, probably less disciplined in that he could let his determination to succeed get the better of him. He was the passionate professional, one of the hardest and most competitive players of his day: the essential football man, a player who, in his later years, revelled in the captain's role. It was no surprise that, after hanging up his boots, he became a manager.

It summed up Langley's attitude that, when he came to Sheffield, many believed Wednesday had signed a 'crock', for the Horncastle product who had learned his football at Boston and Grimsby, was plagued by knee trouble, even though he was only 23. In fact, Aston Villa were keen to sign him, but hesitated when they learned of his injury problems. To cover themselves, they insisted he should have a medical before the deal was completed; but Langley refused and the move was called off. Langley was determined Wednesday would not regret what some regarded as a gamble, and, in over 300 games, proved his point and earned a place among the club's genuine giants.

Fortune smiled on Wednesday on the day Earp and Langley made their Cup debuts in the first-round tie at Woolwich Arsenal, where a Spiksley double saw them through. But there was nothing lucky about their unforgettable third-round home triumph over Aston Villa, who at the time were running away with the

Tom Crawshaw — his 1896 Cup success was the first of two he enjoyed with Wednesday. He also won two League Championship medals in a great career.

League and fancied for the Double. A crowd of 22,100 saw Woolhouse shoot Wednesday in front after ten minutes, but Villa hit back and a Bob Chatt double seemed to have set them on course for victory. With only two minutes remaining, Spiksley collected a pass from Webster, dribbled past two men and pushed the ball beyond goalkeeper Dunning's reach. Then, in extra time, the idol of Olive Grove produced another moment of magic in laying on the winning goal for Woolhouse.

Alas, in the semi-final at Fallowfield, Wednesday ran right out of luck: the black cat that ran across the path of the wagon taking them to the ground from Manchester Station was not, after all, the happy omen they had believed. They felt they would have beaten Bolton had the referee not disallowed two fine efforts by Spiksley, who was adjudged offside on both occasions; but, in truth, they paid for two errors which haunted Allan for weeks. First, the goalkeeper appeared to be blinded by the sun as he lost a dipping shot by Bentley; then, attempting to stop a swerving effort from the same man, he contrived to punch the ball into his own net. Woolhouse subsequently made it 2–1, but his goal was merely a consolation.

That match, incidentally, marked the last Cup appearance of Billy Betts, the defender the fans called 'The Old Warhorse', and at the start of the following season, his place was filled by another local product who would become one of the great Wednesday heroes—Tom Crawshaw. A native of the old Park district, he had played with his brother George in the famous Attercliffe team and had a spell with Heywood Central before moving to

Olive Grove. It says much for the impact Crawshaw made that, by the end of the 1894–95 campaign, he had collected the first of his ten England caps and been chosen to represent the Football League against the Scottish League.

Three Scots also arrived in the summer of 1894—Archie Brash, Bob Ferrier and Bob Petrie—and all four newcomers contributed to a much-improved start to the League programme. However, the fact that Wednesday won only one of their last eleven First Division games served to show the Cup was again the big distraction . . . and, sadly, they again ran out of luck one step from the final.

When they crushed the Cup-holders, Notts County, 5–1, and then hammered Middlesbrough 6–1 (Harry Davis scored a hat-trick), everybody at Olive Grove was convinced this was going to be their year. That view was strengthened by the circumstances in which they clinched a magnificent 2–0 triumph over Everton in a home quarter-final which drew a 28,000 crowd to the Wednesday ground. Brady gave them the lead after 25 minutes, but, almost immediately, Davis retired with an injury; and then Ferrier was so badly hurt that he was no more than a passenger. Yet, hobbling on the wing, he managed to limp into the goalmouth to get the second goal just before half-time.

Some 8,000 Sheffielders made the journey to Derby for the semi-final with West Brom, only to see their heroes fall to a controversial 2–0 defeat. Hutchinson put Albion ahead after twenty minutes, but Wednesday were just beginning to gain the upper hand when they conceded a penalty

which Langley, who was alleged to have tripped Billy Bassett, never tired of recalling as the harshest decision ever given against him throughout his career. Many years after the event, the memory of what he felt was a great injustice still pained him.

In those days, remarkable as it might seem to the modern supporter, the penalty area extended right across the width of the field; and the incident that brought Albion's decisive 36th-minute spot-kick actually occurred close to the corner flag! Bassett, when tackled by Langley, fell as if poleaxed. 'I never touched him; he threw himself down,' the Wednesday man pleaded, but in vain. Bassett, who had already played ten times for England and twice helped Albion win the Cup, was nothing if not a wily professional; and Wednesday paid for allowing the feeling that they had been cheated to put them off their game.

There was an amusing footnote to this story a month later. Two days after Albion had lost to Aston Villa in the final, they went into their last game, a home match with Wednesday, needing to win 6–0 to avoid having to play a Test match. Langley, still bitter, vowed they would get six 'over my dead body'. But they did it . . . which simply added insult to injury in the big defender's book.

In the event, there was ample compensation for Langley and his colleagues in 1895–96 when they finally won the FA Cup; though, as is often the case, two players were to miss out on the glory when it came. Bob Ferrier and Bill Allan both suffered untimely injuries, with Ferrier managing only one Cup outing while Allan's hopes of extending his sequence of sixteen consecutive Cup appearances ended in misfortune shortly before Wednesday embarked on their run to the Crystal Palace.

Allan was unlucky in that it was his courage (and perhaps his fear of not being able to get back in the side) that cost him his place. Playing at Burnley in early January, he took a severe knock on a leg, but did not mention it. A week later he lived up to his 'William the Silent' nickname by not revealing the discomfort he endured in the 3–0 defeat of Blackburn. However, when he turned up for the Aston Villa match, he could barely walk—and it was obvious he could not be risked. It marked the end of the Scot's senior career at Olive Grove, and in the following summer he was transferred to Loughborough.

What made things worse was that his deputy, Jimmy Massey, a Denaby product who had come from Doncaster Rovers a year earlier and played just eight senior games, was nursing a broken finger. He was thrown in against Villa, and though Wednesday lost 3–1 he kept his place, starting on a run of 71 consecutive appearances and being the first-choice goalkeeper for the next five years. In truth, Massey was not particularly impressive in his early games, but his display in the later stages of the Cup final (only his 23rd senior outing), when Wednesday came under intense pressure, made him a lasting favourite with the supporters for whom that famous year will always be synonymous with Fred Spiksley.

It is worthy of note that, in the nineteen FA Cup ties Wednesday played between January 1893 and

April 1896, Spiksley scored fifteen goals; and his contribution to the 1896 triumph was truly that of a very remarkable player, for he was involved in twelve of the team's seventeen goals that brought the trophy back to Sheffield.

Brady, who was now partnering Archie Brash (the smallest man in the team) on the right flank, notched the double that turned the game and helped Wednesday come from behind to win 3–2 at Southampton St Mary's in the first round. Spiksley sealed a home victory in the second round against Sunderland with a peach of a goal and, despite being ill in the dressing room before the third-round tie with Everton, he contributed to the goal of the match from Lawrence Bell in a famous 4–0 success in which Bell (a close-season buy from St Mirren) and the irrepressible Brash each scored twice.

The semi-final against Bolton saw Wednesday avenge the defeat at the same stage in 1894. However, two games were required to settle the issue. When the teams met at Goodison Park, Bob Tannihill gave Bolton the lead after only seven minutes, but Brash equalised from a Spiksley cross eleven minutes into the second half. Wednesday probably knew their luck was in this time round when, late in the game, Archie Freebairn missed an easy chance for Bolton.

In the replay, at Nottingham Forest's ground, Tom Crawshaw shot Wednesday in front with a 25-yard effort in the opening minutes, but former Olive Grove favourite Bob 'Sparrow' Brown equalised soon afterwards, and when a raw young centre-forward called Tom Vail, making his Cup debut for Bolton, clattered Langley and left him limping, the defender feared the semi-final hoodoo was going to strike again. By the end of the game, Langley's knee had swollen to the size of a football, but there wasn't a happier man in the whole of Nottingham, for Davis had headed in a Petrie free-kick on the hour, Spiksley had made it 3–1 a few minutes before the final whistle, and Wednesday were set to face Wolverhampton Wanderers at the Crystal Palace.

Langley remained doubtful right up to the morning of the final. It had been decided that if the pitch at the Palace was heavy, Harry Brandon would play at left-back with John Jamieson filling in at right-half. Spiksley, Langley's room-mate on the overnight stay at an Upper Norwood hotel, was so desperate to see his pal in the side that he kept getting out of bed during the night to check it wasn't raining! The weather remained fine, and Langley played. The full line-up was:

Wednesday: Massey; Earp, Langley; H. Brandon, Crawshaw, Petrie; Brash, Brady, Bell, Davis, Spiksley

Wolves: Tennant; Baugh, Dunn; Griffiths, Malpass, Owen; Tonks, Henderson, Beats, Wood, Black

Skipper Harry Wood (a colleague of Crawshaw's in the England team against Scotland a fortnight earlier), Baugh and Malpass had all been in the Wolves side that won the Cup in 1893, and, though most of the pundits did not feel there was much to choose between the sides, the Midlanders had the edge in the betting. The trophy was a new one

because the original had been stolen from a Birmingham shop window, Aston Villa had been foolish enough to leave it on display there after winning it the previous year.

Contrary to expectations, the 1896 final was an excellent game in which two sides with modest League records rose to the occasion; and nobody shone more than Brash and Spiksley. It was from Brash's throw-in barely thirty seconds into the match that Davis pushed the ball into the path of Spiksley, who stunned Wolves with a superb piece of finishing. Though Scot David Black caught Massey napping when he hooked a splendid equaliser soon afterwards, in the eighteenth minute Spiksley produced another tremendous strike to score the goal that won the game.

Spiksley hit the ball with such force that it rebounded into the goalmouth off a stanchion at the back of the goal; and, amid all the noise and excitement, Wolves goalkeeper Bill Tennant was said to have assumed the ball had hit a post and was still in play, so he kicked it upfield. How he missed noting the game being restarted it is hard to understand, but, anyway, at the final whistle he is supposed to have asked Jack Earp 'When's the replay?', to which the Wednesday captain replied, 'There's no replay, we've won 2–1,' and Tennant said 'You can't have, only one shot went past me.' The lad was convinced only when Lord Kinnaird handed the new trophy to Earp.

Wednesday returned to a joyful reception in Sheffield, where the scenes outside the Midland Station and in the city centre streets were like nothing ever witnessed before at a sporting homecoming. The throng

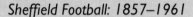
was so great on Sheaf Street that the victory parade was delayed, and the celebration meal at the Royal Hotel in Waingate (it stood where the entrance to the Castle Market is now) began late. A memorable evening ended with the players appearing on the stage of the new Empire Theatre in Charles Street.

Sadly, Wednesday's remaining three years at Olive Grove after the 1896 triumph were to prove an anti-climax. Their Cup form deserted them, and while they finished in the top six in 1897 and 1898 they suffered an astonishing decline in 1899 and lost their top-grade status as well as their home. The irony was that, in the same spell, neighbours United finished second in the table and followed it with a League championship success in 1898 and an FA Cup triumph in 1899—the very year when Wednesday's fortunes were at their lowest ebb. But then, such contrasting circumstances have been common-place in the history of the Sheffield football clubs!

The 1896 FA Cup winning squad (players only) —
Back row: Harry Brandon, Jim Massey, Jack Earp, John Jameson (reserve), Ambrose Langley.
Front row: Tom Crawshaw, Archie Brash, Alex Brady, Bob Petrie, Harry Davis, Fred Spiksley.
In front: Lawrence Bell.

Champions!
United 1897–1898

AFTER their prompt promotion in 1893, United consolidated their First Division status reasonably quickly. They led the table within a few weeks of their arrival in the top grade, and while they were unable to maintain that pace, the graduation from newcomers to League Champions took only five years.

By the time they claimed the title in 1898, only Bob Cain, Rab Howell and Ernest Needham survived from the side that had climbed out of the Second Division. In the meantime, players such as Harry Thickett, Willie Foulke, Tom Morren and Walter Bennett—all destined to write their names large in Bramall Lane history— were recruited with, among others, 'old' Harry Johnson, Fred Priest, Jack Almond and George Hedley.

United began their initial term in the top grade with an impressive 3–2 home defeat of Everton, and winning seven of their first nine games, went top in early October. In December, soon after Thickett returned from Rotherham Town for a £20 fee, they stood second. Unfortunately, five straight defeats saw them slip to ninth, and this slide coincided with the first hints of the problems that led to the capture of Foulke, the giant goalkeeper who became one of the most famous 'characters' in football history.

Charlie Howlett suffered a painful knee injury during United's 2–1 defeat of Wednesday at Olive Grove in November, and when he returned after missing a few matches, he showed an unexpected lack of confidence, conceding fourteen goals in the four games that precipitated the team's slump. Lilley, his deputy, was not enjoying the best of form either, but what alarmed the directors and brought the problem to a head was that, in March, Howlett told trainer Jack Houseley he would prefer to be left out of the team for the trip to Newton Heath. Howlett admitted the Manchester side's reputation for testing the physical endurance of goalkeepers had unnerved him: frankly, he couldn't do with it. George Waller, right-half and coach to the reserves, volunteered to play in goal, and indeed, excelled in the unfamiliar role as United won 2–0; but clearly the sooner a permanent replacement was found the better.

It so happened that a refereeing contact of the club had mentioned a burly young miner from Blackwell, called Foulke, who was the talk of Derbyshire football circles. The tale was told of how, in an exhibition match between the village team and Derby County, the goalkeeper, attempting to punch away a cross, had missed the ball and instead hit the legendary John Goodall so hard in the mouth that the England man lost two teeth! Director Joe Tomlinson and assistant secretary Harry Stones went to watch Foulke in a Derbyshire Cup tie and were sufficiently impressed to try to sign him on the spot; but Blackwell officials wanted to keep their 6ft 2in star until the end of the season. Tomlinson, aware that other clubs were hot on the trail and anxious not to leave without completing a deal, compromised by offering Blackwell £1 for each of the eleven days left in the season if they would then sell Foulke to United.

Foulke, who was then just twenty years old and, at twelve stone, half the weight he was later in his playing career, made his debut at the start of an 1894–95 season in which United finished in the top six but suffered another defensive crisis with the unexpected loss of Bill Hendry. On New Year's Day 1895, during United's now customary mid-season Scottish tour, the influential skipper dislocated a knee at Leith. It was a mark of his popularity that a crowd of 4,000 turned up for his benefit match in February, but his days at the top were clearly over, and it was only after a long battle to regain his fitness that he was able to play on at Bury, Brighton and Shrewsbury. Sadly, within a few years of leaving Sheffield he died, at the age of 32. The irony was that Hendry always seemed so indestructible. Indeed, two months before the accident that finished his playing days with United, he had been one of only six members of the team who had survived unscathed from a First Division fixture played in wet and freezing conditions which had broken the toughest of his colleagues.

The match, against Aston Villa at Perry Bar in November 1894, is shown in the records as a 5–0 victory for the Birmingham side, but the referee was subsequently criticised by the FA for allowing play to continue in wind and sleet that had turned the pitch into a pond even before the kick-off. On one of the coldest days of the year, the downpour lasted all through the game, and the football was a farce compounded by the fact that, at one stage, Villa centre-forward John Devey left the field and returned wearing an overcoat, while team-mate Charlie Athersmith used an umbrella to keep off the rain!

Much more serious was the effect of conditions on the players, principally in United's team. Early in the second half, Needham hobbled off, then Cain collapsed a few minutes later, he was followed off the field by Jimmy Yates and Hugh Morris. Then Foulke, having made several splendid saves, fell unconscious in his goal-mouth immediately after diving at Devey's feet and clearing the ball. Spectators carried hot drinks along the touchline for the Villa players, and, apparently, the only home man who was overlooked was goalkeeper Wilkes, whose frantic calls fell on deaf ears. Nobody bothered about the Sheffield lads.

Four of the five goals came amid the chaos, but, by the time referee Thomas called a halt, the United men couldn't have cared what the score was. Those who completed the game returned to the dressing room to find Foulke and Needham still in a terrible state; and there were some harsh words for the match official when he called in to say he was reporting Yates and Morris for having left the pitch without permission. A month later, Needham was still confined to his home at Staveley and missed the Scottish tour on which Hendry was injured.

Needham, who succeeded Hendry as captain, also filled in for the Scot at centre-half, but as the following season progressed, finding a long-term replacement pivot became an increasingly urgent priority. George Waller, now in charge of the team, found the solution to the problem thanks to a tip from a contact in Middlesbrough, where the United trainer had played a lot of his professional cricket. He learned that Tom Morren, who had helped Middlesbrough win the Amateur Cup, was travelling to Reading with a view to joining the Southern League club; and Waller's informant is said to have confirmed the time that Morren's train would pass through Sheffield.

The story has been told of how Waller went to the railway station in Sheffield, located Morren's compartment, and removed his baggage, ordering the player off the train. We cannot be sure if this is what really happened, and it has been suggested that Morren had stopped off in Sheffield anyway, for he did have a brief link-up with Barnsley. However, it is evident that Waller persuaded him to play in a trial match (ironically against Barnsley St Peter's) in a Wharncliffe Charity Cup-tie on 25th November 1895.

Morren, who stood only 5ft 6ins and was to figure in the smallest half-back line United ever had, made an immediate impact, was signed the same evening, and after playing in the first team against the Corinthians in late December, made his First Division debut at Burnley in a match abandoned after 65 minutes. He was to collect only one England cap (it would have been two but injury cost him his place against Scotland in 1899), but there is not much doubt that Morren was an outstanding player and a key figure in United's climb to the peaks of success in the final years of the Victorian era.

An equally notable signing in 1895–96 was Walter Bennett, a member of the famous Mexborough footballing family that also produced 'Mickey' Bennett, who played for Wednesday in the 1890 final. Walter had scored 168 goals for Mexborough Town in two seasons in the Midland League when United beat several rivals to snap him up for a mere £40. In truth, at the time, while nobody disputed his abilities, many doubted whether Bennett would make the grade in the Football League. He was said to be a man of moods, and when he arrived at Bramall Lane, had a serious weight problem. His 75 goals in some 220 League and Cup games for United, and two England caps (his international partnership with the legendary Steve Bloomer was not a success) did not reflect his merit; but, while there were times when he was the crowd's 'whipping boy', he was amongst the most popular players United ever had. Bennett's goals were invariably gems that the fans treasured and talked about for months afterwards. Amusing as it might seem now, the fact that he was known as 'Cocky' upset the Bramall Lane management, and they tried for years to persuade the press and public to refrain from using the nickname. Remarkably, many supporters never knew he was called Walter.

United's undoing in 1895–96, when they finished twelfth, was poor away form. At home, where a new stand had been erected on the John Street side, they lost only twice and their nine victories included an 8–0 defeat of Bury in which Hammond scored four and Bill Egan three. They did not win an away game until they went to Derby in March, and their first away point, which came at Aston Villa in November, was notable in that the hero of the 2–2 draw was trainer George Waller. When Arthur Watson sent a message that he was too ill to travel, Waller played in borrowed boots and scored a goal.

United were desperate to succeed, but the fact that Waller filled in as often as he did suggests this was still a period when clubs were not always prepared for all contingencies. Indeed, two incidents in 1895 serve to show how relaxed players and officials seemed to be about punctuality. When Stoke visited Bramall Lane, the kick-off was delayed while the teams were photographed; and when Derby came the players were told the referee had not turned up but had sent a telegram in which he said 'Manage 'til I arrive'!

Yet it is evident that some players had a conscience about their responsibilities to the club. Harry Thickett, for instance, made only eight appearances in 1895–96 after falling ill with typhoid fever, he volunteered to accept reduced wages. One cannot imagine a player in the mid-1990s making such a gesture. However, to United's credit, they insisted on paying him in full, and when you consider Thickett's Bramall Lane career as a whole there is not much doubt that the club got full value for their money. Indeed, Thickett helped ensure United enjoyed an early dividend from their investment.

There are two points to notice about the improvement in United's record that led them to the League Championship: the dip in the number of goals they conceded, and the increase in away points. In 1896–97 and 1897–98 they lost only five times on their travels after suffering 29 away defeats in the previous three seasons; and moreover, in home and away matches they conceded an average of only one goal per match.

1896–97

	P	W	D	L	F	A
Home	15	6	4	5	22	16
Away	15	7	6	2	20	13
	30	13	10	7	42	29

1897–98

	P	W	D	L	F	A
Home	15	9	4	2	27	14
Away	15	8	4	3	29	17
	30	17	8	5	56	31

Ironically, in 1896–97, when they finished runners-up to Aston Villa in the title chase, they were let down by poor home form after starting the season in style with an unbeaten run of nine games. In the end they trailed Villa by eleven points, but there were more positives than negatives from the season—not least of which was the immediate success enjoyed by their latest front-line recruits Jack Almond, Kenny McKay and Fred Priest.

Priest, who started on the wing but later had some success as an inside-forward, was an instant hit, and there were few more popular players with the crowd than the lad from South Bank. He made over 230 appearances for United, collected one England cap, and scored some of the most important goals in Sheffield football history. Almond, the son of a Yorkshire brewer and said to be due to inherit a fortune on his 21st birthday in November 1897, scored nine goals in twenty games; while McKay's six goals included point-winning strikes against Stoke, Wednesday and Wolves.

United went into the 1897–98 campaign with just about the best squad of players they had boasted up to that time, and the October arrival of John Cunningham, an experienced Scottish forward from Preston, completed the jigsaw. Cunningham, who earned £3 a week and was said to be United's third highest-paid player after Needham and Foulke, scored seven goals in 24 outings, including the two that completed the crucial double over Aston Villa in January. United's usual line-up was as follows:

Foulke; Thickett, Cain; Howell, Morren, Needham; Bennett, McKay, Almond, Cunningham, Priest

Harry Johnson, Harry Howard and George Hedley were the main deputies, though Ralph Gaudie, Henry White and T.J. Jenkinson figured in the side on several occasions.

From the outset, United displayed a resilience that was to stand them in good stead. They came from two goals down to beat Stoke at home in September, and trailed at Everton before romping to a 4–1 victory; and they did not taste defeat until their fifteenth match, at Stoke in early December. It was at the end of December that they fell at home for the first time, defeated by Liverpool,

Sheffield United 1898.
Standing: Walter Bennett, Harry Johnson, Jack Almond, George Hedley, Willie Foulke, Harry Thickett, George Simpson, Fred Priest.
Sitting: Micky Whelan, Ernest Needham, Tom Morren.
Note: *Whelan arrived after the League title success.*

but they followed that with four straight wins to go seven points clear in the title race.

This was the moment when they suffered their most embarrasssing defeat of the season, being knocked out of the FA Cup at Burslem Port Vale. The Potteries club was then in the Midland League, and, whether or not United were guilty of over-confidence, they never got to grips with a game that was played in a gale-force wind. Vale led after only three minutes, and there were just eight minutes left of normal time when United snatched an equaliser through Thickett, who had been switched to centre-forward in a last-ditch attempt

Harry Johnson: initially a very capable deputy, later a half-back of England class.

to salvage Sheffield's pride. The decisive strike came early in extra-time when, with United putting the home team under incessant pressure, Foulke wandered up into the centre circle, only to be caught napping as Lucien Boullimier latched onto a clearance and raced past the goalkeeper, shooting into the net after running half the length of the field pursued by the huge eighteen-stone figure of 'Little Willie'!

Once again, United bounced back from a blow that might have knocked a lesser side off their stride, but, in early March, when they visited their closest rivals, Sunderland, Needham and his team fell to a 3–1 defeat which seemed to indicate that, with five games left, the pressure was starting to get to them. The circumstances in which the game was played were far from ideal: the atmosphere was perhaps the most intimidating any of the United players had ever experienced, and they always claimed that they were not allowed sufficient time to settle after the crowd was cleared from the pitch before the delayed start of the second half. Sunderland went straight down and scored, that put the top on a dismal day when Rab Howell put the ball into his own net—not once but twice! The man often referred to as the only gypsy to win a Championship medal was completely unnerved by the atmosphere: his lack of composure, while out of character, was to cost him dearly, for the club sold him to Liverpool at the end of the season.

The return match with Sunderland at Bramall Lane on 2nd April was the most important match United had ever played up to that day, and they did not feel their cause was helped by the Football Association's refusal to release Needham from duty with England for the international against Scotland. Sunderland had refused to let two of their men play for the Scots, and, with United having gone four games without a win (and lost three), they felt they had a big psychological advantage. United were also without McKay and, in the light of his experience in the previous game with the Wearsiders, Howell was dropped. Almond, Howard and Johnson were brought in. Johnson especially rose to the occasion, for he claimed the 32nd-minute goal that sealed a famous victory. Cain, United's acting captain, could not have chosen a better way to celebrate having completed 100 consecutive appearances.

The Championship was clinched on the following Friday, Good Friday, at Bolton. It was intended to give young Hedley only his third senior outing in attack but, when the players assembled at Bramall Lane prior to departure, it emerged that his employer would not give him the time off from his full-time job. Needham decided Howard would continue to deputise at left-half and the England man elected to play in attack. It was like something out of schoolboy fiction when Needham claimed the only goal of the match

with a brilliant solo run reminiscent of that with which Jack Drummond had sealed victory in the Test match five years before. It settled a dour, physical game in which several United men finished limping.

At the final whistle, Needham, instead of heading for the dressing rooms, went straight to the Bolton secretary's office, where he borrowed a telephone and made the call which revealed that Bury had beaten Sunderland—and United were the new League Champions! United concluded the most memorable League campaign in their history on the following Monday when they beat West Brom 2–0 at Bramall Lane, with a 9,000 crowd seeing Walter Bennett (who had lost two stone in weight before the start of the season) claim a double that made him the leading scorer with twelve goals.

When their First Division programme was completed and they finished five points ahead of Sunderland, United staged a benefit match which raised £70 for the last of the 'old school'. Dear old Mick Whitham would henceforth concentrate on his trade as a file-cutter in his native Ecclesfield while watching from a distance as his old club chased more glory . . . in the FA Cup!

Willie Foulke

Foulke Tales

WILLIAM Foulke, known to his friends as Bill but generally referred to as 'Little Willie' or 'Fatty', was undoubtedly one of the great characters of his era, the stuff of which myths and legends are made. He has passed into sporting folklore as the heaviest goalkeeper in the history of the Football League and, while there is an abundance of tales about his exploits on and off the field, many of the stories bear only a slight link with the truth.

When he arrived at Bramall Lane in 1894, he was twenty years old and had already attained his full height of 6ft 2ins, but at just under thirteen stone he was much slimmer than he would be in a few years. Indeed, by the time he moved to Chelsea in 1905, he was over 23 stone and still expanding; and moreover, still revelling in his role, as the giant whose presence was guaranteed to add a few thousand to the attendance. Late in his career, when Chelsea began their history in a blaze of publicity, Foulke arrived at a railway station in a northern town to see a line of men carrying sandwich boards that advertised: 'Come and see the 24½-stone Chelsea goalkeeper'. His face was a picture as he cried with mock anger: 'Twenty-four stun! I'll give 'em twenty-four stun!' and, shuffling his feet as if he intended to pursue the men, he induced them to take sudden flight, leaving their boards behind!

Big and heavy as he was, in his prime Foulke was astonishingly agile for a man of his size, and it is not intended as a pun to say that he played a huge part in United's success. For a start, he made the goal look very small to opposing forwards, and there were few who were prepared to stray too close. It was said that he would catch a terrific shot with the ease of a man plucking a cricket ball out of the air and, with forearms the size of huge legs of mutton, he could punch the ball beyond the halfway line. It was tough luck for anybody who got in the way of his fist when he was seeking to reach a high cross into the goalmouth!

Of course, there were many forwards who sought to exploit Foulke's notoriously short temper. He was not fond of attempts to catch him off balance, and when he was in high spirits he revelled in poking fun at would-be assailants. Late in his United career, he came face to face with a young upstart called Harry Hampton of Aston Villa, who announced he was not going to stand on ceremony when he met 'Little Willie'. Hampton kept bouncing off the big goalkeeper, but once, late in the game, Foulke showed such fleetness of foot that the Villa man missed him completely and finished upside down in the goal with his feet entangled in the netting. He pleaded: 'Bill, help us down!' Foulke looked at him and chuckled: 'Tha got thissen up there, tha can get thissen down!'

There is another famous tale of a day in 1899 when United went to Anfield. Liverpool's George Allan, having wagered that he would knock Foulke and the ball into the net, proceeded to barge into the goalkeeper every time he had an excuse—and sometimes when he hadn't. Foulke was not thrilled at the treatment he was getting. Eventually, a shot came in and cannoned off Foulke's fist and into touch. In the same instant, Allen, quite deliberately, collided heavily with the United man. Some say that all that happened then was that, as the goalkeeper got up and sought to untangle his and Allan's legs, the Liverpool man fell to the ground head first. Another version suggests Foulke picked Allan up and stood him on his head in the goalmouth.

Whatever the case (referee Thomas, the man who had been in charge at Villa in 1894, was again criticised for his decision), Foulke conceded a penalty, and was so upset at the award of a spot-kick that he refused to try to save it. (Years later, in his Chelsea days, Foulke was involved in a similar incident at Port Vale, where he was said to have got so angry with one forward that he picked him up and threw him into the net—and then refused to stand in his goal when the resulting penalty was taken. His captain, J.T. Robertson, finally ordered the goalkeeper to take up his position. Foulke did so, but ignored the spot-kick and instead glared at the referee, J.T. Howcroft.)

Howcroft was a linesman at the 1902 FA Cup final in which Southampton, then of the Southern League, held United to a 1–1 draw with a late equaliser; he told the story of how, after the game, a naked Foulke pursued the referee, Tom Kirkham. 'Foulke was exasperated by the goal and claimed it was miles offside. He was in his birthday suit outside the dressing rooms, and I saw F.J. Wall, secretary of the Football Association, pleading with him to rejoin his colleagues. But Bill was out for blood, and I shouted to Mr Kirkham to lock his cubicle door. He didn't need telling twice. But what a sight! The thing I'll never forget is Foulke, so tremendous in size, striding along the corridor without a stitch of clothing.'

Many people have indicated that Foulke, who was born at Darley in Shropshire but grew up in Blackwell in Derbyshire, was a rough diamond. No doubt he could be coarse, and a few journalists from that era reported that, if he didn't like something they had written, he could produce invective which took bad language into realms they had never imagined. Yet Tom Bott, the United director who became a sort of unofficial team-manager, insisted there was never a more gentle man.

Bott said: 'Professionals in those days could be quite a handful, but I never had a minute's trouble with Foulke. A wonderful chap, he was. Intelligent, a good talker, and a marvel for keeping his pecker up when things were running against the team. Mind you, he was often a bit nervy before a big game, and when he was feeling jumpy he'd point to my little whisky flask and say "Now, Father, I'll be better for a drop"; and after a toothful he'd be right as rain.' It was Bott who also said that, for such a huge man, Foulke was never a big eater—at least not on match days.

'Before a game he would eat nothing but a piece of toast and a small beer,' he recalled.

However, one of the most famous Foulke tales concerns his enormous appetite, and the occasion during training for the 1899 semi-final when he is said to have eaten fifteen breakfasts at United's Cup head-quarters. It was the custom for the players to join trainer Waller for a stiff early morning walk before eating, but when he could, Foulke avoided these expeditions. On this occasion he was alleged to have hidden until his team-mates had left, and then, after the waiter had laid out fifteen breakfasts, all under hot covers, he emerged to devour the lot in the deserted dining room. When the players returned, they waited and waited for food to be served, and, finally ringing for a waiter, were told: 'You gentlemen are making fun of me, I cleared away the used plates fifteen minutes ago.' A search revealed a happy Foulke sleeping in a corner!

Foulke was a great favourite in the dressing room, and he was especially fond of little Walter Bennett, partly because the physically contrasting pair were often the butt of critical sections of the Bramall Lane crowd. It was known that Bennett liked a flutter on the horses when there was racing at Doncaster, and the winger once arrived for training with the back pocket of his trousers bulging with £25 he had won the previous day. While the winger was out on the pitch, Foulke removed £15 and hid it, and was surprised when Bennett made no comment on his return. The next day the goalkeeper told his colleague: 'A chap I know says he'll give thee £15 if tha scores two goals on Saturday.' Bennett's eyes lit up, he did in fact, hit a hat-trick (against Manchester City) and collected his 'reward'. It was another week before Foulke revealed he had paid the winger with his own money!

Of the 399 League and Cup games Foulke played in his career, some 340 were with United. First with Thickett and Cain and later with Thickett and Peter Boyle, he and the backs formed a trio of giants who were the cornerstone of the Bramall Lane side's remarkable defensive stablility. It was significant perhaps, that after the departure of Thickett (who went to Bristol City) and Boyle (he left for Motherwell after falling foul of the United directors) in 1904, Foulke suddenly felt exposed and vulnerable. His Lane career took a dip, and it may not have been entirely his own fault.

In 1904–1905, he played in ten of United's first thirteen games, but after conceding ten goals in two games in mid-November, including seven on the visit to bottom-of-the-table Bury, he was dropped. When his deputy Joe Lievesley proved an almost instant hit, it was clearly the end of an era at Bramall Lane. Foulke could have stayed on, but he wasn't prepared to do so as second choice; and when the Chelsea club was formed and gained prompt election to the Football League, it offered the veteran goal-keeper an opportunity to extend his senior career. He later returned to Yorkshire and played briefly with Bradford City.

Foulke played only once for England, in 1897 when he and Ernest Needham lent a little local colour to the international with Wales at Bramall Lane. Whether he should have collected more caps is perhaps a

---

Willie Foulke

matter of opinion. It was a measure of his prowess, and United's success in his time at the club, that he was on the losing side only seven times in 41 FA Cup outings, and United were beaten in only five of the 21 League and Cup derbies with Wednesday in which Foulke played.

He was often to be found around and about Bramall Lane after he hung up his boots, for he kept the Duke Inn in nearby Matilda Street, but at least one player of the next generation who came into contact with him suggested the old goalkeeper tended to outstay his welcome. To some degree it does seem that Foulke fell on hard times. For a while he sought to exploit his fame by appearing in a shooting booth on Blackpool sands, and it was after a visit to the seaside that he fell ill. He was admitted to Sister Tate's Nursing home in Glossop Road, where he died on 1st May 1916, aged 42. He was buried in Burngreave Cemetery.

It is perhaps appropriate here to refer to Foulke's successor, Joe Lievesley, who, despite the fact that his United career coincided with a period when the honours proved elusive, was certainly amongst the best goalkeepers the club ever had. A native of Poolsbrook and a nephew of former Lane man, Harry Lilley, Lievesley was one of the many fine goalkeeping products of the Chesterfield area, and he was said to have been in the mould of the legendary Sam Hardy: never spectacular, always dependable. Indeed, it was a mark of his consistency that he enjoyed one run of 192 consecutive League games, and he made 286 League and Cup appearances before moving to Arsenal. He once played in an international trial and was in the Football League XI that met the Southern League at Chelsea in 1910, but the nearest he came to an England cap was when he toured South Africa with the Football Association.

Remarkably, Lievesley's Cup record at Bramall Lane was in stark contrast with Foulke's, for he made nine appearances in the competition for United and finished on the winning side just once. Yet, ironically, no sooner had he left than the Blades rediscovered their Cup form, and Lievesley's long-term successor, Harold Gough, was to enjoy the ultimate glory when helping United bring the coveted trophy back to Sheffield in 1915.

Gough, who also came from the Chesterfield area, had the kind of luck that eluded Lievesley, and his experience served to show how accidents of fate influence what a man can achieve in the game. Gough only got his chance because the leading man for the goalkeeper's jersey, Ted Hufton, broke his nose just before the start of that 1913–14 season when United reached the semi-final for the first time since 1902. Mind you, Gough himself suffered a setback and missed the chance of completing a Cup double in 1925, he was suspended by United after taking a public house in Castleford.

George Waller—the great United trainer who was a key figure in the Blades' successes between 1898 and 1925.

Cup Glory! United 1899

T HE 1898–1899 season produced starkly contrasting fortunes for the Sheffield clubs. While Wednesday were relegated from the First Division and kicked out of their Olive Grove home, United won the FA Cup for the first time—and the triumph coincided with the opportunity to buy their Bramall Lane ground for £10,134.

United's hopes of retaining the League Championship looked good when they remained unbeaten until late October, but they won only three of the next thirteen games and not only fell out of contention for the top prize, but finished only four points above bottom-placed Wednesday. However, they amply compensated with a memorable Cup run that spanned ten matches including two replays in the earlier rounds and a semi-final 'marathon'.

The loss of Cain, Cunningham and McKay after the title success was a blow, but of the five newcomers recruited by late autumn, Peter Boyle and Billy Beer proved inspired signings. Irishman Boyle, who came from Sunderland, made an out-standing success of solving the left-back problem caused by Cain's move to Spurs; while inside-forward Beer, having been an amateur with Staveley and Chesterfield, not only adjusted quickly to League football but was also a lucky mascot to the team on the Cup trail.

In fact, it was a Beer double (he scored both goals with his head) that earned United a 2–2 draw when they began the run to the Crystal Palace with a tough date at Turf Moor, where Burnley had been beaten only once all season. When that first-round tic was replayed at Bramall Lane, Boyle had the misfortune to concede a penalty from which Ross gave the Lancastrians fresh hope after Bennett had shot United in front. Fortunately, Morren promptly restored the advantage and United held on to win 2–1.

After losing the lead at Preston in the second round, United settled for another replay—and one that looked to be slipping away when Chalmers shot North End in front and Needham missed a penalty. But the fates were kind: first Needham saw a cross fortuitously deflected past the Preston goalkeeper, then United got a second spot-kick and this time the skipper made no mistake.

So United visited Nottingham Forest, the holders, in the quarter-final, and it was a day that began badly but had a happy ending. In between, there was another priceless moment of drama and humour involving Foulke. When the Bramall Lane party arrived at Nottingham, the crowds on the platform and around the station were so dense that the players had great difficulty fighting their way through to the waggon taking them to the ground. Then, no sooner had they reached the dressing rooms than it was discovered the kit basket had been left behind. Fortunately, the railway staff responded to an SOS, and the gear was delivered to enable United to take to the field on schedule.

When Jack Almond, injured in the early stages, was unable to continue after half-time, the omens were far from good. It was fortunate that Foulke was in top form, and when he made one save which could only be described as miraculous, Unitedites roared their approval. A Forest forward's shot was screeching towards the bottom corner, and the ball seemed to have passed beyond Foulke's right arm before he reacted;

but the giant goalkeeper suddenly sprang sideways and astonished everyone by turning the ball round a post. He finished up stretched full length in the goalmouth, it was not until Forest were about to take the corner kick that the referee noticed Foulke was still prostrate on the pitch. It transpired that, in making the save, he had torn a muscle in his thigh and he could barely move. That was the serious part. The funny part came when United's training staff and match officials attempted to get the nineteen-stone goalkeeper off the pitch. An ordinary stretcher was of no use and, after a long delay while the matter was debated, Foulke was slowly raised and asked to stand on his 'good' leg. Then a bearer party of

The Cup heroes of 1899 prepare for a triumphant tour of Sheffield city centre. Ernest Needham (with the coveted trophy) is standing behind director Tom Bott, and the familiar figure of Willie Foulke can be easily identified in the foreground.

six men was organised to carry him off on their shoulders—to applause and laughter from the crowd. Thankfully, there was a pleasing postscript for United, with Fred Priest pouncing to win the game with the only goal four minutes from the end.

The semi-final paired United with Liverpool, who had done the double over United in the League and were on their way to finishing just behind Aston Villa at the top of the table. Moreover, the tie brought Foulke face to face with George Allen, with whom he had been involved in a famous penalty incident early in the season. The first meeting was at Nottingham Forest, and when Allan snatched an early goal and Liverpool led 2–1 there were few ready to believe the Merseysiders could be stopped; but Needham equalised to earn a replay.

The second meeting, at Bolton, was a remarkable eight-goal thriller in which United twice trailed by two goals but saved the day with a typical never-say-die performance from Needham. That man Allan had made it 2–0 to Liverpool six minutes into the second half, but goals from Beer and Bennett levelled the score just past the hour. Then United's world appeared to collapse when Boyle turned the ball into his own net and Morren conceded a penalty which Foulke saved only for Cox to knock in the rebound. Needham decided his team had nothing to lose by throwing caution to the wind and attempting to save the match by going on all-out attack. He ordered everyone except Foulke and Boyle to push forward. Had the policy failed, United might have been trounced, but in the event, Priest scored twice in the last seven minutes to force another replay.

The third meeting, at the notorious Fallowfield ground that had staged the troubled 1893 final, was a chaotic affair. United, who went into the game without the injured Bennett and Johnson, and had Morren off the field for a long spell, were grateful when the referee abandoned proceedings at half-time. To illustrate the problems that stemmed from persistent crowd encroachment; the game, scheduled to start at four o'clock, started thirty minutes late and had only reached the halfway stage at quarter to six. At the time, Liverpool were leading 1–0, the goal having come, as you would have expected, from Allan.

When the fourth attempt to settle the issue was staged at Derby, United were without Morren, but Bennett and Johnson returned and, though Needham was taken ill in the dressing room before the game, he insisted on playing and, filling in at centre-half, ensured Allan did not trouble Foulke. Beer, meanwhile, emerged the match-winner, finally breaking the deadlock five minutes from the end. At the final whistle, the most dejected man on the field was former United hero, Rab Howell, now with Liverpool and keen to punish his old club for axing him after the Sunderland episode of the previous year.

Remarkably, having defeated Liverpool on the Thursday, United played League matches on the Friday and Saturday. Not surprisingly, perhaps, they lost both, at Burnley and Blackburn, but they then had a two-week break before the Cup final. Director Tom Bott and trainer George Waller took the players to Skegness to relax and prepare for the clash with Derby County at the Crystal Palace.

Bott, who was then about 55 years old, was a wholesale fishmonger who, though born in Birmingham, had lived in Sheffield from boyhood. His family home in his early days had been in Fitzalan Square, and he often said that the day he wandered off beyond Pond Street and discovered Bramall Lane was the most important of his life. He had a rare passion for cricket and, later, football, and while he was not an original member of the United football committee, he soon got himself involved. Moreover, he made a practical contribution to the cause of ensuring the club matched the biggest of their rivals by seeking to instil a realistic and professional approach to the management of the team. Thus he was almost single-handedly responsible for instituting a system of bonuses for results when many of his colleagues were opposed to the principle. Moreover, he spent as much time as he could in the company of George Waller, and he became a sort of honorary team-manager in that he made himself available to join the players when they went into special training. On these occasions, he revelled in organising activities that kept the squad amused and occupied and, because he seldom found it necessary to pull rank and earned the trust and respect of the professionals, he enjoyed great popularity.

Of course, one or two of them were difficult to handle and some got up to tricks that tested his patience but, for the most part, he was like an overgrown schoolboy, full of energy and enthusiasm on these trips to the seaside or into Derbyshire. Typically, he once organised a race between the super-fit trainer Jack Houseley and the hefty Foulke. He staggered the other players by saying he was so confident that the giant goalkeeper would win that he promised to take the team to a show if Houseley was first to the tape. Foulke did win, but Bott still laid on a night out for the players.

So, 'Nudger' Needham and his men were in high spirits as they went into an FA Cup final at which the 73,833 crowd included the famed South African statesman, Cecil Rhodes, and Prime Minister A.J. Balfour, with William Clegg, Lord Mayor of Sheffield, sitting alongside his brother Charles in the VIP enclosure. Derby, who had reached the semi-final in 1896 and 1897 and fallen to Nottingham Forest in the previous year's final, were fancied finally to capture the trophy; but they were accused by their supporters of shooting themselves in the foot when they chose to leave out Archie Goodall. The line-up was:

United: *Foulke; Thickett, Boyle; Johnson, Morren, Needham; Bennett, Beer, Hedley, Almond, Priest*

Derby: *Fryer; Methven, Staley; Cox, Paterson, May; Arkesden, Bloomer, Boag, McDonald, Allen*

Thickett, by the way, went into this game still recovering from broken ribs suffered in the semi-final marathon, but it was not true that he played wrapped in forty yards of bandages. This was a story perpetrated by the doctor who attended the United man: he said he made it up to amuse the press and was surprised when they didn't recognise it as a joke. Thickett, like Foulke, was a huge man who captured the imagination and was often the subject of greatly exaggerated tales. Most of them were untrue: as was the one suggesting he drank a bottle of champagne at half-time in the 1899 final.

Jasper Redfearn had travelled from Sheffield to record the game on his cinematograph machine, and match referee Arthur Scragg allowed him to carry the cumbersome equipment to the centre-circle to film the toss-up, which was won by Needham; but, almost immediately, things began to go against United and after twelve minutes John Boag shot Derby in front. It was only towards half-time that United began to get to grips, there were some long faces in the Sheffield dressing room at the interval. Tom Bott recalled later that Billy Beer was the man who cheered everyone up. 'Billy said we were sure to win. He said the Derby lads were all puffing and blowing and he mentioned one opposing player who was calling his colleagues names and causing them to fall out with one another. 'I went back to my seat for the second half a lot more confident,' said Bott.

It took United until the 59th minute to equalise, and, just before they did so, they should have been further in arrears. The legendary Steve Bloomer (he had scored six in a record 9–0 defeat of Wednesday the previous January) shot wide with only Foulke to beat, and then forced a brilliant save from the goalkeeper. But at last, Needham got away on the left, and, just when it looked as if the captain had delivered his cross too close to Fryer in the Derby goal, Walter Bennett nipped in and guided the ball into the net with his head.

The balance of the game suddenly swung United's way, and, with Derby in a panic and missing the cool old

head of Goodall, there was only one team in control. Beer, an amateur musician of some note, really called the tune in the 65th minute when he waltzed through on his own and shot the Sheffield side in front. Five minutes later, Jack Almond made it 3–1 from a Bennett centre; and, after Derby had lost Scot, Johnny May, their influential left-half, with an injury, Fred Priest added a late fourth United goal following Johnson's free-kick.

Minutes after the final whistle, Needham stood on a table in front of the Crystal Palace pavilion, holding the Cup and responding to cries of 'speech!'. He said: 'I think we have earned this cup. We have had to play hard for it, and I'm sure there is no man in this ground more proud than I am now. I am also proud of having such a team to play with.'

As he went to the dressing room, the United captain was approached by Bloomer, and the man who was to finish with 332 goals in 525 games for Derby asked if he might hold the Cup for a moment. The England ace was to play in two more semi-finals, but he knew this was the nearest he would get to the prize he most coveted in the game.

On the way home from the Crystal Palace, Joe Wostinholm confirmed he was to resign after thirty years as secretary at Bramall Lane, but he was retaining his post with Yorkshire CCC and intended to join the new board when the United club became a limited company. With Harry Stones having already relinquished the assistant secretary's duties, United recruited John Nicholson, who had formerly been with Attercliffe FC and was already a prominent figure in the Sheffield & Hallamshire Football

John Nicholson, United secretary 1899–1932 and one of Sheffield football's great characters.

Association. 'Old Nick', as a later generation of players dared to call him (though never to his face), was one of the great football characters of his generation. Nicholson was a very thorough administrator but one with a sharp dash of wit who tended to enjoy measuring the intelligence of professionals by seeing how far they could be pushed before agreeing to any demand that was reasonable.

With the ground (almost twelve acres) finally purchased, the Sheffield United Cricket & Football Club Ltd held its first annual meeting on 18th July 1899 and the first board numbered twenty directors, who were: Lord Hawke, F.S. Jackson, J.C. Clegg, William Chesterman, W.A. Matthews, C.E. Jeffcock, C.E. Vickers, Frank Atkin, Michael J. Dodworth, Charles Stokes, J.B. Wostinholm, David Haigh, Edwin Barber, Alfred Cattell, Arthur Neal, Tom Bott, Harry Lockwood, A.A. Tasker, Arthur Bingham, and Walter Sissons. The number remained twenty until being reduced to sixteen in June 1919, and separate cricket and football committees operated within the framework of the board until they were amalgamated in the build-up to the end of the cricket era at Bramall Lane in the early 1970s. Of the original board Charles Stokes, Tom Bott, Walter Sissons and Alfred Cattell all chaired the football committee at different periods over the next 34 years.

The first decisions made by the new board included planning the erection of a new cricket pavilion (the one that survived until the late 1970s) and the creation of a new John Street stand (the last remains of which were demolished in 1994). The directors intended that big things would happen at Bramall Lane and, indeed, by 1903 the ground had staged a cricket Test between England and

Australia and another England–Scotland soccer international. More importantly, the club went remarkably close to starting the new era by recapturing the League Championship; and, after losing in the FA Cup final in 1901, they lifted the trophy again in 1902.

In 1899–1900, United's first as the owners of Bramall Lane, they relinquished their grip on the FA Cup and the League crown proved just beyond their reach; but it turned out to be one of the most eventful seasons in the history of football in Sheffield. With Wednesday in the Second Division, it was fortunate that the city clubs should be paired in the FA Cup, but what a battle it proved to be!

Ernest Needham

Records and Rivalry: The Epic 1899–1900 Campaign

THE 1899–1900 season ranks as one of the most remarkable in the history of football in Sheffield. It was the year when FA Cup holders United equalled a Football League record by going undefeated through their first 22 games in Division One while relegated Wednesday began their Second Division campaign with a fourteen-match unbeaten run. In the League the clubs lost only one home match between them, but hopes that they might achieve a title double in their separate grades went unfulfilled because, while Wednesday won promotion at the first attempt, United's form faltered just enough for them to finish two points behind Aston Villa in the Championship race.

The supreme irony was that United's season took a dip after they had finally defeated Wednesday in a marathon FA Cup tie which still ranks as perhaps the most bitter Sheffield derby duel of them all, with Wednesday having two men sent off and one carried off with a broken leg while United lost two men injured.

The rivalry between the clubs had peaked following their sharply contrasting fortunes in the previous season, for while United captured the FA Cup for the first time Wednesday endured a period of such trauma off as well as on the field that there was a time when their very existence seemed under threat. Wednesday's lease on Olive Grove was due to expire in September 1898, but they

had assumed renewal was a formality, and it was with disbelief and alarm that they learned they would have to vacate the site by the end of the 1898–99 season at the latest. The Midland Railway Company wanted to extend their lines, and Sheffield Corporation said they aimed to convert the rest of the area to municipal use. To say the prospect of being suddenly homeless sparked a major crisis is probably an understatement.

Whether the circumstances were responsible for the dramatic decline in the team's fortunes is difficult to estimate, but obviously, the situation created uncertainty which affected the players. Everyone at the club believed the fates were conspiring to make life as tough as possible in every direction just when they could use a bit of decent luck. They began the season well enough, and were at one time second in the table; but a subsequent lack of quality and consistency induced a slump that made them favourites to suffer under the new automatic relegation that had replaced the Test match system.

This, by the way, was the season that included the famous 'split' game with Aston Villa, when the first $79\frac{1}{2}$ minutes were played on 28th November 1898 and the remaining $10\frac{1}{2}$ minutes completed on 13th March 1899! On the earlier date, referee Arthur Scragg (who was to take the Sheffield United–Derby

County FA Cup final later in the season) did not arrive until half-time after missing his train from Crewe. The game started seven minutes late, and, towards the end of the second period, with Wednesday leading 3–1, Mr Scragg decided the light was too bad to continue. Villa, naturally, urged the Football League to order the game to be replayed, but, remarkably, the authorities said it would be sufficient to complete the final 10½ minutes. This was done and Wednesday registered a delayed 4–1 victory which did not detract from Villa's push for the Championship nor halt Wednesday's inevitable slide to relegation.

In fact, Wednesday won only eight matches all season, and the win against Villa was one of only two they managed between February and the end of the campaign. When they lost their final home game, against Newcastle, it probably added insult to injury that United were winning the Cup on the same day. If there were any consolations to be found by that time it was that they were set to exchange contracts for the purchase of a new ground at High Bridge, Owlerton.

There was, of course, a certain irony in that, just when Wednesday had been facing the possibility of being homeless, United were set to buy Bramall Lane from the Duke of Norfolk. When there had been some doubt about Wednesday being allowed to remain at Olive Grove long enough to complete the 1898–99 campaign, United had said they would put their ground at their neighbours' disposal to ensure they finished their programme; but there does not seem to have been any discussion about the

possibility of the clubs sharing Bramall Lane on a permanent basis. There was talk of Wednesday using Sheaf House, just up the road from United's headquarters, but it was never a serious contender; the best bet looked to be a site at Carbrook, but the owner accepted a higher bid from a builder while the football club was hesitating over finalising negotiations.

The ten-acre site at High Bridge, alongside the River Don, was acquired in late April at an initial price of £5,000 plus costs, but it had the disadvantage of being a long way from the city centre, poorly served by public transport, and requiring a lot of urgent and costly work to convert it into a football stadium before the start of the new season. The original Wednesday club was formally wound up at a meeting at the old Maunch Hotel and a limited liability company was formed, with the original share issue raising £7,000—income that was crucial in financing the essential work on the new ground.

George Senior, one of the most famous industrial figures of that era and among the greatest of Sheffield's self-made men, was elected chairman and the initial Wednesday board included: Arthur Dickinson (still honorary secretary), Charles and William Clegg, Tom and Herbert Nixon, George Franklin, Herbert Hughes, Bernard Firth, William Turner, Walter Fearnehough, Joe Mastin, Henry Wood, Arnold Muir Wilson, A.G.W. Dronfield, J.R. Wheatley, John and Alfred Holmes, William Tasker, Fred Bye, Joe Cowley, and Herbert Newbould. The Fearnehough and Turner families were to remain connected with the club well into modern times—indeed,

For the first 14 years of its existence, the home Wednesday acquired in 1899 was known as Owlerton, and this picture, featuring the old Olive Grove stand, was taken around the time of the famous FA Cup marathon between the Sheffield clubs in February 1900.

Cecil Turner became a vice-president in 1995 after being a director for some years.

Wednesday's fears that the move to Owlerton (as the ground was called until 1913–14) would see them lose support proved unfounded, but of course, it helped that they made such a splendid start when launching their bid to return to the top grade at the first attempt. They won eleven of their first fourteen games dropping only three points, and it was New Year's Eve before they tasted defeat— at Chesterfield. In the meantime, United dropped just two points in their opening ten games, and while they lost to Wednesday in a friendly on Boxing Day, they reached mid-January having equalled Preston's record of 22 League matches without defeat.

In truth, for a few weeks before they claimed a slice of history, United, though six points clear at the top of the First Division, had been showing signs that the pressure of nearing the record was beginning to inhibit them.

Yet, in retrospect, it is not diffcult to imagine that they might have bettered Preston's 1888–89 feat but for a freak downpour which cost them the chance to equal the record a week before they finally did so.

The whole course of United's season, and perhaps League history, might have been changed but for the heavy rain that fell in Lancashire on the first Saturday in January. United went to Blackburn needing only to draw to complete 22 games unbeaten. The rain never stopped all through their journey over the Pennines. It was so bad that the trains were delayed and United reached Darwen only half an hour before they were due to kick off at Ewood Park. When they arrived at the ground, the pitch resembled a lake, and, after Needham lost the toss, United found them-selves kicking into driving rain and sleet. The match soon degenerated into a farce, and, after 36 minutes, the referee (again it happened to be Mr Scragg) decided he had no choice but to abandon proceedings. When the game was replayed United shared a 3–3 draw, and they were left feeling that, had they emerged with a similar scoreline on the original date and then gone into a home game seeking to extend the record, the odds would have been in their favour.

As it was, they equalled the record in a 1–1 draw with Derby in an exciting duel at Bramall Lane, where the visitors led until late in the game. Then, after the Derby goalkeeper had saved from Bill Barnes (a capture from Leyton), the poor custodian was unceremoniously bundled into the net with the ball. A point left United's statistics reading:

P22 W14 D8 L0 F45 A16

It ensured that United's next match, at Bury, took on the status of a cup final, and a 15,141 crowd packed into Gigg Lane. Because the local railway company refused to authorise excursion trains while the Lancashire people set up special trips from all the main football centres west of the Pennines, Bury had the benefit of overwhelming support in a Roses battle that was no place for the faint-hearted.

Yet United more than held their own in the first half, and, just after the interval, Charley Field, an ex-soldier who had quit the army to become a professional at Bramall Lane, shot them in front, Field, known as 'Oakey', was deputising for Almond.

Members of Sheffield United's committee 95 years ago.

Unfortunately, after 70 minutes, Bury equalised through Wood; five minutes later United lost Priest, who was carried off with a sprained ankle. In the 80th minute, Wood scored Bury's winner. The dream of being the first club to remain unbeaten in 23 League games from the start of a season was over.

That defeat cut United's lead at the top of the table to two points, and with their defence of the FA Cup dominating the next five weeks (during which they played only one League game), they were to lose ground they were never able to make up. Moreover, whilst Aston Villa lost only one of their last thirteen First Division fixtures, United lost four.

The Sheffield clubs both managed 1–0 home victories in the first round of the FA Cup: Wednesday's victims were Bolton, United's, Leicester Fosse. When the second-round draw paired the city clubs at Bramall Lane, the news was greeted with tremendous enthusiasm and excitement and, commented the *Telegraph*: 'No football match in local history has been so heavily (and heatedly) discussed, or so eagerly awaited.' As Wednesday, following three defeats, had conceded top place in Division Two to Bolton, the experts were tipping a United victory.

Saturday 10th February could not come quickly enough for supporters, though in the week preceding the tie there was a good deal of snow and ice about and fears that the weather might prompt postponement. Indeed, though the big day dawned fine and cold, and 32,381 spectators paid £1,183 to see the first-ever FA Cup clash between the Sheffield clubs, the snow returned with a

vengeance and, five minutes into the second half, conditions became so bad that referee John Lewis had little choice but to abandon the match. Attempts were made to re-stage it on the following Thursday, but there was more heavy snow and, when the game was played two days later, it was only thanks to dozens of volunteers who had worked for hours clearing the pitch.

A crowd of 28,374 saw the teams share a 1–1 draw in an ill-tempered clash marred by over-aggressive play and conditions that made good football difficult. Hedley had the ball in the net for United, but his effort was disallowed for handling; then Brash shot Wednesday ahead after twenty minutes. It was in the second half that the mood of the match turned sour. Wednesday, angered when goalkeeper Massey was lamed by an unnecessary kick, were incensed when Spiksley was carried off with a knee injury. There was little but fouls after that, said a local reporter, but, with ten minutes left, Almond snatched United's equaliser.

Because the third round was only a week away, the replay had to be played within two days—not long enough, argued the *Sheffield Independent*, for tempers to cool. The *Telegraph* meanwhile, pleaded with both teams to 'bury the hatchet'. It did not help generate goodwill that, while United went into the Owlerton match at full strength, Wednesday were without three key men: Massey, Spiksley and Harry Millar (a free-scoring centre-forward signed from Bury the previous summer), all victims of the ill-treatment they had received in the first clash. The line up was:

Wednesday: *Mallinson; Layton, Langley; Ferrier, Crawshaw, Ruddlesdin; Brash, Pryce, Lee, Wright, Topham*

United: *Foulke; Thickett, Boyle; Johnson, Morren, Needham; Bennett, Beer, Hedley, Almond, Priest*

A crowd of 23,000 witnessed a match that the local press described as 'a disgrace . . . a game of wild excitement that sadly tarnished the image of Sheffield football.' For 38 minutes it was just a rugged local derby, but then Thickett clattered into young George Lee, and Wednesday's deputy centre-forward was carried off with a broken leg. After that, the play degenerated into a bitter feud in which retribution was the name of the game, the ball almost incidental to proceedings.

Two minutes after half-time, Langley tripped Bennett and Needham scored from the penalty spot; after 71 minutes John Pryce, formerly of Hibernian and Glossop, was sent off for kicking Hedley, the United man having to be helped off; and, five minutes from the end, Wednesday were reduced to eight men and United to nine when Langley was dismissed for a foul that ensured Bennett did not finish the match. Billy Beer then made it 2–0 to United but, as the *Telegraph* commented: 'Under the circumstances, there was no very great glory attached to the victory, with one goal scored when Wednesday had ten men and the other when they had only eight.' (Incidentally, Lee's broken leg marked the end of his League career. He was subsequently released and, sadly, in 1906 he died at the age of 29.)

It was five days later that United faced a third-round date, and though it was at home and only Harry Johnson had failed to recover from wounds inflicted in the battle of Owlerton, the prospect of meeting Bury, the team that had ended their great League run, did not exactly fill them with confidence. Indeed, it was a tired home side that trailed 2–1 at half-time at Bramall Lane, and they were grateful for another saving act by Needham, who earned a replay by equalising from the penalty spot.

This was the point at which circumstances began to conspire against United, for while Johnson was able to resume, now Thickett was troubled with a bad leg, and the decision to take a gamble and keep him in the side was to prove a costly error of judgement. Moreover, when they went to Gigg Lane, the game had not been long in progress when Needham was clattered and reduced to a passenger with an injury that caused him to miss several key games in later weeks.

Bury, in fact, were destined to win the FA Cup, and indeed, on the way they would triumph at Bramall Lane in a semi-final replay against Nottingham Forest, but the double they achieved over United in League and Cup at Gigg Lane was the boost that transformed their season. Their hero in the second defeat of Needham's men was winger Billy Richards, who in the second half, twice exposed Thickett's lack of mobility: scoring the first goal and crossing for John Plant to make it 2–0.

Two days later United faced a top-of-the-table clash at Aston Villa, and considering they were without Needham, Thickett, Morren and Priest, a 1–1 draw was a good result. Subsequent victories over Preston and Newcastle kept them in the title race, but a 4–0 defeat at Nottingham Forest at the end of March was probably the setback that ended their hopes. They had gone into the game without Needham and Thickett, who were injured, and Foulke and Hedley, who were on Football League duty. Foulke's deputy, ironically called Billy Biggar, had a nervous debut against a side which, three days earlier, had been knocked out of the Cup in that semi-final replay with Bury in Sheffield.

Wednesday, having started their Owlerton era with a 5–1 defeat of Chesterfield after trailing to a Herbert Munday goal, maintained a 100 per cent home record in winning the Second Division title, scoring 61 of their 84 goals on their new ground while conceding only seven. Langley and his colleagues did not allow the Cup setback against United to distract them from the aim of a prompt return to the top grade. True, immediately after the United defeat, they lost heavily at Small Heath, but they then suffered only one fall and won ten of their remaining twelve games, in one spell scoring eighteen goals in four matches.

This was the season when they began to fashion the side that would ensure the first years of the Owlerton era began on a note of high achievement. The likes of Willie Layton, a back, and Herrod Ruddlesdin, a half-back, confirmed the progress that had lightened the gloom of the previous season. Bob Ferrier, having been switched from inside-forward, blossomed into an outstanding wing-half; and, in January, another Harry Davis was signed (this one from Barnsley), and it was quickly evident that he was going to make a

very important contribution.

Willie Layton, who had joined the club in 1895 and finally succeeded Jack Earp as Langley's back partner, was destined to make some 360 senior appearances. An intriguing story is told of how, when he was due for a trial at Olive Grove, he took the previous night off from his job as a miner at Blackwell Colliery. In his absence there was an explosion in which seven of his workmates died; Layton always said he saw the hand of fate in this and decided that, if Wednesday signed him, he would never play for anyone else. Ruddlesdin, who came from Birdwell and developed into an England player, was similarly loyal, though in his case his later career was blighted by illness.

Davis, who scored seven goals in Wednesday's promotion run, stood only 5ft 4ins tall and laid claim to being the smallest player in the First Division for the following seven years. From the moment he arrived in Sheffield, supporters applauded not only outstanding talents, that won him three England caps, but a toughness and resiliance that earned him the nickname 'Joe Pluck'.

Like United, Wednesday made sound defence the cornerstone of their success in this phase of their history but, in escaping from the Second Division, they owed much to the marksmanship of John Wright and Harry Millar—not forgetting the inevitable and vital contribution of Spiksley. Wright, who had arrived from Bolton for £200 the previous season and made his debut in that famous unfinished game with Villa, did not enjoy the best of starts in Sheffield, but, when Millar came from

Bury to join him, they established an outstanding partnership. Wright's 26 goals included three hat-tricks, and Millar, who scored in his first three games and finished with fourteen, was the first Wednesday man to score four in a League match.

Millar, however, was not to enjoy the same success on the club's return to the First Division. It was his misfortune that in the summer, they captured another Scot—one destined to become an all-time Wednesday great. His name was Andrew Wilson, who would serve the Owls for twenty years, in which time he made over 500 senior appearances and scored a record 216 League and Cup goals.

Cup Trail and Triumph: United 1901, 1902

20

T HE 1900–1901 campaign passed into Bramall Lane history as another season that ended in disappointment. While United again reached the FA Cup final, they lost in a replay to Tottenham, who were then in the Southern League; and, in finishing fourteenth in the First Division, their League record offered little in the way of consolation.

Of course, the Cup run generated considerable extra income, which was all the more welcome in the light of investments being made in ground improvements; but the lure of the Crystal Palace so distracted United that they had one spell when they won only two of fifteen League games and collected a mere seven points. In fact, they never managed more than three successive League victories all season, and, for the most part, supporters were not impressed with the team's performance.

Yet it was not a term without some positive points, not the least of these were several notable individual successes. Walter Bennett and George Hedley got their first England caps, Peter Boyle played for Ireland, and the form of Charley Field and Bert Lipsham, United's only uncapped players in the Cup final, was a source of great satisfaction. Ironically, at the start of the season the diminutive Field had found his position under threat with the signing of Patrick Gilhooley from Celtic.

The arrival of outside-left Lipsham late in the previous season had enabled Priest to switch inside, and they formed a formidable partnership. Lipsham, who was signed from Crewe (it was said United secretary John Nicholson held up an express train while the forms were completed!), had to give up his job as Official Receiver in Chester to move to Bramall Lane. His speed and shooting power made him an instant hit, and as well as enjoying one run of over 100 consecutive appearances, he eventually gained international recognition.

However, if Lipsham quickly became a favourite with supporters, there were others who were the target of constant criticism. So much so that the following amusing note appeared in United's official programme:

> The attention of the Committee has been drawn to a most iniquitous and scandalous treatment of our players by certain sections of the crowd behind the Bramall Lane goal. Their language is most dirty, to say nothing of the bitterness with which they taunt Foulke and Bennett. It has become so warm that today a large staff of detectives has been engaged to catch the delinquents, and it will go hard with the wrongdoers.

Foulke, in fact, was dropped for the first time in December and when he returned after missing four games, he conceded four goals on a dismal day for the team in the home match with Stoke. But, a week later, the giant goalkeeper retained his place when United started on the Cup trail with a daunting date at Sunderland. Cooks organised a 5s 6d (27½p) excursion for Sheffield fans, who saw goals by Lipsham and Priest seal a notable success. Everton were disposed of in a 2–0 home victory at the next stage, and United romped to a memorable 4–0 triumph at Wolverhampton in the third round.

Bennett, having notched doubles against both Everton and Wolves, was answering his critics in style: indeed, after the Everton game, he was called into the England team against Wales, and, after Wolves had been defeated, he was named for the Scotland match. Needham, who captained England against Wales, knew the full International Committee was at the Wolves tie and according to Tom Bott, he said he was going to ensure Bennett got so much of the ball that afternoon that he could not fail to be selected for the Scotland fixture. Bennett's only misfortune was that his England partnership with Steve Bloomer failed to fulfil expectations, largely because the Derby man tended to play for himself on these occasions.

A much greater personal misfortune befell Harry Thickett ahead of United's semi-final with Aston Villa at Nottingham. While the players were in special training at Skegness, the defender learned his wife had been taken seriously ill. He dashed home, but she died a few days later. Naturally, he was told to forget football for a while. In his absence,

despite leading twice through Priest and Lipsham, United had to settle for a 2–2 draw. But Thickett insisted on making himself available for the replay the following Thursday, when Priest, who scored two goals and Bennett were on target as Villa were beaten 3–0 and the Bramall Lane men celebrated reaching their second final in three seasons.

Tottenham, having won the Southern League title the previous year, had developed a skilful, cultured side under player-manager John Cameron, he was one of four internationals in the team. One of the others was skipper Jack Jones, who had gained the first 9 of his 21 Welsh caps in three years in Sheffield from 1894. Indeed, United helped him get a coaching appointment at a public school and they had been dismayed when he repaid them by encouraging Bob Cain to leave—all the more so as Cain later regretted following Jones to Tottenham.

Much is made of the fact that Spurs were the first and only non-League side to win the FA Cup after the creation of the Football League; but at the time, they were as good as the majority of First Division teams. That is evident when it is noted that, en route to the final, their victims included Cup-holders Bury, Preston and West Brom. Their star performer was a dashing young centre-forward called Alexander Brown, known as Sandy, he was one of five Scots in the team. Brown had claimed twelve of the fifteen goals Spurs had scored in their Cup run, including three in the semi-final.

A staggering attendance of 114,815 was officially recorded by the Crystal Palace authorities at the 1901 final, and it was soon evident that a huge majority of the spectators were Spurs supporters. A contemporary report noted:

> There was not much cheering when Priest, collecting a pass from Field, shot Sheffield in front after ten minutes; but there was a deafening explosion of noise twelve minutes later when Brown headed the London team level. Then there was another great roar just after half-time when Brown put Spurs in front. If Tottenham had not been deserted, they would have heard the cheering there!

However, United salvaged a draw, and it was an equaliser that sparked controversy. Lipsham's shot was not collected cleanly by George Clawley, the Spurs goalkeeper, and with Bennett challenging, the ball was turned behind. Most people anticipated a corner, though some felt Bennett may have got the last touch. Remarkably, referee Kingscott signalled a goal, insisting Clawley had let the ball slip over the line before putting it round the post.

In the final analysis, the incident did not have long-term consequences for Spurs. They won the replay 3–1, the only controversy concerned the choice of venue. Why it was staged at Bolton was a mystery, though it was suggested that some powerful FA official mistakenly believed the Lancashire town was halfway between Sheffield and London—and none of his minions dared to say he was a duffer at geography! In fact, it had been intended to replay the game at Goodison Park, but Liverpool, the Champions-elect, were at home to Nottingham Forest on the same day,

and their objection was upheld.

Tom Bott, the United director, speaking many years later, said the replay would never have been necessary if United had not put a stale team into the first game. He explained that the players' accommodation in London had been in a loft and few got a decent night's sleep. His excuse for their failure at Bolton was that the hotel where the team stayed had been next to a manure works. 'The smell all night was frightful. No wonder Tottenham beat us!' he said.

The day of the replay was wet and miserable, and the weather, combined with the fact that the railway authorities had refused to put on special trains or cut fares, reduced the attendance to barely 28,000, of whom 19,905 paid at the gate on the day. (Bolton were not enjoying good gates for their own matches, and only 2,000 had watched them play United a few weeks earlier.) Local caterers had been told to expect at least 50,000, and, having produced food to meet that level of demand, they were left with thousands of meat pies they couldn't even give away. The occasion is still remembered in Lancashire folklore as 'Pie Saturday'!

In the week ahead of the trip to Bolton, United, because of injuries, had to face Liverpool with a weakened team and they lost: but they were grateful to neighbours Wednesday for agreeing to postpone a midweek League match. This gave injury victims Needham, Field, Hedley and Bennett time to recover whilst resting at Lytham. United, like Spurs, went into the replay with an unchanged side. The teams were:

United: *Foulke; Thickett, Boyle; Johnson, Morren, Needham; Bennett, Field, Hedley, Priest, Lipsham*

Spurs: *Clawley; Erentz, Tait; Morris, Hughes, Jones; Smith, Cameron, Brown, Copeland, Kirwan*

Needham was the inspiration when United grabbed the initiative five minutes before half-time for, at the end of a typical forward run, he fooled the Spurs defence into thinking he was going to shoot. Instead he laid the ball wide to Lipsham, whose hard, low cross was turned into the net at close range by Priest. However, Spurs took control after the interval. Cameron equalised after 50 minutes, a lucky rebound left Tom Smith the easiest of chances to put Spurs in front on 73 minutes, and, 10 minutes from the end, Brown scored a third.

The majority of the journalists praised Spurs for giving them a good yarn from a poor match, but one made sure his piece included this paragraph: 'A word of pity is due to the reporters, who had been placed in the open air. They had to work with water pouring onto their notebooks. It was a shoddy arrangement for the Press.' Today, in the late 1990s, media facilities have greatly improved, though some clubs still treat newspapermen (but not radio or television) with contempt. However, in this context, one notes that, in the summer of 1901, United completed the new John Street stand—it incorporated a rooftop press box offering comfort and an excellent bird's-eye view of play.

The ground improvements at Bramall Lane did not coincide with a notable start to the 1901–1902 season, for United won only two of their first nine games and stood next to bottom of the table in late October. It was typical of the ill-luck that dogged them for much of the season that they lost Bennett with a broken arm in the third game of the campaign. Later, Needham, Priest and Lipsham all had spells on the sidelines. Things took a turn for the better following Alf Common's arrival from Sunderland

A view of Bramall Lane around 1901 showing the new rooftop Press box (so handy for the pigeons who carried the football writers' reports to the local editorial offices) in the old John Street stand. This stand, which was demolished in 1994, was originally built in 1895 and redeveloped after United bought the ground in 1899.

for £325 in late October, and at one stage, the Blades climbed as high as fourth: but a nine-game run with only one win (a 3–0 defeat of Wednesday) saw them finish tenth in the table.

This time, however, their season ended on a high note when they returned to the Crystal Palace and, at the second attempt, defeated Southampton, another Southern League club. There was, perhaps, a touch of irony in that Bennett missed out on the final glory (as did Field and Beer, who both joined Birmingham in February), while Common, in his first season, and Barnes, who made only eighteen appearances in his United career, shared in the success. Barnes, however, scored the goal that won the Cup—though he promptly elected to return south for family reasons, joining West Ham. Incidentally, this was the year when Morren fell out of favour and Bernard Wilkinson, another diminutive centre-half, but so strong and commanding that he was known as 'the pocket Hercules', consolidated his position and went on to make nearly 400 senior appearances.

United's triumphant Cup run began at Northampton, where they won 2–0 with goals from Bennett and Common (a bonus was the discovery in the home side of a fine young inside-forward called Herbert Chapman, who was signed a few months later). In the second round, Needham's men came from behind to beat Bolton at home, Priest scoring the winner with a shot that went through the legs of the legendary goalkeeper J.W. Sutcliffe, (his brother was to play for the Blades in a Cup final 23 years later). A goal by Priest

earned United a draw at Newcastle in the third round, and the replay, a magnificent affair played in muddy conditions, saw the Blades pegged back after Needham had given them the lead, but Common sealed victory with a late strike.

The semi-final paired United with Derby, the team they had beaten in the 1899 final, and many fancied Bloomer and Co. would avenge that defeat. Three games were required to settle the tie, and as if they were fated never to succeed in the FA Cup, Derby conceded the initiative in each of the first two matches. The first meeting was at West Brom, where Derby outplayed United in the first half-hour and led after twelve minutes, Warren pouncing when Foulke failed to hold a hard shot from Bloomer. United had an astonishing escape when Bloomer headed against the bar, and fortune again favoured them when they equalised just after half-time. Fryer, the Derby goalkeeper, aided United's cause when he appealed for an infringement, didn't bother to try to stop Hedley scoring, and was left red-faced when the referee signalled a goal.

In the replay at Wolverhampton, Derby again took an early lead, Wombwell scoring, and poor Fryer was again at fault when United levelled on 37 minutes. The goalkeeper stopped a shot but let the ball slip from his grasp, and Priest nipped in to slot it into the net. However, it was Fryer's subsequent brilliance that denied United a winner in normal time; though Derby had reason to regret not capitalising in extra-time when Needham was forced to retire injured.

*United 1901–1902. The men who brought the FA Cup home for the second time in three years —
and note how hefty 'Fatty' Foulke has grown!*
Back row: Johnson, Thickett, Foulke, Boyle, Bernard Wilkinson, Needham.
Front row: Barnes, Common, Hedley, Priest, Lipsham.

Billy Parker, formerly of Sheffield Boys and the Boys' Brigade (also a future United director), deputised for Needham in the second replay at Nottingham. He had only played in one League game, but performed like a seasoned veteran: he eclipsed Bloomer and was involved in the move that brought the only goal of the afternoon, seven minutes before half-time. Collecting a pass from Bennett, he fed Lipsham, and the winger teed up the ball for Priest to hammer hard and low past Fryer.

Meeting Southampton in the final, United faced another lethal Southern League centre-forward called Brown: this one Albert 'Jigger' Brown, who claimed 29 goals that season. He was a key figure in astonishing triumphs at Bury and Liverpool and in the defeats of holders Spurs and, in the semi-final, Nottingham Forest. Southampton's team included the double international C.B. Fry (that summer he played in the only Test match ever staged in Sheffield); their captain was Harry Wood, who was playing in his fifth final and had been in the Wolves side beaten by Wednesday in 1896; while one of their most influential men was Edgar Chadwick, who had figured in two finals with Everton.

The 1902 final had been in progress only ten minutes when United suffered a cruel blow, with Bennett reduced to a passenger after a fearsome tackle by hardman Bert Lee. The same Southampton man later made Lipsham see stars, and indeed, the outside-left was so roughly handled at one stage that his shorts were virtually ripped from his body— and the other players hurriedly surrounded him while he was fitted with a new pair!

Johnson was the hero when United took the lead after 55 minutes. Aware of Bennett's handicap, he ignored the winger and instead dribbled to the by-line before delivering the centre from which Common scored. If the former Sunderland man was a picture of joy at that moment, two minutes later he was writhing in agony after that man Lee had produced another crunching tackle. Common, moreover, was kicked on the shin (albeit accidentally) by a spectator when he went to retrieve a ball from touch. Thinking it was deliberate, Common apparently clipped the man with his hand, and was soundly booed through the rest of the first-half. During the interval he was persuaded to apologise to the fan, and, thereafter, that section of the crowd cheered every time Common touched the ball.

Three minutes from the end, Southampton equalised with astonishing simplicity. There was a scramble, the ball was half cleared, and then, somehow, it was at the feet of Wood, who stood unmarked six yards away from the unguarded goal. When he put it into the net, United promptly appealed for offside, but, after consulting with linesman Jack Howcroft, referee Tom Kirkham signalled a goal. Howcroft, as is mentioned elsewhere, later described how this incident so incensed Willie

Foulke that, after the game, the giant goalkeeper, totally naked after having a bath, went chasing through the dressing room area in search of the match officials!

Foulke, of course, had calmed down by the time of the replay, and, as often happens, the second meeting was decided by a controversial decision which, going in United's favour, more than compensated for the ill-fortune they believed they had suffered the previous week. Moreover, while they were denied the services of Bennett, the man they brought in, Bill Barnes, emerged the hero. After Hedley had poked in the opening goal within two minutes of the start, United were grateful for two moments of brilliance from Foulke and a desperate clearance when Thickett walloped the ball over his own bar. Southampton's persistence paid off after 69 minutes when, with the Blades defence at sixes and sevens in a desperate goalmouth mêlée, Brown struck the equaliser.

It was ten minutes from the end that Wood was penalised, harshly he felt, for he argued that the ball had bounced against his elbow and there had been no intent. Needham, taking the free-kick from forty yards out, sent the ball into the goalmouth, where Fry headed it out. It again reached Needham, and he attempted a dipping shot. Robinson, the goalkeeper, seemed to try to punch the ball, failed to connect properly, and it dropped at the feet of Hedley. The United centre-forward was so taken by surprise that he slipped with the goal at his mercy, but Barnes rushed in and thumped the ball into the net.

Needham, after collecting the

SHEFFIELD TURN OUT PUNCTUALLY WEARING THEIR COLOURS

AND QUICKLY NET A GOAL

COMMON HAS A LITTLE DIFFERENCE WITH ONE OF THE CROWD

WHICH IS AMICABLY SETTLED AT HALF-TIME

NEEDHAM, WHEN SHEFFIELD SCORED THEIR SECOND GOAL

SOUTHAMPTON'S GOAL

FRANK GILLETT

trophy from Lady Beatrice Villiers, made a short speech: 'We lost it, so it's fitting that we should win it back,' he said. Later, at a celebration dinner at the St Pancras Hotel, the captain made public reference to Bennett's misfortune in missing the replay. 'I think it's very hard lines on Walter. He has done so much for the club in all the matches up to today's, and it is sad that at the last he should be deprived of his medal. I hope the committee will do their best to recompense him.'

Charles Clegg admitted that Bennett's was a rather special case and promised that the club and the FA would look into the matter. A few weeks later, permission was given and Bennett got his medal. Unfortunately,

the winger was to enjoy few more golden moments in his remaining three years with United, and after a brief and miserable spell at Bristol City, he astonished everyone by returning to South Yorkshire to play Midland League football with Denaby. Alas, in 1908, at the age of 33, he died in an underground tragedy at Denaby Colliery.

The 1902 Cup finals teams were:

United: *Foulke; Thickett, Boyle; Johnson, B. Wilkinson, Needham; Bennett (Barnes in replay), Common, Hedley, Priest, Lipsham*

Southampton: *Robinson; Fry, Molyneux; Meston, Bowman, Lee; A. Turner, Wood, Brown, Chadwick, J. Turner*

THE WEDNESDAY
FOOTBALL CLUB.
LIMITED.

Banquet

* * AT THE * *

MASONIC HALL,

· ON ·

Friday, May 20th 1904.

To Commemorate the winning of the

Football League Championship

for the second year in succession.

Chairman:

Ald. GEO. SENIOR, J.P.

Champions Twice!
Wednesday 1903, 1904

WEDNESDAY followed their Second Division title triumph of 1900 with a couple of seasons in which their record was satisfactory rather than spectacular. They finished eighth in the top grade in 1901 and ninth in 1902, and if United's run to the FA Cup final in both years gave the Bramall Lane club the limelight, the consolation down at Owlerton was that at least they had ended up higher in the table than their neighbours.

While they were never serious Championship contenders, they would certainly have been in with a shout had their away form not been so dismal. In 1900–1901 they did not win once on their travels, and in fact, went nineteen months without an away victory until the sorry sequence was ended at Liverpool in October 1901. In contrast, their home record was good, and they had one spell between mid-February 1901 and early March 1902 when they were unbeaten in eighteen games at Owlerton and won all but four.

In truth, it was a phase during which the team was being re-shaped, although some half-a-dozen members of the promotion side of 1900 survived to make a significant contribution to the Championship 'double' of 1903 and 1904. Crawshaw, Davis, Ferrier, Layton and Ruddlesdin were to remain key figures over a long period; while Langley and Spiksley starred in the first title triumph. Langley was still there when

the second one was clinched, but had spent most of the season on the injured list; and with great reluctance, he finally accepted his playing days were over. (In April 1905 Langley became Hull City's first manager, and in fact, played in a dozen or so of their early Second Division games. Around 1913 he returned to Sheffield and had a spell helping out as Arthur Dickinson's assistant before re-launching his managerial career at Huddersfield. Here he preceded Herbert Chapman, and might have remained much longer but for his support of a plan to move the Town club lock, stock and barrel to Leeds.)

Most notable of Wednesday's new men were goalkeeper Jack Lyall, back Harry Burton, and forwards Andrew Wilson, Harry Chapman, Jock Malloch and George Simpson; though it was in this period that the likes of Bill Bartlett and Jimmy Stewart, who came to the fore later, were recruited. Lyall, who was to make some 300 senior appearances over eight seasons, was a Dundee product who arrived from Jarrow and became the first Scot to play for his country while on Wednesday's books. His chance came unexpectedly, for when Massey got injured in the first season back in the top grade, Frank Stubbs was the initial deputy; but Stubbs never recovered from a nightmare experience at Notts County, where he took a heavy blow on the head and, quite literally, handed the home side five goals in a 6–1 defeat because he didn't know what he was doing!

Burton, though born at West Bromwich, was a Sheffield product who joined Wednesday from Attercliffe FC and, in some 200 games, proved an able and popular successor to Langley; while Malloch, a Scot who came via Brighton, and Simpson, a Geordie, created a notable left-wing partnership. In having to step into Spiksley's boots, Simpson faced an unenviable task, but he rose to the challenge and his pluck as well as his skills made him popular.

Wilson, as was mentioned earlier, earned a special place in Wednesday's hall of fame by scoring a record 216 goals in 540 games. He was barely 20

Andrew Wilson

when he arrived, and though he took time to settle, his talents were evident from the outset, the club has had few players who gave longer or more consistently high service. His popularity was such that when, towards the end of the second title-winning season, he missed several games because of a serious head injury suffered in a match at Nottingham Forest, a rumour spread through the city that he had died. Indeed, one shopkeeper went so far as to announce the 'news' in his window. However, the reports were greatly exaggerated! It took Wilson until 1907 to win favour with the Scottish selectors, and the former Clyde man was unfortunate not to gain more than six caps.

A player who made as big and immediate impression as Wilson, and also gave Wednesday excellent service, was Harry Chapman, a small but solidly built and extremely clever inside-forward from Worksop Town. It has often been said that, but for Bloomer's brilliance, this Kiveton Park product would surely have played for England. He scored over 100 goals in some 300 games for Wednesday, and he and Harry Davis, who were known as 'the marionettes', formed one of the finest wing-partnerships in League football. Like Davis, Chapman suffered his share of rough treatment, but, coming from mining stock, he was tough and resiliant. His biggest problem was persistent knee trouble—it was not uncommon during a match to see him sit on the ground and push his cartilage back into place.

Harry was the brother of Herbert Chapman, whose place in the history of football is assured by virtue of his

Harry Chapman

achievements as manager of Huddersfield and then Arsenal in the 1920s and early 1930s. However, when they were both playing League football, it was Harry who was the star; though Herbert was no mean performer indeed, he made quite an impact when he joined Sheffield United from Northampton in the summer of 1902. By coincidence, he made his United debut in the derby match at Bramall Lane at the start of the campaign in which Wednesday lifted the League title for the first time. Wednesday won 3–2 that day, but United had their revenge a few weeks later when they became the first team that season to succeed at Owlerton, where, by the way, the Chapman brothers formed the right-wing pairing when Sheffield met Glasgow in the first inter-city match at the Wednesday ground.

That 1902–1903 season produced an exciting chase and a dramatic finish to the Championship race. West Brom were the early pacemakers, but in the end, Sunderland and Aston

Villa were Wednesday's chief rivals, though United finished fourth only three points adrift of their neighbours. In the final analysis, Wednesday's most important victories were a 4–0 defeat of Villa in January and an Andrew Wilson-inspired 1–0 success at Sunderland in late March when the Sheffield players were stoned as they left Roker Park. Wearside fans were not keen to see their favourites relinquish the title they had won the previous year!

Wednesday, having left it late in the season to claim top spot for any length of time, found it difficult to consolidate. A solitary win in their final four games left them with a one-point advantage over Sunderland, who still had one match to play and looked a fair bet to collect full points at Newcastle. The Roker men had never lost at St James's Park, but they fell that day, to a Bob McCall goal— and the title was Wednesday's.

In the event, Wednesday were away on a southern tour at the time they learned they had won the Championship. On the afternoon when Sunderland slipped up, Langley and his colleagues were facing Notts County in a match at Home Park, the headquarters of the newly-formed Plymouth Argyle. The game was all part of a campaign to promote football in South Devon, and, after beating County with goals by Malloch and Ruddlesdin, they claimed the Plymouth Bowl—a trophy that is still in the club's possession.

From Plymouth they travelled to Bristol and South Wales before returning to Sheffield, where they were met by an enthusiastic crowd on their arrival at the Midland Station. After the customary victory parade, they held a celebration dinner at the Carlton Restaurant and finished up appearing on the stage of the Empire Theatre. As well as winning the League Championship, Wednesday had captured the Sheffield Challenge Cup, the Midland League Trophy and the Wharncliffe Charity Cup (all won by the reserves), this unique collection was put on display at the formal banquet held at the Masonic Hall in Surrey Street.

Langley, Ruddlesdin and Wilson had been the only ever-presents, though Lyall, Crawshaw, Ferrier and Malloch each missed only one game and Chapman and Spiksley just two. With Layton and Davis absent on only a handful of occasions, consistency of selection was a key factor. The team's strength had been in defence, for only Sunderland could match their record of conceding only 36 goals. Several clubs—including Sheffield United!—managed more goals than Wednesday (54), whose leading scorers were Davis (13), Chapman (12) and Wilson (12). It is intriguing to note that when Wednesday retained the League title in 1903–1904, they were the lowest-scoring side in the First Division's top seven, but nobody could match their defensive record of 28 goals. Of their seven defeats, all in away fixtures, the heaviest were 3–1 at Stoke and 4–0 at Newcastle.

This was a remarkable and memorable season for several reasons. One was that Wednesday had never been as close to a League and Cup double; another was that between September and late January the top two clubs in the First Division were Wednesday and United. Sadly, this state of affairs was too good to last and United, for whom teenager

Arthur S. Brown excelled with 17 goals, fell away after a five-match run without a win. They finished seventh, and their consolation was that Brown, at 18, had, along with Common, been capped by England in February; so when Bernard Wilkinson was called up to face Scotland in April the Bramall Lane fans could claim they had a full team of internationals.

Wednesday lost only one of their first eleven games, while United kicked off with an astonishing eight successive victories—the best of which was a 7–2 drubbing of Wolves, who a week earlier had become the first side to defeat Wednesday. When Wednesday suffered their second defeat, at Stoke in early November, they relinquished the table leadership they had finally wrested from United a few days earlier; and they did not claim it back until the end of January. A seven-match unbeaten run between late January and the end of March, which included a 1–0 defeat of Manchester City (who had emerged their chief rivals), was crucial to Wednesday's title hopes. However, three defeats in four games threw the race wide open again until victory in their last home match, against Aston Villa, meant the Owls had finally edged beyond City's reach. That was a great relief and amply compensated them for having their dream of a League and Cup double shattered by the Manchester club.

In the FA Cup, Wednesday had needed two attempts to dispose of Southern League Plymouth in the first round, but a superb 6–0 crushing of Manchester United at the next stage induced visions of another trip to the Crystal Palace. This triumph was inspired by amateur Vivian S. Simpson, who turned in a dazzling display and scored a memorable treble. Unfortunately, after he had helped Wednesday beat Tottenham in a replay of their quarter-final, it was discovered that he had suffered the injury that prematurely ended his season. This was a cruel blow to Simpson, for he had also helped Sheffield FC reach the final of the FA Amateur Cup, but had to miss the game (at Bradford) in which they beat Ealing 3–1. His consolation was that he was awarded a special medal.

However, it was Wednesday who missed Simpson the most. The amateur had compensated for the loss of Andrew Wilson, sidelined for several weeks with a head injury; and now, with a semi-final looming, the backroom staff at Owlerton committed a tactical blunder. They rushed Wilson back when he clearly was still far from fit, and with the rest of the team playing well below par, they could not complain at falling to Manchester City in the semi-final at Goodison Park. Wednesday went behind after 20 minutes when Lyall, having done well to stop a fierce effort from the legendary Meredith, couldn't hold the ball and Scot Bill Gillespie pounced to score. Sandy Turnbull made it 2–0 before half-time and added another goal after the interval.

The Owls would not get that close to a League and Cup double again until 1930, for though they reached the semi-final in the following season

Wednesday 1904.
Back row: W.E. Hemmingfield, J. Stewart, T.L. Jarvis, W. Bartlett.
Middle row: J. Davis (Ass. trainer), R. Ferrier, A. Langley, J. Lyall, T. Crawshaw, W. Layton, H. Burton, H. Ruddlesdin.
Front row: H. Davis, H. Chapman, A. Wilson, J. Malloch, G. Simpson.

(they lost to Newcastle), it coincided with a slide to ninth in the First Division —this after they had kicked off the 1904–1905 campaign with seven successive victories and led the table until early November.

Chapman, an ever-present for the only time in his years with Wednesday in that second title-winning season, was leading marksman with 18 (16 League). Andrew Wilson chipped in with 12, while Harry Davis's 10 included 5 in the Cup run. Apart from Chapman, only Willie Layton played in every game. Thus nobody had the distinction of figuring in all the League matches in both Championship seasons.

Wednesday 1904 League Championship banquet menu card — the function was held at the old Masonic Hall in Surrey Street.

Wednesday: FA Cup-Winners, 1907

AFTER their 1896 FA Cup triumph, Wednesday's fortunes in the competition fell into sharp decline. In the next seven years they never managed to get beyond the second round. But then in 1904 and 1905, they reached the semi-final and, although they fell at the quarter-final stage in an exciting duel in 1906, supporters sensed that another slice of Cup glory was looking likely sooner rather than later. However, when it came in 1907 it proved to be the last time the club won a major trophy for many years; indeed, it marked the end of a remarkable phase in Sheffield football history.

As has been noted, in 1904 the prospect of a League and Cup double faded with painful suddenness when Wednesday succumbed in the semi-final with a tame show against Manchester City. Then, in 1905, just when the Cup looked to offer compensation for a slide down the First Division after an excellent start, the Owls ran out of luck when they fell to Newcastle one step from the Crystal Palace. (Ironically, Wednesday did go to the Palace late in that season and came home with a trophy, the Sheriff of London's Charity Shield, but it wasn't the same as *the* Cup! Indeed, there was so much dismay amongst club shareholders that the annual meeting that summer was a rather stormy affair.)

There was a big improvement in Wednesday's form in 1905–1906. This was the season when membership of both grades of the Football League was increased to 20, and, in a 38-match First Division, Wednesday finished third. They lost only one of their first eleven games and had a spell at the top, but then five defeats in seven matches and another six-match run without a win early in the new year left them with too much ground to make up. In the end they were seven points adrift of champions Liverpool.

For long enough, it had looked as if, at last, the Cup was going to provide an alternative route to glory. A George Simpson goal gave Wednesday a narrow first-round win over Bristol Rovers, and Simpson was on target in the victories over Millwall (3–0 after 1–1) and Nottingham Forest (4–1) at the next hurdles; and then came a famous quarter-final clash with Everton at Goodison Park on 10th March 1906.

It was a date that evoked memories of the unforgettable 5–5 thriller the teams had produced in a League match the previous season, when the Owls had hit back to salvage a point after trailing 5–1 with less than half an hour left. Once again, in this quarter-final, Everton began with a tremendous burst, Jack Sharp and Jack Taylor putting them 2–0 up within six minutes of the kick-off. In the next four minutes, Wednesday missed a penalty when Harry Davis's spot-kick was saved, but Simpson reduced arrears; then, alas, before half-time Bolton and Booth made it 4–1 to the Merseysiders. Wednesday, however, were far from finished, and after 55 minutes Bill Bartlett jinked his way past four Everton men before beating goalkeeper Billy Scott. Ten minutes from the end it was 4–3 after Davis compensated for his earlier failure by scoring with a second penalty. Though the home goal was under intense pressure in the final stages, Everton held out to push the Owls off the Cup trail.

However, 1905–1906 provided plenty of positive points, not least the development of Bartlett at left-half and Jimmy Stewart at inside-left, and the arrival of Frank Bradshaw on the scene: a trio who would have key roles in the 1907 Cup triumph. Bartlett, whose Wednesday career spanned some 200 games, was initially seen as Ruddlesdin's deputy, but he did so well that 'Ruddy' was switched to right-half and it was Bob Ferrier who lost out. Stewart, who had arrived with Bartlett from the North East, really came into his own in 1905–1906, when he was leading marksman with 22 goals. Those who tipped him for England honours did not have long to wait to see the prediction fulfilled.

Bradshaw, in fact, only played once in 1905–1906 and, indeed, he was to make it into the Cup final side after only thirteen senior outings, but he has passed into club history as a local lad with a remarkable story. A big, well-made inside-forward, he looked destined for great things in his early days, and marked his England debut in 1908 with a hat-trick against Austria in Vienna. Unfortunately, he had to pull out of the next international

because of an injury, and he was never selected again. In fact, he was plagued with knee trouble for some time after this, and Wednesday, fearing his best days were behind him, sold him to Herbert Chapman's Northampton for £250. Chapman sent Bradshaw to a specialist, the lad recovered his old form, and he moved to Everton at a profit. Later he had a fine run with Arsenal, and the man they said was finished in 1910 did not finally quit the League scene until 1923!

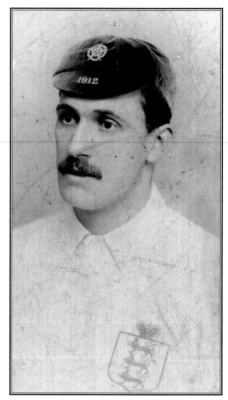

Tom Brittleton

The other main difference between the Championship side of 1904 and the team that won the Cup in 1907 was at right-half, where, because of Ruddlesdin's ill-health, Wednesday

were relieved to have a player of the
stature of Tom Brittleton. He came
from Stockport in January 1905
and went on to make over 370
appearances and collect five England
caps, taking over as captain around
1912. Brittleton still has a place in
club records as the oldest man to play
League football for the Owls. He was
41 when he bowed from the
Hillsborough scene in 1920, and yet
he still went on to help Stoke win
promotion. It was said that nobody
loved the quiet life more than
Brittleton, he was never happier than
when he was off fishing, but on the
field his strength was his
dependability: he was a ball-winner
par excellence, and he was one of the
earliest exponents of the long throw-in.

The Cup triumph of 1907 coincided
with Wednesday finishing in their
lowest League position since their
move to Owlerton. Ironically, they lost
only one of their first sixteen games
and stood second in the table in
December, but then managed only
four League victories in the remaining
months of the season. At home they
suffered six defeats and dropped
seventeen points, their poor away
record included an 8–1 drubbing at
Aston Villa. They reserved their best
for the Cup games, in which they
showed skill and grit and enjoyed
several crucial moments of good
fortune. For instance, in the home tie
with Wolves in the first round they
trailed 2–0 at one stage but hit back
to claim a dramatic 3–2 victory with
goals from Oliver Tummon
(deputising for Davis), Stewart and
Simpson. Then, in the second round,
Wilson snatched an equaliser at
Southampton with twenty seconds
left, and the Owls won the replay 3–1

at Owlerton, with goals from Wilson,
Stewart and Chapman.

It was in the third-round game with
Sunderland at Owlerton that
Bradshaw, deputising for Wilson,
made his Cup debut in a tense, tight
duel which produced no goals.
Wilson returned for the Roker replay,
but Bradshaw stayed in because
Stewart was unfit. This was the day
when George Simpson's 67th-minute
strike sealed a famous 1–0 victory in a
game that skipper Tom Crawshaw
always described as the hardest he
ever played in. It was a triumph
touched with sadness, for, soon after
Simpson's goal, little Harry Davis was
brought down by McConnell and
suffered the broken leg that not only
ended his season but finished his
playing days. Crawshaw recalled:
'When Harry fell, the crack was heard
all over the ground. I ran across and
he held up his foot. "It's broke," he
said, without a trace of emotion.
Later, in the dressing room, when
they were getting him ready to take to
the hospital, he said only one thing:
"Give us a cigarette, captain." I think
he sensed that his playing days were
over.'

How Wednesday survived the
pressure that Sunderland forced them
to endure in the last twenty minutes
of this tie was a mystery to everyone
in the ground, and it might be said it
was the moment when they first had
the look of Cup-winners. It would
have been so easy to succumb, and
they sensed they had defied the fates.

In the quarter-final, against the
reigning champions Liverpool, a
38,000 Owlerton crowd saw Vivian
Simpson take Davis's place, and
Stewart returned. But the hero was
Harry Chapman, who notched the

Action from Wednesday's 1907 FA Cup semi-final tie with Arsenal at Birmingham.

game's only goal early in the second half, after the final whistle he was carried from the field on the shoulders of supporters delighted to see their heroes through to their third semi-final in four years.

Nobody was more determined than Crawshaw to ensure Wednesday would go all the way this time, and when they went to St Andrew's, Birmingham, he believed they could overcome Woolwich Arsenal, even when the North Londoners' cocky captain, Jim Ashcroft, told him: 'I feel sorry for you fellows today—you simply won't be in it.' He may not have been quite so sure after Garbett had given the Gunners the lead in the ninth minute, but his confidence flooded back when Wilson grabbed an equaliser after 21 minutes. Early in the second half, Wilson put Wednesday in front, and Stewart made it 3–1 in the last minute. No wonder Crawshaw said to Ashcroft as the teams left the field: 'I'll bet tha'll be feeling sorry for us now, eh?'

Crawshaw told an amusing story about Dr and Mrs Bishop of Buxton, who were great Wednesday fans. Mrs Bishop always carried an old umbrella to matches, and it had come to be regarded as a lucky mascot. 'I thought it wasn't going to help us today,' Crawshaw commented to Mrs Bishop after the Arsenal game. 'I thought we weren't going to get here,' she said. 'By the time we reached the ground, Arsenal had scored. Fortunately, you got an equalising goal soon after we were in our seats!'

Wednesday's opponents in the final at Crystal Palace were Everton, who had beaten them in that exciting fourth-round game the previous year and gone on to lift the trophy. The

Goodison side was strongly fancied to triumph again, but Crawshaw, the only survivor from Wednesday's 1896 Cup-winning side, refused to be drawn into a debate about the opposition's strengths. He admitted it would be a tough game, and added: 'Now look here, I'm not going to say we are going to win, and I'm not going to say we shall lose. We are going to try to win. We shall go all the way, and while the ball is rolling you can bet we have a chance. We shall keep going to the end.'

Wednesday went into the match with the same line-up as was chosen to face Arsenal in the semi-final. Thus Chapman was switched to outside-right and young Bradshaw came in for only his fourth Cup appearance. The teams were:

Wednesday: Lyall; Layton, Burton; Brittleton, Crawshaw, Bartlett; Chapman, Bradshaw, Wilson, Stewart, G. Simpson

Everton: Scott; W. Balmer, R. Balmer; Makepiece, Taylor, Abbott; Sharp, Bolton, Young, Settle, Hardman

Wednesday went in front after twenty minutes, with Stewart and Chapman involved in a move that put the Everton goal under pressure. Twice Scott, the goalkeeper, punched clear, but Chapman hammered the ball straight back at the target. Scott stopped but didn't hold it, and, while Chapman was appealing that the ball had crossed the line, Stewart nipped in and nodded it into the net. After that, the Sheffield team had to defend in depth for a long spell, and once Bartlett cleared the ball off the line when Lyall was beaten. Then, just before half-time, Jack Sharp equalised. In a fairly even second half, the game swung Wednesday's way with barely four minutes remaining: Wilson chased a long pass down the wing and, just managing to keep the ball in play, turned it into the goalmouth where Simpson, at the back post, headed it past Scott. The Cup was bound for Owlerton!

Some years later, Crawshaw, reflecting on that triumph, remembered how Chapman twice had to stop playing while he slipped his cartilage back into place. The old skipper also recalled taking the team to a London music hall on Cup final night. The legendary comedian, George Robey, was the star of the show, and when he invited the Wednesday lads onto the stage he promised Crawshaw he would not have to speak. Then, however, Robey turned to the audience and said: 'And now Tommy Crawshaw will tell us all about how Wednesday did it!' The occasion was one the captain never forgot. 'Honest,' he said, 'I was lost

for words, but I managed somehow. Mind you, I think they were mostly amused by my Yorkshire accent and probably didn't understand much of what I said!'

It was to be 28 years before Wednesday won the FA Cup again, and their record in the competition in the next few years was embarrassingly poor, for they fell in the first round four times in the next five seasons. Moreover, three of those defeats were at the hands of non-League sides, two of whom had the satisfaction of winning at Owlerton. It was probably of little consolation that United's Cup record in this period was as dismal. The Blades went out in the first round every year from 1907 to 1913. However, when success in the most famous knockout tournament of all finally came Sheffield's way again, it was the Bramall Lane club who claimed it.

FA Cup winning squad of 1907.

Steps to a 'Khaki'
Cup-Final Success, 1915

WHEN United reached the FA Cup semi-final in 1914 and then finally captured the trophy in 1915, it marked the end of a long phase during which their fortunes faded and the triumphs of the golden age became a distant memory. The sense of anti-climax was evident in that, in nine seasons between 1905 and 1913, the Blades got beyond the first round only once—and that was the year they fell at the next hurdle after persuading Second Division strugglers Blackpool to forego home advantage and play the tie at Bramall Lane for a £250 'consideration'! Later United's Cup woe was compounded when they suffered the embarrassment of being dumped by non-League Swindon and Darlington in front of their own supporters.

Yet if this was a grey period, that is not to suggest it lacked interest and incident, and of course, some of the men who would bring a touch of glory back to Bramall Lane began to appear on the scene. Even some of those who did not stay to help in achieving that ultimate success did at least do enough to gain the respect and lasting affection of supporters.

The case of goalkeeper Joe Lievesley was mentioned in an earlier chapter, but there were others such as Bob Benson and Walter Hardinge who left just before United's fortunes took a sudden upturn. By coincidence, all three went to Arsenal. Benson (273 League appearances,

1905–1913) was an outstanding back who, ironically, had played for England six months before he lost his place to Jack English. Hardinge, too, was capped by England while at Bramall Lane, and his merit as an inside-forward is confirmed by a record of 48 goals in 152 games. While Hardinge has passed into sporting history as a double international (he made his Test debut in 1921), Benson is remembered as the man whose unique penalty-taking technique (someone placed the ball on the spot and he would run half the length of the field to hammer it into the net) made him a great favourite; it will not be forgotten, either, that in 1916, he died in the Highbury dressing room after leaving the field during an Arsenal–Reading wartime fixture.

Of course, in those lean years that followed the triumphs between 1898 and 1902, there were players who gained and then lost the affection of the fans. A classic case was provided by Arthur Brown, the brilliant centre-forward who scored 101 goals in only 185 League and Cup games after arriving at the age of 17 from Gainsborough in 1902. He was still two months short of his 19th birthday when he was capped by England in February 1904, and the Bramall Lane fans loved him. But, after having a benefit match in 1908, he refused to re-sign, claiming the death of his father made it necessary for him to leave to concentrate on running the family business in Lincolnshire. Almost immediately, he joined Sunderland, and while United collected a £1,600 fee (a huge sum in those days) the Blades followers were dismayed by Brown's actions.

By coincidence, Sunderland had been involved in another controversial transfer from United four years earlier, when Alf Common (signed from the Roker club in 1901) suddenly announced he wanted a move—and had no intention of going anywhere but back to Wearside because he was homesick. United always said they had received better offers from other clubs, but they talked to Sunderland and while the man who had cost them £325 ultimately returned to Roker for £520, the main consideration had been the player's insistence that he could play on only if he went 'home' to his previous base.

Barely six months later, in February 1905, Sunderland sold Common to Middlesbrough for the first £1,000 transfer fee in League history. People in the game were staggered by the size of the fee, and Common was berated as 'the wandering Jew of football' (not an expression one would be allowed to use in describing a player in 1995!). United felt cheated because they had sold Common in good faith for less than they could have got elsewhere—and Sunderland had made a rapid 50 per cent profit on the deal. It was not the first time a club would feel 'used', and of course, it would certainly not be the last. That, however, was not the end of the matter, for there was a painful footnote. Common made his debut for Middlesbrough (who were bottom of the First Division and had not won an away game for nearly two years) at Bramall Lane. Middlesbrough beat the Blades 1–0 and Common got the goal—from the penalty spot. United, incidentally, missed with a spot-kick—the culprit was Arthur Brown!

Brown's successor was another Gainsborough Trinity discovery whom United signed at the age of 17, Joe Kitchen was destined to score more League goals (106) for the club than his predecessor. Moreover, Kitchen, a native of Brigg, was the first of the signings that were to re-shape the Blades' fortunes. At £350, he proved a bargain buy, and while he was never a good header of the ball, he thrilled

Alf Common

supporters with his electrifying
dashes and lethal shooting.

The next capture of note was Albert
Sturgess, one of the most remarkable
characters ever to wear a Blades shirt
and a player whose hallmarks were an
indomitable spirit and a versatility
that astonished his colleagues. United
got him from Stoke in June 1908 two
days before the troubled Potteries
club resigned from the League.
Making nearly 380 appearances in
fifteen years at Bramall Lane, he
repaid a modest fee many times over.
Tall and thin with very long legs (he
was nicknamed 'Hairpin'), there were
few more consistent performers, and
he was an obvious choice as captain.
Sturgess played twice for England and
served the Blades until he was 40; and
when he was released in 1923 it was
no surprise that he went on to make
over fifty appearances for Norwich.

Early in 1908–1909 United recruited
R.E. 'Bob' Evans, a winger whom
Aston Villa had rather neglected after
signing him from Wrexham. Evans has
a unique place in football history as
the man who played ten times for
Wales before it was discovered he was
English; and he subsequently
collected four England caps. In fact, it
was John Nicholson, United's
secretary, who, noting the player had
been born in Chester, alerted the
English FA. Evans was to make some
216 appearances for United, scoring
36 goals. Jimmy Simmons and Bill
Brelsford, who also arrived around
this time, from Blackwell and
Doncaster respectively, were a
contrasting pair. Simmons was a
dainty little winger who might have
achieved more but for injuries,
whereas Brelsford was a tough
defensive half-back who proved a

particularly significant piece in the
jigsaw of success. Another key recruit
was Bill Cook, a miner signed from
Hebburn Argyle, who got his big
chance at right-back soon after his
arrival in 1912 at the age of 21. He
never looked back and boasted nearly
300 senior appearances (including 32
in the FA Cup) in a Lane career that
extended into the mid-1920s.
(Incidentally, many years later Cook's
son-in-law, Albert Winter, was
President of Sheffield Chamber of
Commerce.)

Of course, with the benefit of
hindsight, it has to be said that in the
long term, the most significant
capture United made in the years
leading up to the 1915 Cup success
was Billy Gillespie from Leeds.
However, though he made an instant
impact after his arrival in 1911 and
figured in the 1914 run to the semi-
final, he broke a leg in the opening
game of 1914–15 at Sunderland, and
so missed out on the glory. His finest
hour was postponed for another ten
years, and, with that in mind, he will
be featured in more detail in a later
chapter.

It was between March and November 1913 that the jigsaw was all but
completed with the introduction of
Stan Fazackerley, Harold Gough, Jack
English and George Utley in that
order. Fazackerley, who cost £1,000
from Hull, was a tall (6ft), intelligent
inside-forward of such grace that he
never got a mark on his shirt on the
muddiest day; Gough was one of the
coolest goalkeepers in the business;
and English, who cost £500 from
Watford, arrived as the best back in
the Southern League.

There was an element of luck in the
way both Gough and English got the

chance to forge a place in the team, and Gough, a Chesterfield product who was signed from Castleford, profited from the misfortune of Ted Hufton, who had to move to West Ham to make his name. Joe Mitchell was the man who had initially displaced Lievesley in goal, but then Hufton, a product of the local Atlas & Norfolk Works team, had staked a claim. Indeed, in a thirteen-match run at the end of the 1912–13 campaign Hufton had so impressed that he looked certain to start the new season as number one choice. Unfortunately, he broke his nose in the public practice. Gough stepped in, and, although conceding fourteen goals in his first five outings, survived to make some 260 senior appearances and gain an England cap.

English, like Gough, was always going to make the grade, but his chance also came through another's misfortune, that of Bob Benson. When Benson recovered from a slight injury, he was unable to displace his fellow North Easterner. Ironically, English only spent two seasons in United's team (he didn't return after the Great War because of a dispute over a benefit), but the fourteen Cup games in which he played just happened to coincide with the club's best runs in the competition since 1902.

The one problem still plaguing United as the 1913–14 season progressed into the autumn was the lack of an 'old head', and they found the ideal man when they splashed out £2,000 for George Utley from Barnsley. His departure from Oakwell in mid-November provoked uproar in the mining town, but United had been so determined to get him that they not only paid a record fee but gave the Elsecar product the best contract any player had managed to negotiate at Bramall Lane. Remarkably, he was said to have taken a pay cut and agreed to accept ten shillings (50p) a week less than he had earned at Barnsley, but his five-year deal compensated in other ways; a subsequent source of additional income came when he took over a sports outfitter's shop near the ground from trainer George Waller. (This was later known as Jack Archer's, and stood on Bramall Lane, near the John Street end of the ground.)

Utley, who had collected his only England cap earlier in the year, had already played in two FA Cup finals with Barnsley (including the 1912 triumph over West Brom at Bramall Lane) and, at 26, was at the peak of his form. A big, well-built man, he was a battler in the true Barnsley mould, but he had great ability and tactical awareness (he was also a fine exponent of the long throw). He was a natural leader who inspired his colleagues. Tom Bott, who had succeeded Charles Stokes as Football chairman only shortly before Utley's arrival, knew he had achieved a major scoop, and having been closely involved in those famous earlier Cup triumphs, he believed the new captain would help write a new golden chapter.

In truth, with such an outlay, United needed some success to boost income and crowds. Utley's mere presence boosted attendances (his debut, against Manchester United, attracted a 27,249 gate, nearly double that at the previous match), but what was needed was a dramatic revival of

Sheffield United group in 1914. George Utley, the costly new signing and the team's great inspiration, is on the left of goalkeeper Gough on the back row.

the club's Cup fortunes. Bott was delighted when the Blades reached the semi-final within less than six months of Utley's arrival.

Ironically, United started on the Cup trail that season without their new captain, yet romped to a 5–0 first-round victory at Newcastle, where the home side finished with eight men and three of United's goals came after they had lost their goal-keeper. A record 51,006 crowd packed into Bramall Lane to see Utley return and produce an outstanding two-goal display in a 3–1 defeat of a Bradford City side that was outclassed in the second round.

Utley also struck at the double in a 4–0 win at Millwall at the next stage, but three meetings were required to dispose of Manchester City in the quarter-final, Jimmy Revill, deputising

for injured Evans, set up the goal with which Simmons broke the deadlock. (Revill, a product of Sutton-in-Ashfield, was an immensely plucky and popular little winger who could play on either flank but never gained the recognition he deserved. He made some seventy senior appear-ances between 1910 and 1915 and never earned the maximum wage even when he had a long run in the senior side. His dedication was such that, when there was no public transport one holiday weekend, he walked all the way from Chesterfield to Bramall Lane to play. Tragically, he died on active service during the Great War.)

United's semi-final with Burnley went to two games, the first at Old Trafford and the other at Goodison Park, and critics complained about the quality of the football. 'The curse of modern cup football is the belief that defence is not just the best policy but the only policy,' moaned one writer. He said of United's display: 'This is Barnsley playing in red-and-white stripes'—no doubt meaning that Utley had instilled an Oakwell philosophy into the Sheffield dressing room. The irony was that, after a goalless draw, Burnley won the replay with a single goal headed by Tom Boyle . . . once of Barnsley!

The Blades hoped for better things in 1914–15 but suffered a major setback in the opening League match at Sunderland, for Gillespie broke a leg and missed the rest of the season. Wallace Masterman, yet another capture from the Gainsborough club (though, in fact, he was a native of Stockton-on-Tees) and a tall, fast forward, was the lad who profited from the Irishman's misfortune; but it has to be said that he took his promotion in his stride.

Masterman, indeed, was the hero of a hard-earned 2–1 victory at Blackpool in the first round, when, in the absence of the injured Gough, Hufton made his only Cup appearance for the Blades. Masterman gave United the lead, but Blackpool soon equalised, and the First Division side were grateful when Masterman settled the tie with a second-half goal. United's other ex-Gainsborough man, Joe Kitchen, was the scoring star in each of the next three rounds as United disposed of Liverpool, Bradford and (in a replay) Oldham.

Once again Utley led by example in the semi-final, in which United met Bolton at Blackburn. After Simmons had put the Blades in front, the skipper added a memorable second

goal just before half-time: collecting the ball near the halfway line, he embarked on a tremendous dribble and, just when the opposition expected a pass, he hammered a fine shot past the Wanderers' goalkeeper. Obviously someone told him that Ernest Needham had specialised in notable solo runs! Bolton reduced arrears, but United refused to surrender their initiative.

The final, watched by a 49,557 crowd at Old Trafford on 24th April, was a curious affair in that, since the previous August, a World War had been raging in Europe. There were many who believed it was immoral that football should continue to be played in such circumstances, but throughout the season, the presence of many soldiers at games indicated they revelled in the opportunity to forget what lay ahead, at least for ninety minutes. The spectators who went to see United face Chelsea on that wet, murky spring afternoon in 1915 included thousands of men from the Sheffield City Battalion (many of whom would die on the Somme in July 1916) whose presence, along with that of other soldiers, ensured the occasion would always be remembered as 'the khaki final'.

Because of the war, United's special training was confined to a couple of excursions into Derbyshire on the Thursday and Friday before the game. They were taken out in cars and required to walk the ten miles or so back to Bramall Lane, where their reward was a rub-down by George Waller.

Chelsea, having struggled in the First Division, were not much fancied, and in the event United always had the edge and dominated in every area of the field. Utley was responsible for the penetrating cross into the goalmouth that enabled Simmons to give the Blades the lead after 36 minutes; and two goals in a three-minute spell shortly before the end of the game, from Fazackerley and Kitchen, sealed a comfortable victory. In a splendid all-round performance, many considered the hero of the day to be Simmons, who had delighted the crowd with a succession of dazzling runs. The teams were:

United: Gough; Cook, English; Sturgess, Brelsford, Utley; Simmons, Fazackerley, Kitchen, Masterman, Evans

Chelsea: Molyneux; Bettridge, Harrow; Taylor, Logan, Walker; Ford, Halse, Thompson, Croal, McNeil

The trophy was presented to Utley by Lord Derby, who said the clubs and their supporters had seen the Cup played for and it was now 'the duty of everyone to join with each other and play a sterner game for England'. It was a sentiment that reflected the mood of the moment, and, indeed, this was one of those triumphs which, although it was savoured by United supporters, lost much of its significance because it was overshadowed by events of greater magnitude. However, when the Blades party held a rather subdued celebration in a Manchester hotel that evening, Charles Clegg responded to anti-football comments that had been made throughout the season.

Bill Cook — he played in both the 1915 and 1925 finals.

> There has been some talk of disgrace being attached to winning the Cup this year, but I do not hold with that opinion. I take the victory to be an honour to Sheffield.
>
> So far as I am concerned, I take responsibility for the statement that the action which the Football Association took at the outset would be repeated were the same crisis to arise again. We have suffered more than usual from ill-judged criticism, and people who criticise sometimes get popularity in proportion to their ignorance; but I think, after all, we acted wisely, having regard to our knowledge of all the circumstances when we had to come to a decision.

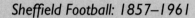
That, at all events, was the opinion of the Sheffield United club, and we did not trouble about the opinion of critics. I am as pleased as anyone that we have won the Cup. It is sheer twaddle talking about disgrace. The disgrace lay with those who made such a suggestion.

However, this was the last season of 'normal' League and Cup football until the war ended, and these competitions did not resume until 1919. Two days after they had beaten Chelsea, United (whose League season had included a twelve-match unbeaten run between late December and the end of March) concluded their programme with a 1–0 defeat of Bolton to finish in sixth place but only three points behind Everton, the Champions.

Wednesday: Fall and Rise, 1919–1926

THE years following the end of the Great War were a painful time for Wednesday. The first post-war campaign of 1919–20 was one of the most traumatic in the club's history, for they won only 7 of their 42 First Division games and lost 26. With a paltry 23 points they finished the season stranded at the foot of the table far below even their relegation companions, Notts County, it took six troubled years to regain their place in the top grade.

The eight years between the Cup triumph of 1907 and the suspension of League football in 1915 had hardly been outstanding, but viewed from the gloomy depths of the early 1920s, that pre-war phase must have seemed almost golden, for at least Wednesday had finished outside the top seven only twice and the club had boasted some colourful performers who had lent enchantment and excitement to the scene. All but two of the senior players who contributed to the 1914–15 campaign survived to figure in the side after 'normal' football resumed in 1919, but significantly perhaps, only three remained twelve months later. Indeed, only one, goalkeeper Teddy Davison, was still there in 1921.

Perhaps the mistake Wednesday made in 1919 was keeping faith with so many pre-war players. Davison apart, the only men who still had much to offer were the Scots, centre-forward David McLean and left-back Jimmy Blair, and ironically, both were unsettled and desperate to leave. In fact, McLean made only three appearances in 1919 before joining Bradford in a £2,000 deal; while Blair remained barely fifteen months and moved to Cardiff for a £3,500 fee.

McLean's departure was a serious blow, for between 1911 and 1915 he scored 100 goals in 144 games following a £1,000 move from Preston. However, after establishing a club record by hitting 38 in 40 League and Cup matches in 1912–13, the Scottish international rejected Wednesday's terms for the following season. He went so far as to return to Scotland and play with an obscure junior side, and though he came back, his relationship with the Owls had been permanently damaged. McLean and Blair both went to Scotland for the duration of the war, and neither was happy about being made to return.

The likes of Andrew Wilson, fellow-Scot George Robertson, Tom Brittleton and Jimmy Spoors—all key men in the pre-war team—were past their peak. In different circumstances, each might have been able to exploit his experience, but the 1919–20 season was one that started badly (they won only one of their first thirteen games) and got worse (one win in the last sixteen), and, with Wednesday calling upon no fewer than 41 players in a desperate but vain attempt to find a winning formula, the situation was more a handicap than a help to the 'old hands'.

Poor Arthur Dickinson had never known such frustration in all his 28 years as honorary secretary. He scoured the length and breadth of Britain for players. He bought a centre-forward called Fletcher Welsh from Raith to replace McLean, but the newcomer, despite a big reputation, was a flop; and John Edmundson and Arthur Price, snapped up for a joint £1,750 fee at the famous auction following the sensational expulsion of Leeds City by the Football Association, failed to make an impact. In that bleak season, the only newcomer who was to prove a success in the following years was George Wilson, a centre-half who cost £3,000 from Blackpool. But his arrival in March 1920 came too late to save Wednesday's status. While Wilson was to remain another five seasons, make nearly 200 appearances, and collect nine England caps, he left a year before the club finally gained promotion. Wilson captained England, as well as the Owls, and he was often described as one of the finest players Wednesday ever had; yet in his time as skipper the Hillsborough dressing room was fraught with friction. Many insiders felt that when Wilson left in 1925 after failing to agree terms, it was no coincidence that the atmosphere suddenly improved, and Wednesday went on to reclaim their First Division status within a year. Meanwhile, Wilson's career fell into an unexpected decline.

Relegation in 1920 prompted Wednesday (with a £5,000 deficit on transfers and an overall loss of £1,677 5s 3d in the season) to take drastic

action; and 20 players were either released or listed. Meanwhile, Dickinson, having been trying to resign since mid-season, finally persuaded the board to engage a professional manager; and, although it did not seem to be so at first, the choice of Bob Brown to fill this role was an astute piece of business. When Brown's appointment was announced at the annual meeting in June 1920, few shareholders had heard of him. He had never played League football, for an injury suffered on duty with Hebburn Argyle had dashed his hopes. However, he had compensated by becoming a scout in his native North East, and it was in this capacity that Wednesday had first employed him. Later he had been brought to Hillsborough to help Dickinson in the office, but when he left to join Portsmouth in 1911 nobody could have predicted that he would develop into a first-rate secretary-manager and achieve considerable success at the Southern League club.

In fact, Brown had resigned his post at Portsmouth in March 1920, and it seems possible that he was lined up for the Sheffield job months before he moved in. Curiously, the last signing Dickinson made before handing over to Brown was from Portsmouth: the player in question was a Sheffield lad whom Brown had acquired from Hallam—Fred Kean. A future England player and Wednesday captain, Kean signed the transfer forms that brought him home, and on being invited to meet the new Owls manager, was astonished to see his old boss walk through the door!

That Brown was unable to transform the club's fortunes overnight was hardly surprising, but he was no doubt dismayed when it proved such a persistently difficult task. Early in his first season, after Wednesday had kicked off with three goalless games and it was clear a major problem was the lack of a marksman, the new manager showed the first signs of what would later be seen as one of his key characteristics—a talent for switching a player's role with profit. Johnny McIntyre, who arrived from Fulham as a half-back, was converted into a centre-forward and promptly hit ten goals in six games. Unfortunately, his success provoked added attention and increased rough treatment from defenders, and after being sent off against Birmingham for retaliating, McIntyre's form took a sudden dip. Moreover, Wednesday won only one of fifteen games.

Brown solved the problem by signing Sam Taylor, a Sheffield-born centre-forward, from Huddersfield for a substantial fee, and playing McIntyre as his supporting inside man; and Wednesday eased into a run of thirteen matches in which they lost only once—and one or other of the new partners scored in ten of those games. Unfortunately, it did not enable Wednesday to finish higher than tenth in 1920–21.

Wednesday also had to settle for a mid-table placing in 1921–22, but, though it was not immediately apparent, they made a number of signings that would prove significant. Charlie Petrie (Stalybridge), Arthur 'Darkie' Lowdell (Ton Pentre) and Frank Froggatt (Denaby) were notable recruits, but by far the most successful in the long run was Jimmy Trotter, who cost £2,500 from Bury. It took the Geordie centre-forward four

Frank Froggatt (left), who was destined to captain Wednesday's 1926 Divison Two championship side, is welcomed to Hillsborough by manager Bob Brown. Note the old Leppings Lane corner of the ground behind them.

seasons to come good, but that was because he was plagued with injuries; then he scored 112 goals in 148 games, including 77 in a two-season burst. Trotter had the distinction of scoring five goals in a League game on two occasions for the Owls.

However, in 1922–23, it was Taylor and two more new forward recruits, Andy Smailes and Sid Binks, who took the scoring honours, sharing 39 League goals. Binks, who came from Bishop Auckland after helping them win the FA Amateur Cup, was an instant hit with the fans. He was a big, bustling front man with a terrific turn of speed, and his exciting dashes delighted supporters. In 1923–24 he was leading marksman with 16 goals, and Petrie, who scored 15, had a good run after regaining his place following Smailes' move to Bristol City.

In both 1923 and 1924, Wednesday finished eighth. In the earlier season, another six points would have seen them up, and they paid for inconsistency; while in the later campaign they never quite made up for a bad start when two wins in the opening eleven games provoked a long and aggressive public debate about the sorry state of the club. Once again Brown's consolation lay in certain individual successes, such as Kean gaining a first England cap, and further newcomers who would pay big dividends in the longer term—notably a future England back and captain, Ernest Blenkinsop (Hull), goalkeeper Jack Brown (Worksop) and Rees Williams (Merthyr). This trio were to figure prominently in Wednesday's eventual climb out of the Second Division.

Unfortunately, Brown had little to console himself with in 1924–25, for

Wednesday, rather than moving nearer the top of the table, slumped towards the bottom and only wriggled out of the relegation zone with nine points from fourteen in their final seven games—a run in which late-season buys Sam Powell (six goals in eight games) and Matt Barrass made crucial contributions. If there were plusses in a poor term, they had to be the belated emergence of Trotter (sixteen goals) and the initial success of the diminutive inside-forward Harold Hill, signed from Notts County. But Billy Marsden, who had been brought from Sunderland, failed to make an early impact—and he would not do so until manager Brown made another of his inspired switches and converted him from inside-forward to wing-half.

Wednesday's relegation struggle of 1925 coincided with an FA Cup triumph for their city rivals, and, moreover, United had defeated the Owls on the way to Wembley. As preparations began for the 1925–26 campaign, the decided lack of optimism among Hillsborough regulars was hardly surprising: even total commitment to the cause could not induce realists in the blue-and-white camp to believe Brown's boys had any hope of promotion. Anyone who might have dared to predict Wednesday would be Second Division champions would have been regarded as plain daft.

There was still evidence of unrest in the dressing room, and about half a dozen players rejected terms for the new season. Fred Kean and Rees Williams were the only 'rebels' who eventually re-signed, and the most notable of those who didn't was George Wilson. Remarkably, the man

Wednesday 1925. Back row (players only): Kean, Lowdell, Felton, Brown, Froggatt, Blenkinsop, Marsden. Front: Williams, Barrass, Trotter, Hill, Prince. The trainer (in the cap) is Chris Craig.

who had so recently been England's captain joined Wigan in the Third Division (North). His departure, however, gave Frank Froggatt an unexpected chance to step from the shadows and become the first Sheffield-born player to skipper the side on a permanent basis since Tom Crawshaw—and, like his son was to do 33 years later, he led them into the First Division.

It is sometimes difficult to pinpoint the various elements that can transform a modest team into a successful one. Of course, it cannot be done unless the basic ability is there, but, even in the mid-1920s, the importance of confidence and self-belief was widely appreciated. For too long Wednesday had lacked that vital extra few ounces of conviction. At last, in 1925–26 they began to get the

chemistry right, and a particularly significant signing that Bob Brown made was not a player but a key newcomer on the training staff—Chris Craig.

George Utley, the former Sheffield United captain, had had a year at Hillsborough as coach, and when he left to join Fulham, Brown invited Craig to join him. Craig came from Forfar, but Brown had known him well at Portsmouth when the Scot was serving in the Royal Army Medical Corps and had guested with Pompey as a tenacious half-back. What had impressed Brown was his knowledge of the treatment of injuries and his ability to handle people. Craig had been Aberdare's trainer for some time when Brown took him to Hills-borough in 1925. Brown was rather remote from the players in day-to-day team matters and training, and Craig took charge of the dressing room, restoring discipline and spirit; and while there were to be occasions in 1925–26 when things did not go quite as planned, a good start (they lost only one of their first ten games) boosted morale and laid the basis of success. Their only real hiccup in a promotion chase in which Derby and Chelsea were their main rivals came late in the season, when they won only one in six games and a 5–1 drubbing at Darlington set the alarm bells ringing. On that occasion it was Brown who rebuilt confidence with several changes that revived the team's flagging hopes.

Jack Brown, Marsden (now at left-half) and Froggatt played in every game, while Blenkinsop, Trotter and Williams missed only one and Matt Barrass (he scored thirteen goals) only two. Felton was right-back in the first 35 games until Tommy Walker came in, and Prince was at outside-left from October to March, when Jack Wilkinson

Billy Felton

took over. Lowdell and Kean made important contributions; and Hill, though he missed the start and the end of the season, scored twelve vital goals, including a hat-trick and three doubles. Finishing top of the table with sixty points, three more than Derby, was essentially a team triumph, but it was an especially memorable season for Trotter, whose record 37 goals included one five and a four as the Owls bagged a haul of 88, with 61 coming at home.

There was a touch of irony in that the defeats in March that unnerved Wednesday involved Port Vale and Darlington—and the opposition's heroes just happened to be a couple of lads who would later be Hillsborough favourites. Alf Strange was the star when Port Vale inflicted Wednesday's second home defeat; and Mark Hooper (Bob Brown had once said he was too small to make the grade!) gave Blenkinsop a real runaround as Darlington sent the Owls to their heaviest defeat of the season.

It was then that Bob Brown axed Felton, Lowdell, Hill and Prince. Walker, who had cost £1,900 from Bradford City in February, and veteran Brough Fletcher (who had come from Barnsley as player-coach to the reserves) were brought in, and Kean was recalled. However, the most unexpected change saw Jack Wilkinson, a teenage winger, play his debut—and the lad from Wath played like a seasoned campaigner, proving a key figure as the Owls won six of their last seven games to land the Second Division title.

There was some disappointment when, on the Monday after the last League game, Wednesday went to Bramall Lane and lost 3–1 to United in the final of the Sheffield & Hallamshire County Cup; but, of course, the important thing was that the club had finally emerged from the shadows. The fans were at last beginning to feel some golden days were just around the corner.

Hillsborough Heroes of the Early 1920s

DESPITE all the problems that Wednesday endured in the early 1920s, it was a period when several of the most famous names in Hillsborough history arrived on the scene—and some, such as Jack Brown, Ernest Blenkinsop, Tommy Walker and Billy Marsden, remained to figure in that golden phase which spanned the last years of the decade and the early 1930s.

Goalkeeper Brown, once a miner at Manton Colliery, had enjoyed his first taste of fame in 1923 when he helped Worksop Town hold mighty Tottenham to a goalless draw at White Hart Lane. The Midland Leaguers were crushed 9–0 in the replay, also in London, but Brown was still the hero and Wednesday paid £300 for a man who went on to make over 500 appearances and collect six England caps. He is remembered as something of a rough diamond, but also as one of the most consistent and coura-geous men who ever guarded the Owls' goal.

However, Brown did not imm-ediately displace Teddy Davison, and, until the season before Wednesday finally climbed out of the Second Division in 1926, his predecessor was generally considered to have the edge. Davison, who had been at the club since 1908, stood only 5ft 7in, but he could match the best in terms of agility and anticipation, and clocked up 424 appearances in eighteen years at Hillsborough. He was unfortunate in that his long Owls career did not coincide with club honours, though it said much that, in 1922, for all that Wednesday were struggling, he collected an England cap, and in fact became the smallest goalkeeper to play for the national side.

Davison could not have been more different from the man who eventually succeeded him, for there was probably never a more gentle professional footballer. He was often referred to as 'Honest Ted' and it was said he could never tell a lie. One story that has passed into local football folklore concerns an incident in a Sheffield derby when United's Joe Kitchen put the ball in the net with his hand, and Davison, normally the model of reserve, was so incensed that he chased after the referee. Alas, the official did not believe the goalkeeper, which prompted a local writer to comment 'If Teddy says it is so, then it must be so, for he could never lie about anything.' A few days later, Davison received a postcard addressed to George Washington!

When Wednesday paid Hull City £1,100 for Ernest Blenkinsop in January 1923, they captured one of the finest backs the club ever had: a man destined to make over 420 appearances and become the club's most-capped player with 26 games for England, some of these as captain. The story of his move to Hull and the circumstances that led to his transfer to Hillsborough serve to show the part luck can play in a player's early development.

Ernest Blenkinsop

A product of Cudworth, 'Blenkie' was working at Brierley Colliery when the opportunity knocked for him to become a professional footballer. H.P. Lewis, the Hull manager, is reputed to have paid £100 plus 80 pints of ale to get his man; but the lad, who was earning 30 shillings (£1.50) for a 48-hour shift at the coal face, did not have his head turned by the prospect of a £10 signing-on fee and his first week's wage (£5) in advance, and he insisted on working out his notice at the pit. However, the colliery boss wouldn't hear of it. 'Nay, lad,' he said, 'Thee go now. Owt might 'appen down t'pit in a week.'

Remarkably, Hull tried to convert him into an inside-forward, and he was limited to less than a dozen senior outings before the accident of fate that set him on course for bigger things. When he played at left-back in the Hull reserve team against Wednesday at Hillsborough, Owls manager Bob Brown nearly didn't make it up into the directors' box to watch the game because of other duties. However, as he intended looking at Hull's other back, Matt Bell, he decided to take in the first half—by the interval had decided it was Blenkinsop he wanted.

Tommy Walker, the Scot who became Blenkinsop's best-known partner, arrived from Bradford City for £1,900 in February 1926, and was one of the men given his debut the following Easter weekend after Wednesday's promotion push looked to be faltering. Over the next nine seasons he made over 280 appearances, and while many felt he could have gone on longer and was unfortunate to lose his place, he was to remain with the club right until the mid-1960s as a member of the backroom staff.

Billy Marsden is assured of a lasting place in the Hillsborough Hall of Fame as a member of one of the greatest half-back lines Wednesday ever had: old-timers never cease to enthuse about the Strange–Leach–Marsden combination. Marsden was the first of the trio to arrive, coming from Sunderland in 1924, and, like Leach and Strange, he was signed as an inside-forward. All three owed much to manager Brown's perception in switching them into roles in which they were capped by England. Marsden would have made many more than 221 appearances for the Owls and played more than three times for his country but for the misfortune that occurred while playing for England in Germany in 1930. He and colleague Roy Goodall (Huddersfield) collided when both going for the ball, and the Wednesday man suffered a spinal injury that ended his career.

Fred Kean was the Sheffield lad who, ironically, joined Wednesday from Portsmouth, following Bob Brown to Hillsborough in 1920. Over nine seasons he made nearly 250 appearances and had his share of ups and downs; he collected seven of his nine England caps while with the Owls and had a spell as captain after the promotion success of 1926. Incidentally, it was following the return to the top grade that he switched from his more familiar role as wing-half to centre-half; he ultimately lost his place to young Leach. It was his misfortune that he insisted upon leaving early in the 1928–29 season when Wednesday

Fred Kean

won the League Championship, but his consolation was that he helped his new club, Bolton, win the FA Cup.

By all accounts, Kean was a forthright character, and it is said that there was often friction in the dressing room because he and George Wilson didn't see eye to eye in that bleak spell in the early 1920s. One tale involving Kean concerned the famous Christmas Day match of

1924 when Blackpool came to Sheffield and won 6–2. The game was a nightmare for Kean, who couldn't do anything right, and afterwards stories were circulating in the city that he had been drinking heavily the previous night. 'It was too daft to laugh at, really,' he said some years later, 'but the rumours wouldn't go away. It got so bad that, in the end, the directors called a special inquiry, and I had to attend. I told Charles Clegg I wanted to know who had said he had seen me drinking. Clegg asked why I wanted to know, and I said because I was going to sue the man. Clegg told me to forget it, and as far as the club was concerned it had never happened.'

Jimmy Trotter, with 114 goals in 160 games, will always have a place among the scoring heroes in Wednesday's history, but the Newcastle product endured a long and frustrating struggle in the early years after his £2,500 move from Bury in February 1924. He had wretched luck with injuries and managed only twelve outings in his first $2^{1}/_{2}$ years in Sheffield. Then, in late 1924, soon after Sid Binks had been sold, Trotter suddenly rediscovered the form that had made him look such a fine prospect at Gigg Lane. He had barely established himself when he hit five against Portsmouth, and, within the year, he bagged another five against Stockport as the Owls raced to the Second Division title in a campaign in which Trotter's 37 League goals was a club record.

Jimmy Trotter

Trotter also scored 37 in the First Division in the following season (his full tally in League and Cup over the two seasons was 77 in 86 games), and he contributed 16 in 1927–28, that famous year when Wednesday made an astonishing escape from relegation after looking doomed. But his luck ran out later in 1928 when the injuries began to recur and, in his absence, Bob Brown made another of his inspired switches. Jack Allen was converted into an emergency centre-forward and did so well that Trotter could not get back. He concluded his career with Torquay and Watford before beginning a long and impressive spell as right-hand man to his former Wednesday colleague Jimmy Seed at Charlton. Trotter also had a long association with England as a member of Walter Winterbottom's backroom team.

Students of Sheffield football history will know that the finest pair of wingers Wednesday had in the years between the wars were Mark Hooper and Ellis Rimmer, who both arrived in the period soon after the club's return to the First Division in 1926, However, two flank men, who each made a distinguished contribution just prior to the era of Hooper and Rimmer, were Rees Williams and Jack Wilkinson.

Williams, who came from Merthyr in June 1922, was often described as one of the best outside-rights in the game. He gained four of his eight

Jack Wilkinson

Welsh caps in the five years during which he made 173 appearances and touched a peak in the 1925–26 Second Division Championship campaign. Williams, unlike many players, did not have a weaker foot, and this was one of his strengths, for, no matter from which direction he received the ball, he had instant control, and his special talent for dribbling at speed enabled him to create many chances.

Wilkinson, signed from Wath Athletic in October 1925, had a remarkable start to his Football League career. Thrown in at the deep end on the last lap of the 1926 promotion run, he was an 18-year-old who played like a veteran, showing no sign of nerves and making an immediate impression with half a dozen fine displays. He also did well in his first term in the top grade, but when Wednesday's fortunes subsequently dipped, so did Wilkinson's, and he lost his place following Rimmer's arrival. In 1930 he joined Newcastle and later played with Lincoln, Sunderland, Hull and Midland League Scunthorpe, finally returning to the Dearne valley area where he had learned his football.

Frank Froggatt was a player who served Wednesday well from late 1921 until November 1927, and, while limited to 95 senior outings, had the satisfaction of being both an ever-present and skipper when the Owls won promotion in 1926. He had learned his football in the old

Attercliffe Alliance, but it was from Denaby that Wednesday signed him. Initially, the defender was kept out of the side by George Wilson, but siezed his chance when the England man left for Wigan. Remarkably, after leading the team back into the First Division, he lost his place when Fred Kean was switched to centre-half, and he eventually joined Notts County. A happier footnote that, sadly, Frank did not live to enjoy came in 1959 when son, Redfern, completed a family double by captaining Wednesday to the Second Division title.

There were others for whom 1926 marked a turning point in their Hillsborough careers, and one was Billy Felton, who arrived from Grimsby in 1923 and stayed until 1929. Felton was a full-back who could play on either flank, and there was a time when his partnership with Blenkinsop was regarded as the best in the Second Division. It said a lot that his only England cap came in 1925 at the end of what had been a dreadful season for Wednesday. The following term, having played a significant part in the team's push for promotion right up to Easter, he was displaced by Tommy Walker and thereafter was cast in the role of occasional deputy for either Walker or Blenkinsop. He later played for Manchester City and Spurs.

Gillespie shakes hands with Cardiff skipper Jimmy Blair (the old Wednesday player) before the 1925 Cup final.

Billy Gillespie:
A Great Captain

BILLY GILLESPIE played his first League game for United in December 1911 and his last in August 1931, and in seventeen seasons clocked up over 493 senior appearances spanning both sides of the Great War. However, his name will always be synonymous with that phase between 1923 and 1928 when he captained a team that re-established the Blades' reputation as great FA Cup fighters.

The fact that this son of a Londonderry police sergeant claimed 139 goals for United reminds us that, while he emerged as one of the best inside-forwards of his era, he started out as what we would today call a striker. As such he made his debut with Leeds City in 1910 and joined United a year later; but, subsequently, United's need for a schemer was greater, and Gillespie, who developed

Billy Gillespie comes home with the FA Cup, 1925

a rare talent for knitting a team together and making it tick, was ideally suited to the challenge.

Gillespie was spotted when playing against the Blades in a reserve game in which he gave Ernest Needham such a torrid time that the old international urged United to sign him, a step that surprised the youngster. 'In that match,' he once said, 'I didn't think Needham had been too impressed, for I was getting stuck in, and when he kept saying "You'll get nowhere playing like that, young lad" I clobbered him all the more. I was surprised when I was told United wanted me.'

Negotiations survived a typical John Nicholson ploy when the Blades secretary pretended to refuse to pay the lad more than £3 a week (the maximum then was £4); and United had no regrets when Gillespie scored 14 goals in his first 17 games, including a hat-trick against Manchester City and four against Bradford City. Moreover, within little more than a year, he made his Ireland debut against England in Belfast and claimed a double in an historic 2–1 victory. He was to collect 25 caps, the last when he was 40, and score thirteen times for his country; and, much as Gillespie is famed for what he achieved at Bramall Lane, in the wider perspective he has a place in the folklore of international football as one of Ireland's all-time greats.

Gillespie was involved when United reached the FA Cup semi-final in 1914, but a broken leg suffered in the opening game of the following season not only cost him a place in the 1915 final, it threatened to end his playing days. It was a particularly bad injury, and a silver plate was fitted to aid

recovery, with the player spending endless hours in the early years of the war training alone on an Irish beach in a bid to repair the damage.

When 'normal' football resumed in 1919, Gillespie returned to a United team badly in need of rebuilding, and in the first two seasons after the war they struggled to stay in the First Division, beating the drop by a mere four points in 1920 and 1921. In 1921 the situation was once so desperate that Gillespie stood down from Ireland's match against Scotland to play in a vital relegation duel with Derby—a gesture that did no good because United lost. However, the signing of Villa veteran Jimmy Harrop, a Sheffield product, helped the Blades scramble to safety.

United's consolation was that while the early 1920s were difficult, things were never quite as gloomy at Bramall Lane as they appeared to be over at Hillsborough. Moreover, several younger players came into the side who were clearly destined to make a major contribution as a 'new' United emerged. Among those who were already at the club in 1919 were Harold Pantling, a defensive half-back who had come from Watford just before the war; Harry Johnson, a small but effective centre-forward who, as the son of the old international of the same name, had been given his chance during the war years; and Ernest Milton, another local product who had also come to the fore during the war and filled the left-back spot that threatened to be a problem when Jack English refused to return.

Even when the outlook seemed bleak in that poor 1920–21 campaign, some good things developed: such

Harry Johnson, who became United's record aggregate scorer, early in his career.

as the signings of Fred Tunstall for £1,000 from Midland League Scunthorpe and David Mercer for a record £4,500 from Hull. Wingers with contrasting styles, both would soon play for England; with the tricky Mercer making some 240 appearances on United's right flank, and the more direct Tunstall chalking up over 470 games and 136 goals on the left.

Of this group, Johnson was probably the most interesting. He was never a star and always regarded himself as nothing more than a 'trier', but he deserves more attention than he has often been given. In his career he scored over 300 League goals for United and Mansfield, and he is probably the only player to achieve that without having been a full-time professional. For United he bagged 225 League and Cup goals in 332 matches, scoring twenty hat-tricks and hitting four in a match seven times and five in a game once; yet,

though he was leading scorer in ten of his 12 seasons at Bramall Lane, the club always seemed to be looking to replace him. Johnson, whose full-time job was that of a metallurgist in Hadfields' steelworks, was the epitome of the man who played football simply because he loved it. He once said that if he had a secret it was in compensating for his lack of inches and ability with sheer effort and total commitment. 'I never stopped trying,' he commented. 'If I lost the ball, I was up and chasing it within seconds. I was always waiting for opponents to make mistakes, and when they did I pounced. I never felt myself clever enough to beat anybody with skill.'

In 1928 he brought a dash of colour to a grey February afternoon at Bramall Lane with a hat-trick scored in the space of eighteen minutes to send rivals Wednesday to defeat in an FA Cup replay. He was the first man to perform the feat in a major Sheffield derby fixture, and a local writer enthused:

> Harry Johnson—they ought to call him Harry Hotspur—may not be the ideal centre-forward. He may not be able to 'kill' the ball as Billy Gillespie does; he may not distribute adroitly: but, like Her Majesty's Jolly, once in a while he can finish in style, and it is his electric, deadly finish which makes him a matchwinner.

Johnson, naturally, hoped he might emulate his father by playing in a United Cup-winning side, and Gillespie, when he became captain in 1922–23, no doubt dreamed of compensating for what he had missed in 1915 by leading the Blades to a Cup triumph. They both must have felt

A Sheffield United team from the early 1920s

they were going to get their wish in the Irishman's first term as skipper . . . until the team's luck ran out in the 1923 semi-final against Bolton.

When United finished fifth in 1924 they reached fifty points in a season for the first time, and it took their total tally of First Division points past the 1,000 mark (the Blades were then one of only five clubs to have achieved this distinction, the others being Aston Villa, Sunderland, Everton and Blackburn). However, the most significant development that year was not just the capture of George Green from Nuneaton but the decision (which may have been Gillespie's) to switch him from right- to left-half, thus creating the legendary Green–Gillespie–Tunstall 'triangle' which did so much to

transform United's fortunes. Incidentally, some forty years after all this happened, Ernest Milton insisted that if it had not been for Green's arrival, Gillespie might not have lasted as long as he did. 'Mind you,' added Milton, 'Green and Tunstall owed a lot to Gillespie, but the skipper profited from Green's resilience and strength. George was not very tall, but well made and solid, robust if you like. He was what you would call a brilliant ball-winner, and his distribution was excellent; so with Gillespie's brain and Tunstall's speed, it added up to a very effective combination.'

It was a triangle that paid a big dividend when United won the FA Cup in 1924–25, and that Green's part in the success was widely recognised came when he was also awarded the first of the eight England caps he would collect by mid-1928. Green stayed at United until around 1934 and made some 420 appearances.

The team that won the Cup was certainly not one without weaknesses, as their modest form in the First Division in the same season serves to confirm. However, when you look at the following term, when the only changes of real significance were in goal and at left-back, it serves to emphasise the potential of the side, for they recovered from a start in which they won only one of their first nine games to shoot up to fifth. They hit 102 League goals in 1925–26, including 72 at home, and Bramall Lane regulars feasted on a record-breaking 11–2 spree against Cardiff, an 8–3 defeat of Manchester City, and a 6–1 victory over Burnley.

In 1927–28 United were again in the semi-final of the FA Cup, and once more the coveted prize eluded them, but it was another year when Johnson claimed more records, notching 43 League and Cup goals, including the first five-goal feat by a United man since the days of Harry Hammond. He did this against West Ham on Boxing Day and followed up with a four against Arsenal two weeks later— and incidentally, he was to get the goal that sealed the points to ensure United's safety in a season when the local football scene was dominated by a relegation scramble involving both Sheffield clubs.

Curiously, the 1928 semi-final marathon in which United were pipped by Huddersfield was Johnson's last Cup appearance for the Blades, and, though he had another good season in him, the subsequent rise of Jimmy Dunne signalled the end of an era. Moreover, when United escaped relegation on goal-average in 1929–30, some fans began to sense that perhaps the age of Gillespie was nearing a conclusion, too.

Tom Sampy

The Cup Fighters: United 1923–28

SHEFFIELD UNITED'S proud tradition as famous FA Cup fighters was revived in an eventful six-year spell in the 1920s. Though they fell at the first hurdle twice and at the second stage once, they also reached two semi-finals, in 1923 and 1928, and enjoyed a memorable triumph in 1925 on their first appearance in a Wembley final.

This was a phase during which, because of a tendency to excel in heavy conditions, United were often dubbed 'the mudlarks'. It was also a period that will always be associated with certain key players: the likes of Billy Gillespie, Fred Tunstall, Harry Johnson and Tom Sampy are the outstanding examples. In fact, Cup-winning skipper Gillespie and Wembley goal-hero Tunstall were the only men who played in every one of the 27 ties between 1923 and 1928, though Johnson missed just three, and Sampy, the man who learned he wasn't going to play in the 1925 final only half an hour before the game, was absent only five times. Sampy's disappointment, all the more painful in being purely a choice the directors made based on their opinion and judgement, provided another of the many stories that show how some players drop lucky at the right moment—and some don't.

As we shall see, Harold Gough, who had luck on his side in getting his chance ahead of the 1914 and 1915 Cup runs, experienced the other extreme twice in the early 1920s. His first setback was being injured just before the 1923 run to the semi-final; and there were those who felt that if he had been fit the Blades, not Bolton, would have figured in the first Wembley final (when, of course, the West Ham side included ex-Blade Ted Hufton in goal).

Gough only played for England once, in 1921, but he was the best goalkeeper United had in the ten years he spent at Bramall Lane. He had the right build and the ideal temperament: big, fearless and never troubled by the rare mistake, he was a happy-go-lucky fellow whose person-ality was in sharp contrast with that of his 1923 deputy Ernest Blackwell. The latter was a good goalkeeper and regarded with affection by his colleagues, but a very serious chap whose tendency to dwell on his errors did not always inspire confidence in team-mates.

Blackwell actually made only 56 League and Cup appearances in six seasons, and the 1922–23 campaign was the one in which he enjoyed his longest run. But while this began well, it ended in such emotional pain that he actually asked to be left out of the team after the semi-final defeat against Bolton at Old Trafford.

The 1923 Cup run began with a seven-hour marathon, United requiring four games to overcome Nottingham Forest and finally doing so with a fortuitous winner when the ball spun into the net off Gillespie's shin late in the third replay at Hillsborough. The Blades only needed one replay to dispose of Middlesbrough in the second round, and enjoyed a comfortable 3–0 victory. It was the first game, however, that earned a place in history because United's attempts to deny Andy Wilson taking a long run-up at a penalty kick induced the FA subsequently to add an arc to the marking of the eighteen-yard box.

United's memorable 2–1 win at Liverpool in the third round was probably the triumph that signalled a revival of their reputation as Cup fighters, and it may also have been the moment when they were first dubbed 'mudlarks'. The defeat of Liverpool, reigning champions and well set for another title, was a sensation, and United's mastery of the mud was typified by Mercer, whose display was dazzling. The Blades, facing similar stamina-sapping conditions in the quarter-final at Queen's Park Rangers, squeezed through with a most curious goal—Sampy scored with his nose!

The Old Trafford semi-final attracted a paid attendance, officially given as 72,600, which was then a record for any game outside London, with the £7,593 receipts a record for any match other than a Cup final; but several thousand got into the ground without paying when the gates were broken. Some have suggested that as many as 100,000 were present to see Bolton win 1–0. Unfortunately, even those who watched the match in comfort saw little to excite them, for neither side played well. Jim Plant, the Whitwell product—known as 'the miracle man' at Bramall Lane because

he had been seriously wounded four times while serving in the war but survived—never had the same luck in his football. On the biggest day of his United career, the wing-half was reduced to the role of a passenger after being clattered. However, all the misfortune in United's defeat surrounded poor old Blackwell, though, in later years, it was generally stressed that he was not to blame for the goal that David Jack scored. What happened was that Bolton's Joe Smith did not connect properly when attempting to meet a Ted Vizard cross, and his effort was spinning wide of a post until the ball unexpectedly clipped Jack's toe. Even then, everyone thought the ball was looping over the bar, but at the last moment it dipped just under and into the net.

In those days they didn't have the benefit of television, let alone action replays, and initially the United goalkeeper was heavily criticised, so much so that he begged the club to leave him out of the team. Blackwell, a lay-preacher, was such a kindly chap that team-mates were upset to see him as distressed as he was for months after the game, and it was only their support that persuaded him not to quit football immediately. In the event, Blackwell did hang up his boots within less than eighteen months, and the irony was that his decision was taken just when circumstances had made him United's first-choice goalkeeper. Indeed, his retirement heightened a crisis that blighted the start of the 1924–25 campaign.

The drama began on the eve of the season when the directors discovered that Gough had broken club rules by becoming licensee of the Railway

Hotel, Castleford. The Football League cancelled Gough's contract, the FA suspended him, and he was ordered to repay the £84 he had received in summer wages. He could play for no other club, and United would not have him back unless he gave up the pub. At 33, Gough felt he had simply taken steps to secure his future, and, while admitting he knew of the clause in his contract that prevented him becoming a publican, he argued that relatives would be actually managing the place and he could not see that living on licensed premises would affect his abilities as a footballer. At a distance of seventy years, United's attitude no doubt seems unduly harsh, for the goalkeeper lost three years of his career and though he returned to the League with Oldham (later Bolton and Torquay), he was then past his best; but United officials were angered that Gough had defied them by taking the pub without discussing the decision with them first. Anyhow, Blackwell played in the first five games of the new season.

Strange as it might seem, Blackwell was not very thrilled to suddenly find himself first choice. Colleagues always felt he was quite content to play in the reserves, but his ambitions were further dulled by the after-effects of an appendicitis operation. It was noticed that he had put on some weight, and this may explain why the stitches in his wound came loose and he had to return to hospital. When he was told that a knock in the wrong place could kill him, the goalkeeper, never fond of a hard challenge at the best of times, decided the safest thing was to retire from football.

United promptly bought Arthur Robinson, of Rotherham County's reserves, but, when he had a nightmare afternoon in the 5–0 home defeat against Manchester City, they went back to Millmoor and paid £2,400 for County's senior goalkeeper, Charles Sutcliffe, who had previously played with York and Halifax and been acquired by Rotherham from Leeds City at the famous 'auction' that followed the FA's expulsion of the Elland Road club in October 1919.

Charles Sutcliffe

A novel fact about Sutcliffe was that he and his oldest brother, Jack, the legendary Bolton and England goalkeeper, made their Football League debuts 31 years apart: one in 1889, the other in 1920. However, it is also fair to suggest they were far apart, too, in ability and confidence. Lane colleagues of Charles, asked for their memories many years after that 1925 Cup run, all agreed that he was the most nervous goalkeeper they had known. It was even said that United trainer George Waller used to let Sutcliffe have a pipe of tobacco before a game to soothe his nerves. (What with Sutcliffe puffing a pipe and Harold Pantling invariably needing a cigarette, the Blades' dressing room must have been rather foggy just before kick-off!)

Yet Sutcliffe emerged from his only season as a United regular with a Cup-winner's medal, and, as Ernest Milton once commented, it could not be said that the new goalkeeper did not do all that was asked of him on the run to Wembley. It might be added that Seth King, too, got into the team through someone else's misfortune and similarly rose to the challenge and therefore deserved his moment of glory. In King's case, he was a full-back thrust into the role of emergency centre-half when Jimmy Waugh (who had just completed 100 consecutive games) suffered a neck injury; and the Penistone product did so well the regular man couldn't regain his place.

When United started on the Wembley trail, they were drawn at home for the first time in fourteen years and celebrated with a comfortable 5–0 win against the Corinthians, Johnson getting four goals. The only surprise was that the 38,167 crowd was 3,000 more than the gate at Hillsborough, where Wednesday beat Manchester United the same afternoon.

In the event, the next stage paired the Sheffield clubs in the competition for the first time since the notorious battles of 1900; but this occasion produced a memorable match despite continuous rain and a pitch ankle-deep in mud. Indeed, conditions were so bad that the teams did not leave the field at half-time but turned straight round. Wednesday, with the wind and rain behind them in the first half, were two goals up in the first nine minutes, Trotter scoring both; but barely ten minutes later United were level through Sampy and Green—and Sampy sent home fans in the 40,256 Bramall Lane crowd wild with delight when he scored again a minute into the second half. The Blades held on to win 3–2.

United were also drawn at home in the third and fourth rounds, and a 51,745 crowd saw Tunstall score the only goal of the tie with Everton, while 57,197 packed in to see Tunstall and Johnson seal a 2–0 victory over West Brom, a success that gave Gillespie and his gang a semi-final date with Second Division Southampton at Stamford Bridge. This was the 100th FA Cup tie in the club's history, and while the milestone did not coincide with a memorable game, it did see United enjoy the kind of luck a team invariably needs on the Cup trail. It was not a day Tom Parker, the Southampton captain, remembered with any pleasure, for he conceded an own-goal and then, after Pantling was penalised, contrived to hit his spot-kick straight at Sutcliffe. Tunstall later punished a moment of defensive hesitancy, and a 2–0 victory earned United a Wembley date with Cardiff City.

It is often forgotten that Cardiff enjoyed a remarkable rise from obscurity after their election to the Second Division in 1920. They won promotion in their first season and in 1924 were only denied the League Championship on goal-average (and that after missing a penalty in their last game). Now they were playing in what proved to be the first of two FA Cup finals in three seasons. They didn't win this one, but in 1927 they were to cause a sensation by taking the Cup out of England with a famous victory over Arsenal. However, Blair and Gill, the two Cardiff players with Wednesday links, had left before the later success.

There were several points of particular interest in United's Wembley line-up: notably that the lone survivor from the 1915 Cup-winning side was right-back Bill Cook; the only Sheffield-born player in the team was Tommy Boyle, son of the back who had helped United win the Cup in 1899 and 1902; and the team had a new England man because George Green had just been named in the side to face Wales.

Harry Johnson once told me that, as their modest League form would indicate, United's 1925 team was far from being the best the club had in the years between the wars. Someone had said that, apart from the vulnerability of Sutcliffe and King, they had two of the slowest backs in the First Division. However, in those days it was the half-backs rather than the backs who marked the wingers, and Cook and Milton were both exceptionally good at their main

task—getting the ball out of their own penalty area with the minimum delay. Milton, known to his team-mates as 'Daddy', was particularly adept at making first-time clearances even when facing his own goal—and, incidentally, he had a fine game in a final that was to be his last Cup outing.

Ernest Milton

Boyle's selection at inside-right in preference to Sampy was the major surprise in United's team, and Sampy (at the time he was less than halfway through a Lane career that spanned over 370 games) was subsequently regarded with great sympathy by supporters. Many felt he had been harshly treated, especially in learning of his omission barely half an hour before the game. It was claimed by some that the directors were influenced by the novelty of having two players on duty whose fathers had helped United win the Cup, but this was always denied.

Sampy admitted he had taken his Wembley place for granted and so played to avoid injury in the weeks before the final. Boyle, meanwhile, had a good run and his determination shone through, and that, rather than any sentiment, earned him the vote. Indeed, Milton once told me that one reason Sampy was omitted was because he went missing in Scarborough just as the players were about to return to Sheffield following a few days in special training by the sea. Anyway, Sampy's consolation in later years was that, no matter how badly he played, he was never given the bird by fans who always remembered his 1925 misfortune.

Green's England call-up served to pinpoint the area from which Cardiff

Sheffield United, FA Cup winners 1925.
Back row: A. Neal (director), C.F. Carr (director), A. Cattell (director), A.J. Platt (director),
W. Sissons (chairman), Tom Sampy, Charles Sutcliffe, J.C. Clegg (President), John Nicholson
(secretary), E. Cattell (director), G.E. Marlow (director).
Middle row: P.G. Stokes (director), Harold Pantling, David Mercer, Tommy Boyle, Billy Gillespie,
Harry Johnson, Fred Tunstall, George Green, George Waller (trainer).
Front row: Ernest Milton, Seth King. Inset: Bill Cook.

suspected United would create the most danger. The Green–Gillespie–Tunstall link was considered the key to United's success. Gillespie made that final a personal triumph because, knowing Cardiff were preoccupied by the threat from the left, he deliberately 'starved' Tunstall all through the first half-hour. With everything so consciously fed to the opposite flank, Cardiff were lulled into a false sense of security. Then, in the 32nd minute, Gillespie suddenly played a pass that brought Tunstall into action; though some have suggested that had Wake, Cardiff's right-half, been more alert he could have reached the ball first. This, of course, overlooks Tunstall's speed and the accuracy of Gillespie's pass. Anyway, Tunstall pounced and scored the game's only goal, the one that won the Cup! It was widely acknowledged that the game was not a classic, yet it lacked little in excitement, and pundits agreed United were much the better side. Some felt United were more relaxed, and the credit for this was given to trainer George Waller, who ensured the players did not arrive at Wembley Stadium until twenty minutes before they were due on the field. Ernest Milton recalled: 'When we got to the ground, we could see the Cardiff lads were already stripped and waiting, while we didn't have any time to think or get nervous. Waller said he had never forgotten the mistake Wednesday made when he played for them in the 1890 final and they arrived so early that they were nervous wrecks by the time they went out to play.'

The Cup final teams were:

United: *Sutcliffe; Cook, Milton; Pantling, King, Green; Mercer, Boyle, Johnson, Gillespie, Tunstall*

Cardiff: *Farquharson; Nelson, Blair; Wake, Keenor, Hardy; W. Davies, Gill, Nicholson, Beadles, J. Evans*

There were moments in the 1927–28 campaign when United seemed a fair bet to win the Cup again despite struggling in the First Division. The fifth round was the one when those who seek omens sensed the Blades had that Wembley look, for the circumstances in which they survived to beat Wednesday at the second attempt featured the kind of turning point often associated with a team that goes on to lift the trophy.

The first game, at Hillsborough, ended in a 1–1 draw, Albert Partridge having equalised Jack Wilkinson's earlier goal for Wednesday. However, twelve minutes from the end, United

Gillespie

had an astonishing escape in what has passed into local football folklore as the 'lost ball' incident. Following a Wednesday corner-kick on the right, the ball fell to home captain Jimmy Seed, who, at close range, hammered the ball so hard against the body of United goalkeeper Jack Alderson that it ricocheted into the air and nobody was quite sure where it had come down. For a few moments, which seemed like minutes, the ball was, quite literally, lost. But then the fans at the Leppings Lane end spotted it stuck in the muddy goalmouth, almost touching the heel of Seed's boot, and he was standing inches from the United goal with his back to the net! It seemed impossible for him to fail to knock the ball in by accident, but, incredibly, he looked everywhere but behind him. Meanwhile, quicker than it takes to describe the incident, Len Birks, the United back, suddenly saw the ball and rushed to hit it clear.

In the replay, United won 4–1 in a Bramall Lane duel assured of a lasting place in the records because of the unique Harry Johnson hat-trick mentioned in the previous chapter. United then beat Forest in the quarter-final and so faced Huddersfield in a semi-final which, to everyone's surprise went to three games. At the time Huddersfield were top of the table, United were next to the bottom, and when Town had gone to Bramall Lane in the previous November they had thrashed the Blades 7–1.

In the first match, at Old Trafford, United twice led and were the better team but were held 2–2. The replay, at Goodison Park, ended goalless; and Huddersfield won the third meeting at Maine Road with Alex Jackson's 54th-minute header. It was no consolation to United that neutrals in the 69,360 crowd felt they didn't deserve to lose and rated Huddersfield lucky to be going to Wembley.

In the event, Huddersfield lost in the final and then were pipped in the title race, and, ironically, their Championship hopes were shattered when United went to Leeds Road in late April and won 1–0. What made the victory really satisfying was not that it avenged the semi-final defeat, but that it ensured the Blades were safe from relegation. It also meant that, with one Saturday programme remaining in the season, Bramall Lane regulars could watch without fear while half the clubs in the First Division were still in danger of going down. And one of the clubs who had to win to be sure of staying up was Wednesday!

Wednesday: The Seed of Success, 1928–1930

28

JIMMY SEED often claimed he never surpassed himself in the four years he spent as a Sheffield Wednesday player from 1927 to 1931, yet he has gone down in local sporting legend as one of the greatest captains in the club's history. His name will always be associated with the 'Great Escape' of 1928 and the League Championship triumphs that followed in 1929 and 1930—the latter year being the one in which the Owls not only clinched the title by a margin of ten points, but were denied a shot at a League and Cup double by a controversial defeat in the semi-final.

The circumstances in which former England inside-forward Seed, then 32, moved to Sheffield in the summer of 1927 were unusual in that, after 254 games and 77 goals for Tottenham, he really wanted to hang up his boots and become a manager. The North London club had upset him by cutting his wages from £8 to £7 a week, and as they obviously considered him finished, he lined up a job at Aldershot. But Spurs refused to release him because, they said, he was being transferred to Wednesday— as makeweight in a deal that would enable them to take Arthur 'Darkie' Lowdell from Hillsborough.

Many years later, Seed, a product of County Durham, admitted he travelled to Sheffield with a heavy heart and was far from keen about the job that Wednesday manager Bob Brown had earmarked for him. Brown had seen the Owls struggle in their first term back in the top grade after the 1926 promotion, and while capturing the likes of Alf Strange (Port Vale) and Mark Hooper (Darlington) proved successful long-term investments, the side desperately needed an 'old head'.

Jimmy Seed leads out Wednesday in their change strip.

Seed recalled: 'Wednesday wanted my experience, and I gave it all I'd got and so enjoyed an unexpected lease of life as a player, but I was fortunate in having a bunch of boys who were as loyal as I could wish for. Their keenness was a joy to watch.' However, the veteran did not enjoy the best of starts. In only his fourth game he fractured a cheekbone. It took some months to settle and find form and fitness, and it was not until late in the season that he began to exert the influence that was to make him a Hillsborough idol and prompt Brown to say the former England man had only to throw his shirt onto the pitch to inspire the team.

Wednesday won only one of their first twelve games, and managed only 4 victories in 24 matches up to early January. In this spell they conceded five goals at Liverpool and Aston Villa, and in the home game with Huddersfield. By mid-March, when they were bottom of the table and seven points adrift of their closest rivals (remember it was only two points for a win then), few people gave them much hope of avoiding the drop into Division Two. Yet, just when the outlook was bleakest, there were faint hints that things were starting to slip into place. Brown was a great one for experimenting with his resources: some of his permutations paid off, some flopped. In February and early March, however, he made several changes that not only succeeded in the short term and inspired an astonishing recovery, but had long-term benefits in helping to create a team capable of bringing the League Championship to Sheffield for the first time in 25 years.

The key decisions were: the signing of Ellis Rimmer, an outside-left, from Tranmere; the conversion of Tony Leach into a centre-half and Alf Strange into a wing-half; the recall of Jack Allen and Jimmy Trotter into attack; and, most significant of all, the appointment of Seed as skipper after Fred Kean was dropped.

Rimmer was an inspired signing, a man who would claim 140 goals in 418 games and become one of the all-time Hillsborough favourites. With little Mark Hooper on the opposite flank contributing 136 goals in 423 matches, Wednesday probably had the best pair of club wingers in the First Division over the next ten years. Moreover, the positional switches affecting Leach and Strange led to the creation of one of the finest half-back lines Wednesday ever had, and the trio would all play for England—as would Rimmer.

Initially, many were saddened to see Kean displaced by Leach. Intriguingly, despite losing his first-team job, the ever-popular Kean captained the Football League against the Scottish League in Glasgow. A few were disappointed when he was allowed to

Jimmy Seed

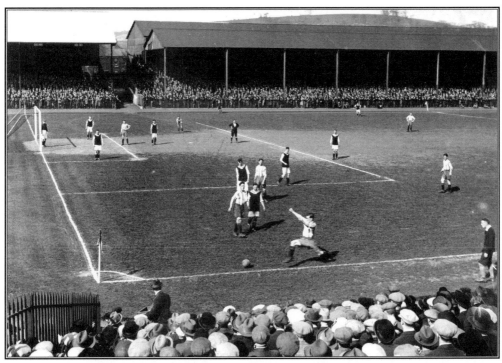

Action at the Leppings Lane end during the famous last match of 1927–28 against Aston Villa.

join Bolton, but in the final analysis they could have no complaints about Kean's successor as pivot—or about the new skipper.

The great revival began on 24th March with a 4–0 defeat of Liverpool, and the Owls went on to collect 17 points out of 20, with seven wins and three draws from their final ten matches. The real turning point came at Easter when they claimed their first League double for two years, and Seed rather enjoyed the fact that the victims were his old club Spurs. Seed scored in both games, and Hooper (some years earlier Bob Brown had said the Darlington product was too small to make the grade!) contributed five goals in 3–1 and 4–2 victories.

The last day of just about every season invariably throws up all sorts of dramatic possibilities, but in May

1928 the final First Division fixture list abounded with so many ifs and buts that it made fans dizzy trying to work them out. Only two points separated twelfth-placed Liverpool and bottom club Manchester United. The only way Wednesday could be sure their remarkable push for safety ended in triumph was by completing their programme with a defeat of Aston Villa at Hillsborough.

They did this, with second-half goals from Jack Allen and Jimmy Trotter, and at the final whistle Owls fans invaded the pitch and hailed Seed as the hero among heroes. The skipper was a happy man, but, when he returned to the dressing room and studied the afternoon's results, there was one final ironic twist to his season. Spurs, who had won only two of their last twelve games, were down! (In fact, Seed's old club had finished their First Division pro- gramme a week earlier, and were on tour in Holland when they learned the bad news.)

Few Wednesday fans who celebrated that Great Escape in May 1928 could have imagined their favourites would win the League Championship not once but twice in the next two years, but this is exactly what happened—and it was achieved more or less with the same players. Hooper was an ever-present in both title-winning seasons; Brown and Strange missed only one game; Allen, Blenkinsop, Leach, Marsden and Rimmer were seldom absent; and if Walker and Seed missed a few more games than the others in the second campaign, the pattern of success was not affected.

The secret was that Bob Brown had found the ideal blend, and consis-

tency of team selection and form were the keynotes, with confidence growing apace as success bred success. The only changes of significance from the side that had beaten the drop were the capture of Bob Gregg from Darlington and Harry Burgess from Stockport. Both were inside-forwards: Gregg enjoyed a 30- match run in 1928–29 and was superseded by Burgess (a great favourite who was to score 77 goals in 234 games) in 1929–30.

Wednesday's dramatic rise was reflected in the England team, for in this spell Blenkinsop, Strange, Marsden and Rimmer were all capped for the first time (all four were in the England side when Scotland were defeated 5–2 at Wembley in April 1930), while Jack Brown, who had been called up five times in 1927, was recalled. It might be appropriate to add that, when England played

Six England Owls — Strange, Rimmer, Marsden, Brown, Blenkinsop and Seed.

Ireland at Bramall Lane in the autumn after Wednesday's second title win, the team included Blenkinsop, Strange, Leach and Burgess (with United's Gillespie in the Irish line-up); while the Owls had four men in the side that lost to France in Paris in 1931.

It was often said that Hooper was desperately unlucky not to gain international recognition in this period, but there was another man who made a major contribution to Wednesday's title double yet was never considered for honours. Jack Allen scored 66 League goals (plus 8 in the FA Cup) in those two seasons, and there is little doubt that his conversion to centre-forward was the masterstroke that did as much as anything to convert the Owls into a Championship side.

Allen began his career with Leeds United and joined Wednesday from Brentford as an inside-forward in March 1927. Initially, he made only a modest impression, though his recall to the side late in 1927–28 had been one of the changes that paid off. Yet the turning point in his career came when, with Harper and Trotter both injured early in 1928–29, he was switched to centre-forward. In his first game in the new role, at Portsmouth, he scored, but the Owls still lost. However, a week later he grabbed a hat-trick in the home match with Birmingham, followed up with four goals at Bury, and when his tally from his first 16 games as a centre-forward was 22, Hillsborough regulars had discovered a new hero.

Wednesday, who did not lose at home throughout 1928–29, hovered near the top of the table from September until early November, and

in late November they became First Division leaders after a seven-match run in which they dropped only one point. Between mid-December and early January they extended their lead to as much as five points, but poor away form prevented them from consolidating their place at the top. They managed only three away wins, all coming before Christmas, and defeats on six of their last seven trips meant the destiny of the title was in doubt until late April. In the end, they pipped Leicester to the prize by a single point and Aston Villa by two points—and they could even afford to lose their final game, at Villa.

Apart from Allen, with 33 goals in 35 games, the only marksman in double figures was Hooper (15), while Seed claimed 8 and Rimmer and Gregg 7 each. It was to be a very different picture in 1929–30 when Allen again claimed 33 and Burgess (19), Hooper (18) and Rimmer (15) all excelled as Wednesday broke the First Division scoring record with 105 goals—bettering the 102 of Sheffield United (1925–26) and Everton (1927–28). Indeed, when Wednesday retained the League Championship in 1930, they did so in great style, finishing ten points clear of runners-up Derby County. The difference from the previous season was a dramatic improvement in away form with double the number of points and eleven victories on their travels. They even won 3–1 at Liverpool in April when four men were away playing for England.

Although the Owls began 1929–30 with an impressive 4–0 win at Portsmouth, they lost two of their first three home games. However, they promptly embarked on a run of

Wednesday's directors, management, training staff and players in the triumphant 1928–29 campaign.

six successive Hillsborough victories which produced 24 goals, including ten for Allen, who claimed a hat-trick against Leicester and four in a 7–2 defeat of Manchester United. In fact, after falling to Leeds in Sheffield in late September, Wednesday lost only two of their next 22 First Division fixtures. By late December they had claimed top place in the table, and in early February they held a six-point lead.

Defeats at Huddersfield and Leicester, combined with an increasing preoccupation with the FA Cup, saw the Owls concede the leadership to Derby briefly, but, in the end, with eight wins and only one defeat in their last twelve games, they romped to a memorable Championship triumph. Symbolically, perhaps, Wednesday clinched the title when they defeated their main challengers Derby 6–3 on 22nd April—and they still had four games left to play.

If there was one major disappointment in this season it was not so much that Wednesday went all the way to the FA Cup semi-final and lost, but the circumstances in which they were defeated by Huddersfield at Old Trafford on 22nd March. Huddersfield, first under Herbert Chapman and now with Clem Stephenson at the helm, were probably the outstanding team of the 1920s: they had won the Championship three times in succession between 1924 and 1926, and reached the FA Cup final in 1928 and the semi-final in 1929—but the Owls felt their Yorkshire rivals had all the luck going in this 1930 meeting.

Wednesday's best Cup run since 1914 began with a 1–0 home defeat of Burnley, and they followed this with a 4–3 victory at Oldham. In mid-

February a 53,268 crowd at Hillsborough saw them crush Bradford Park Avenue 5–1 (their biggest Cup win for seventeen years); then they overcame Nottingham Forest at the second attempt in the quarter-final, winning 3–1 at Hillsborough (attendance 59,205, goals by Seed, Allen and Burgess) after the teams had shared a 2–2 draw at the City Ground. Incidentally, at this stage Jack Allen had scored in every round.

Wednesday went into the semi–final as First Division leaders, and a 69,292 crowd saw Hooper give them the lead with a spectacular shot after 21 minutes; but, two minutes before half-time, the first of two controversial incidents occurred when Huddersfield equalised. When winger Billy Smith broke down the left and crossed into the middle, Town centre-forward Wilf Lewis, failing to reach the ball with his head, fisted it towards Alex Jackson, and as the Owls waited for the whistle to sound the Scottish international went forward and shot past Brown. Even Jackson had hesitated because he had seen what had happened, but neither he nor his team-mates were complaining when referee Lines signalled a goal.

Despite this setback, Wednesday continued to have most of the play, but, midway through the second half, Jackson got away and scored what nobody could doubt was a perfectly legitimate goal. Sheffield's dream of Cup glory was fading fast when, with seconds left, Hooper burst down the right wing and found Allen with a perfect centre. Allen hammered the ball beyond goalkeeper Turner, and just as it flashed towards the net the referee's whistle sounded. The official said later: 'The ball had not crossed the line at the moment I began to blow for full-time.' Wednesday's dismay was compounded after the game when someone who had used a stopwatch to time the match said Mr Lines had played only 43 minutes in the second half. It didn't matter: for the second time in three years, Huddersfield had defeated a Sheffield club one step from Wembley. (In 1928 Town had beaten United at the third attempt, then lost to Blackburn in the final: on this occasion, after beating Wednesday, they fell to Arsenal at Wembley.)

Allen, who scored six goals in the Cup run, was at least to have the consolation of benefiting from a referee's decision two years later when he was involved in the famous 'over the line' goal that helped Newcastle defeat Arsenal in the 1932 Cup final; but, of the Wednesday team defeated in that 1930 semi-final, only Brown, Hooper and Rimmer survived

to play in the Owls side that won the trophy in 1935.

The semi-final teams were:

Wednesday: *Brown; Walker, Blenkinsop; Strange, Leach, Marsden; Hooper, Seed, Allen, Burgess, Rimmer*

Huddersfield: *Turner; Goodall, Spence; Fogg, Wilson, Campbell; Jackson, Kelly, Lewis, Raw, Smith*

There was a touch of anti-climax when, with the Championship won and the League season over, Wednesday went to Bramall Lane and lost to Sheffield United in the final of the County Cup. United had not had the best of seasons and indeed had just escaped relegation on goal-average after concluding their programme with an astonishing 5–1 victory at Manchester United. No doubt they felt that two goals from Jimmy Dunne and another from Jack Pickering served to show the gap between the top and twentieth place was not really all that wide!

Wednesday in the 1930s

AFTER beginning the 1930s as League Champions and retaining the title in the early months of the new decade, Wednesday maintained high standards over the next five seasons, apart from one term when they slipped into mid-table. However, while remaining in the First Division's leading pack, the big prize proved elusive and they finished third in four out of five campaigns. The consolation came in 1935 with their first FA Cup triumph in 28 years.

The Cup success came less than eighteen months after Billy Walker had succeeded Bob Brown in December 1933, but unfortunately, while the new manager's era began so well, it ended badly in November 1937, and in the meantime the Owls had fallen into the Second Division—joining Sheffield United. Moreover, the Blades made it back to the top ahead of the Owls, pipping them to promotion by a single point in 1939

Wednesday finished third in each of the first three seasons after the 1930 Championship success, and in two of them they again topped a century of goals: 102 in the League in 1930–31 and 109 in League and Cup in 1931–32. The new scoring hero in this spell was Jack Ball, bought from Manchester United. Hooper and Rimmer also continued to excel as marksmen, and other stars included newcomers George Stephenson, from Derby, and the man who would captain the Owls to their 1935 Cup

triumph, Ronnie Starling, bought from Newcastle for £2,500.

Ball had a sensational start with 17 goals in his first 14 games, and his arrival coincided with one of the most remarkable scoring sequences in club history: between 1st November and 13th December 1930 Wednesday hit 36 goals in 7 games which began with a 7–2 defeat of Sunderland and ended with a 9–1 crushing of Birmingham. They also beat Blackpool 7–1 and won 5–2 at Leicester. Ball's eleven goals in the run included two hat-tricks, and Hooper claimed two trebles. While Ball's tally in 1930–31 was 29 in 38 League and Cup games, Rimmer hit 24 and Hooper and Burgess 15 each.

Wednesday began 1931–32 with another goal-rush, scoring twenty in their first four games. Stephenson got four in a 6–1 victory at Blackburn on the opening day, and he was on target in the 4–1 and 7–1 defeats of Grimsby and Bolton. The Owls managed two more fives and a six in that season (and bagged seven in the FA Cup against Bournemouth), but they also suffered a few heavy defeats: notably a 9–3 drubbing at Everton and a 6–1 setback at Huddersfield.

It was in the summer of 1932 that Wednesday signed Starling, a ball-playing inside-forward, who, like Blenkinsop, had started at Hull. In 1930 he had helped the Tigers reach the FA Cup semi-final and stagger the football world by taking Arsenal to a

Ronnie Starling

replay. Initially, his £4,000 move to Newcastle was successful, but, failing to figure in their triumphant FA Cup run of 1932 (ex-Owl Jack Allen was a Geordie hero that year), he gladly embraced a challenge that would make him a great Hillsborough idol—though at the outset, he admitted fearing his talents would not suit Wednesday's direct style.

In fact, the only time Starling was absent in his first term at Hillsborough was when he made his England debut against Scotland in Glasgow. He began with eight goals for the Owls, though the scoring hero was again Jack Ball, whose 33 included a record 11 penalties. Alas, though they again finished third, 1932–33 was a season that ended with a greater sense of disappointment than the club had known for some years. One win in their last nine games shattered any hopes of stopping Arsenal's title push; and it said a lot for how the fans felt that barely 5,000 turned up for the final home match against Bolton.

With the benefit of hindsight we can see that the end of the Bob Brown era was at hand, and in the event, it was a sorry conclusion to the managerial career of a man who had achieved so much for the club. Brown suffered a personal tragedy in July when, while holidaying at Blackpool, his wife Mary died suddenly and he was never quite the same after that. In September, he fell ill at a match. His doctor ordered complete rest, and within two weeks he resigned. Remarkably, Brown's departure did not rate a mention in the club's official programme: perhaps the fact that the Owls had made their worst start in eight seasons had something to do with the oversight. Even then, directors lived for the present; past achievements counted for nothing!

The fans wanted Jimmy Seed brought back, but the old hero had just got the Charlton job following a traumatic initiation into management at Clapton Orient; and when the club went for Scot, Tom Muirhead, his club, St Johnstone, refused to release him—after his appointment had been announced! Finally, the post went to Billy Walker, who had completed 531 appearances and scored 244 goals for Aston Villa and collected the last of his 32 England caps exactly a year earlier. He had all the right credentials— except managerial experience.

Before Walker's arrival, Wednesday had won only two games in eleven,

and the slump had led to Starling being dropped by acting boss Joe McClelland. Walker did not long delay the return of the man he made his captain, and the new manager kicked off with four successive wins at the start of an unbeaten thirteen–match run that helped the Owls finish the season in the safety of mid-table— despite a modest record in the final weeks. However, they also reached the fifth round of the FA Cup, losing in a replay to eventual winners Manchester City after a 2–2 draw in a Hillsborough tie assured of a permanent place in the records because the attendance was 72,841.

One of the first things Walker said when he arrived in Sheffield was that he fancied leading them to an FA Cup

Manager Billy Walker gives his men a tactical talk.

triumph, but few expected the words to be turned into deeds within eighteen months. In fact, when the new manager dispensed with the services of Blenkinsop, Leach and Burgess, some fans feared failure rather than success lay around the corner. The sudden death of trainer Chris Craig was another break with the Brown era, which supporters felt might prove significant in the longer term. On the positive side, two of the younger players signed by Bob Brown began to come into their own in 1933–34: wing-half Horace Burrows and Walter Millership, the forward turned centre-half.

Walker's first signing was Neil Dewar, a centre-forward obtained in an exchange deal that took Ball back to Manchester United; and later he acquired Scottish international back, Joe Nibloe (Aston Villa), wing-half Wilf Sharp (Airdrie) and another centre-forward, Jack Palethorpe (Preston). He also signed winger Bernard Oxley from Sheffield United and gave Jack Surtees, an inside-forward from the North East, a trial that proved successful.

It is forgotten now that, in his first months with the club, Walker also tried to sign two youngsters destined to become legendary figures in the game; alas neither Stanley Matthews nor Tommy Lawton came to the club. Walker did however, spot a youngster who would become one of the great Hillsborough favourites: Jackie Robinson. The kid from Shiremoor, then 17, made only one League appearance in 1934–35, but he was to score some 130 goals for the club and only those who saw him can appreciate what a wonderful player he was: great body swerve, superb ball

control, a tremendous turn of speed and lethal shooting power. It was sad that his peak years coincided with the war.

The main talking point in the early stages of Wednesday's 1935 Cup run was the decision to drop Tommy Walker for the fourth-round tie at Wolverhampton. The back, who had been at Hillsborough since 1926 and missed only one of the previous 29 ties, always claimed he was only told he wasn't playing when he was in the dressing room getting ready for the game. Joe Nibloe, who had come as a left-back, was equally at home on the right, and the manager felt that Nibloe and South Bank product Ted Catlin made the better partnership. Tommy Walker hardly played in the first team again, but he was to remain at Hillsborough as a member of the training staff until the late 1960s.

Wednesday, having enjoyed a comfortable 3–1 home victory over Second Division strugglers Oldham in the third round, found the going much tougher at Molineux, but goals from Palethorpe and Rimmer each side of a strike by Harthill for Wolves saw them through, though they were grateful for some good work by Brown. The goalkeeper was again a hero in the fifth-round victory at Norwich, where a lone goal from Rimmer was sufficient to dump the Second Division side.

The background to that tie in East Anglia provided an early example of Billy Walker's attention to detail. The Norwich ground in those days was a tight and peculiar venue known as 'The Nest', and, to familiarise his players with the kind of conditions they would face, the manager arranged a public practice match on a

Hillsborough pitch reduced in width by five yards; and, at his request, 8,000 supporters turned up to crowd along the touchlines. The experiment paid off.

Arsenal, Division One leaders and set fair for a third successive League Championship, were Wednesday's quarter-final opponents at Hillsborough on the first Saturday in March, and a 66,945 crowd saw the Owls come from behind to win 2–1 in a memorable match in which the visitors failed to consolidate the advantage of a seventh-minute goal from Ted Drake. The Arsenal centre-forward subsequently wasted two easy chances, and, after a stunning piece of finishing by little Hooper they levelled the scores, Wednesday sealed victory with a typical opportunist strike by Rimmer.

So they were in their first semi-final since 1930 and faced Second Division Burnley at Villa Park, where a 56,600 crowd saw them register a 3–0 success which was not as easy as the scoreline might suggest. An early headed goal from Rimmer settled the nerves, but it was not until twelve minutes into the second half that the same man got a second—and he owed it to the tenacity of Hooper, for the little man's audacity in charging custodian Scott so surprised the goalkeeper that he dropped the ball!

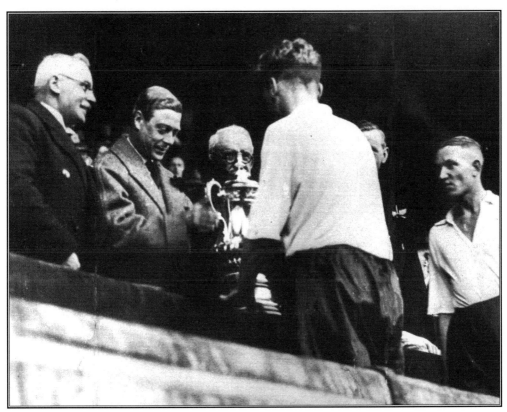

1935 Starling collects the FA Cup from the Prince of Wales.

1935 Starling with FA Cup, protected by trainer Irwin and two constables on the pitch after the final.

Palethorpe completed the scoring.

In the six weeks between the semi-final and their Wembley date with West Brom, Wednesday were clearly preoccupied with thoughts of the FA Cup, and two wins in the seven League games played in this period were not enough to boost their hopes of catching Arsenal in the title race. In the end, the Gunners finished nine points above the Owls and Sunderland took the runners-up spot by a five-point margin.

Although West Brom were below Wednesday in the table, they were considered to have the edge in attack and were made favourites—though the pundits got it wrong in predicting a dour game, for it turned out to be one of the best Cup finals for many years. On the day, Wednesday profited from superior stamina, a slice of fortune, and, perhaps, a couple of errors of judgement made by West Brom ahead of the match. There was some surprise when Albion omitted Arthur Gale from their attack, playing Tommy Glidden instead; and the decision to recall veteran Joe Carter, who had been absent since the semi-final with knee trouble, was clearly a gamble. Within ten minutes of the start Carter was limping, and later, when the score was 2–2, he missed two chances he would have taken with ease if he had been 100 per cent fit.

The 93,204 Wembley crowd, which included old Wednesday heroes Billy Betts and Tommy Crawshaw, witnessed a sensational start when the Owls took the lead after only two minutes. Referee Fogg— whether deliberately or not, it doesn't matter now— allowed play to continue even though Ted Catlin lay injured, and, when the ball was swept upfield, Hooper contrived to push it into the path of Jack Palethorpe, and the big centre-forward steered his shot wide of Pearson and into the net. West Brom's equaliser, after twenty minutes, was the best goal of the game, and ironic- ally it came from the only Sheffield-born player on the field— also the smallest and youngest. Wally Boyes, who had gone to The Hawthorns as a 16-year-old, took a pass from Carter and hammered an unstoppable rising shot beyond the diving Brown.

The second half was the best part of the match: fast, exciting, and full of drama. Starling missed a chance for Wednesday and had another effort cleared off the line, but the Owls

regained the lead after sixty minutes when Hooper, taking a pass from his skipper, sped past two defenders and scored with a shot that went in off a post. However, West Brom were level again within five minutes when Teddy Sandford's shot was deflected in off Millership. West Brom's second equaliser looked as if it might be the turning point in the game, for as Wednesday lined up for the restart they were arguing with each other and the smiles of a few minutes earlier had turned to frowns. But then Carter put one shot against a post and another wide. Boyes set up a perfect chance for W.G. Richardson, and the man with eight Cup goals to his credit that season managed to put it inches the wrong side of the target. The Owls were grateful for the let-offs.

It was later claimed that Wednesday's good fortune held out because Ellis Rimmer's lucky horseshoe was belatedly delivered to the team's Wembley dressing room. Someone had given it to the winger at the start of the Cup run, and he had taken it with him to every tie. Alas, when the Owls went to their Bushey Wood headquarters two days before the final, the horseshoe was left at Hillsborough, and was spotted by

The 1935 FA Cup winners.
Back row: Nibloe, Brown, Catlin, Millership, Irwin (trainer), Burrows.
Front row: Sharp, Hooper, Surtees, W.H. Walker (manager), Palethorpe, Starling, Rimmer.

reserve team trainer Sam Powell just before he travelled south for the game. But he didn't manage to get it to Rimmer until half-time.

The truth was that, in the first period and well into the second half, Rimmer, who had scored in every round on the way to the final, did not make much of an impression. However, in the closing minutes, just when everyone was starting to anticipate extra-time, the winger suddenly found his touch. There were four minutes left when he chased a long, speculative ball that Sharp had directed towards the West Brom penalty area. The odds were very much in favour of Pearson reaching it first, but, as it bounced, Rimmer got his head there a fraction before the

goalkeeper's fist . . . and the ball spun into the net.

Within two minutes, Pearson had stopped but failed to hold a shot from Hooper, and Rimmer pounced to make it 4–2. Soon afterwards, Starling collected the most romantic football trophy of them all from the Prince of Wales, and Rimmer was the toast of Sheffield. The teams were:

Wednesday: Brown; Nibloe, Catlin; Sharp, Millership, Burrows; Hooper, Surtees, Palethorpe, Starling, Rimmer

West Brom: Pearson; Shaw, Trentham; Murphy, W. Richardson, Edwards; Glidden, Carter, W.G. Richardson, Sandford, Boyes

Within a year of the 1935 Cup triumph, Wednesday were in the doldrums, struggling to beat the drop into the Second Division, and, although they succeeded on that occasion, the fall came at the end of the following season—and they were to remain out of the top grade from 1937 until 1950.

Wednesday began 1935–36 with only one win in the first seven games and in one spell conceded seventeen goals in three matches. However, their chief problem was up front, even though Dewar scored nineteen goals after displacing Palethorpe in October. In fact, when the pressure was on in the late push for safety, they failed to score in seven of their last eleven games; and were grateful that Aston Villa, having invested heavily in the transfer market (one of the men they bought was Palethorpe), managed only two points from their last four games.

Unfortunately, the Owls' fortunes worsened in 1936–37, and with only 4 wins in their last 22 matches they went down with Manchester United. At the season's halfway stage they had 18 points from 21 games and were better placed than at the same time in the previous campaign, and when they beat Champions-elect Manchester City 5–1 just before Christmas, hardly looked a relegation side. The main problem was inconsistency in selection caused by injury troubles, and once again the forward-line was the area in which weaknesses proved costly. The decline in the goals-for column continued with a drop to 53.

Surtees (Forest) and Starling (Villa) left during a season when the only individuals who had much to shout about were Catlin and young Robinson, who were both called up by England, and young Jackie

Thompson, who began to look an excellent prospect. Catlin's consistency earned him five caps between October and May, while teenager Robinson made his international debut in the 8–0 defeat of Finland in May.

The 1937–38 campaign saw both Sheffield clubs in the Second Division for the first time since they joined the League in 1892, but while United were to be denied promotion only on goal-average the Owls' slide continued—and though they finished sixth from the bottom they were only two points better off than relegated Barnsley and owed survival to victories in their last two matches.

Wednesday's visit to Barnsley in early November brought their eighth defeat in fourteen games and left them bottom of the Second Division. The situation provoked angry scenes at Oakwell, and Billy Walker was involved in an incident with an Owls shareholder. Whether it was a direct result of this is not clear, but, before the weekend was over, the manager had resigned. His successor, Jimmy McMullan (famed as one of Scotland's Wembley Wizards in 1928), took charge on New Year's Day 1938 after being released by Notts County. Under McMullan the Owls averaged a point a match to the end of the season, which proved just enough to save them from the Third Division (North); and, of his early signings, Douglas Hunt (Barnsley), with six goals in twelve games, and Charlie Napier (Derby), an instant success as new skipper, made the most significant contributions.

Things could only get better in 1938–39, and fortunately, they did, though in the end Wednesday's

A Wednesday group from around 1938, early in the Jimmy McMullan era.

promotion dream faded a week after they completed their programme—for United, with a match remaining, thumped Spurs 6–1 to pip the Owls into second place by a solitary point. Ironically, they had taken three points out of four from the Blades, and beaten them 4–1 (Hunt got a hat-trick) in a pre-season game staged to celebrate the Football League Jubilee.

Nine points from ten in their opening five League games was an almost perfect start, and, in this spell, young Arnold Lowes marked his debut with a goal; but one win in the next nine matches undid all the good work, though another peak came in late November when Norwich were crushed 7–0 and the Owls then romped to a 5–1 victory at Luton.

Hunt wrote himself into the record books with a unique six-goal show against Norwich and followed up with a treble at Luton.

Confidence was restored and, though losing home games against Plymouth and West Ham, they enjoyed another sparkling run in which they won ten matches out of thirteen. The sequence was ended at Coventry in late February, but a week later the Owls narrowed the gap between themselves and the second-placed Blades to two points (with two games in hand) thanks to a 1–0 defeat of United with a goal from Bill Fallon.

In truth, Wednesday's promotion push was a brave one. They lost only one of their final twelve games, but home draws with Chesterfield and

Forest, and three points from six over Easter, made the crucial difference. Wednesday also drew two of the last three away dates. So after beating Spurs 1–0 at home in their final match, they stood second in the table with 53 points from 42 games, but knew United had only to win their outstanding fixture to overhaul them. And, of course, that is exactly what the Blades did.

Sid Gibson

Harry Hooper

Jock Dodds

United in the 1930s

SHEFFIELD UNITED started and ended the thirties on a note of high drama. In May 1930 they escaped relegation from the First Division on goal-average with a stunning 5–1 victory at Manchester United on the last day of the season; and in May 1939 local rivals Wednesday were pipped to promotion by a single point as the Blades concluded their Second Division programme with a 6–1 home defeat of Spurs.

In the meantime, there was probably more pain than pleasure, for, in 1934 their unbroken stay of 41 years in Division One came to an end; and frustration was often the name of the game during their five years in Division Two. They twice just missed promotion, failing only on goal-average in 1938; and in 1935–36 they fell three points short despite equalling a club record with an unbeaten 22-match run in League and Cup. Moreover, if the consolation that year was an FA Cup final date, Wembley proved an anti-climax as Arsenal just did enough to beat the Blades by a solitary goal.

Several factors induced United's slip into this lean phase. Most significant were the retirement of trainer George Waller in 1930; the tragic death of secretary John Nicholson in 1932; and the departure of Gillespie, Tunstall and certain other key players. It was, indeed, the end of an era, and nothing served to emphasise this more than the loss of

Waller and Nicholson. No two men better illustrated the character and spirit of Bramall Lane, and their influence had been so crucial over such a long period that, once both had gone, perhaps it was inevitable that the club should struggle to adjust under new leadership.

The circumstances of Nicholson's death were especially traumatic. He was a man constantly preoccupied with his work, and, when he left the ground on that April morning in 1932 to board a tramcar in Shoreham Street, he was probably dwelling more on some club matter than the short ride to the Midland Station, where he was due to meet the team for the rail journey to Birmingham. On reaching Sheaf Street, he jumped from the platform and, with his head down, dashed round the back of the tram—straight into the path of an oncoming lorry. Tom Sampy recalled the incident:

> He never had a chance and was killed instantly. Most of the players were sitting in a café opposite the railway station, and we all saw it. It is impossible to describe the shock and horror we felt, and, after that, the last thing we felt like doing was playing in a football match. We went to Aston Villa, but our hearts weren't in it, and we lost 5–0. Perhaps it was fortunate we only had two games left after that. We lost them both, and, frankly, we were just glad to get the season over because I

think we all sensed that Nicholson's death was the end of something for the club, and, somehow, it would never be quite the same again.

The irony was that the season in which John Nicholson had died had seen United climb into the top seven after finishing 20th and 15th in the previous two campaigns, and there was a feeling at Bramall Lane that the problems of the earlier spell were gradually being solved. Even when the Blades escaped relegation by the skin of their teeth in 1929–30, Nicholson had felt there was cause for

Jimmy Dunne

optimism. This was the season in which Irishman Jimmy Dunne and local product Jack Pickering, who had both been on the staff for several years, suddenly 'came good', and Harry Hooper, a teenager signed from Nelson, suggested he was going to prove another astute capture at full-back. Dunne's dramatic success, which signalled the end for Harry Johnson, saw him claim 36 goals in 39 games, and in one thirteen-match run in early 1930 he bagged 20 in 13 outings. Pickering chipped in with 14 goals.

Unfortunately, United had serious problems in defence, and all their good work in attack was so often undone by failings at the back. For instance, Dunne's hat-trick at Leicester gave United a 3–0 lead but they ended up drawing the game; and, while he later hit four to turn a 2–0 deficit into a 4–2 win over West Ham, his treble against Blackburn at Bramall Lane proved to be in vain because United lost 7–5! The most traumatic experience in the Spring of 1930 came with an 8–1 thrashing at Arsenal, where poor defending was compounded by bad luck when new goalkeeper Jack Kendall was injured and full-back Birks had to wear the green jersey in the last 35 minutes (no substitute goalkeepers then!).

It was ironic that, just as Wednesday were racing to a second successive League Championship triumph, United, having lost nine games in twelve, reached the final day of the season on the brink of relegation, knowing only a miracle could save them. They had to win their last game, at Manchester United, to have any hope of staying up, and when the home side cancelled out

Dunne's early goal the situation didn't look promising. The turning point was probably when Manchester hit a post early in the second half, but it was not until the 66th minute that Gillespie restored United's lead.

That was the signal for Sid Gibson, a £5,000 buy from Nottingham Forest who was in his second term with the Blades, to produce ten minutes of sheer magic which transformed the scoreline. The winger got the third goal himself, and then, after Tunstall had converted a penalty, Gillespie made it 5–1. The miracle had happened!

Dunne, who had developed into the complete centre-forward, had an outstanding season in 1930–31, for he not only scored 41 goals in 41 League games, but claimed five in the FA Cup, four in the County Cup, and two for Ireland—a remarkable haul of 52. He was a good team-man in that he led his line well, and he had a hard, accurate shot in both feet; but his most notable quality was his ability to score goals with his head more readily than most forwards could with their feet. In his Blades career he scored nearly 170 goals, and the bulk of these came from headers. He profited from Tunstall's crosses, so much so that the big catchphrase at Bramall Lane was 'Tunnie Dunnit—again!'

Yet, as before, Dunne's personal success did not prevent the team from finishing in the lower half of the table. Improvement was only slight and hardly enabled Gillespie to bow from the side on a high note. However, in that summer of 1931 United made another excellent signing when they paid Derby £3,500 for Bobby Barclay. In his first term with the Blades he made such an

Robert Barclay

impact that he became the first United inside-forward for over twenty years to play for England—pipping Pickering to the honour by just twelve months.

Barclay was a neat player in the Alex James mould. He and Pickering complemented each other, for while Barclay excelled at the short-ball game, Pickering's penetrating long passes gave the team's style a touch of variety. Pickering, with over 100 League goals (albeit over a longer period), had the edge in marksmanship, but

Barclay, who made some 250 appearances, was one of the all-time favourites with supporters. It was a source of widespread dismay when he was allowed to move to Huddersfield in 1937, and it was not until a young 1938 signing, called Jimmy Hagan matured into a star that Bramall Lane regulars had an idol to compare with Barclay. By the way, in Barclay's second term, United introduced an outstanding local product at wing-half called Ernest Jackson, who came from Heeley.

Teddy Davison, the former Wednesday goalkeeper, was the man chosen as secretary-manager after the death of Nicholson. He had served his managerial apprenticeship at Mansfield and Chesterfield, and indeed, was destined to spend twenty years at Bramall Lane. However, he had a tough start, and the team's away form was the cause of a slide that sent them down into the Second Division. In Davison's first two seasons they won only four times on their travels, and they had one spell when they won only two of 32 away games and collected a mere eight points.

Davison knew a good goalkeeper when he saw one, and he was very appreciative of Jack Smith, who had emerged the number one choice just before the new manager came; but United still had problems at the heart of their defence, and, in truth, these would not be solved until Tom Johnson became established at centre-half. Consequently, Smith was often left exposed, and he had one especially unhappy game at Arsenal on Christmas Eve 1932 when the Gunners put nine goals past him, with Jack Lambert scoring five.

In that relegation campaign of 1933–34, only one other club in the bottom six won more home games than the Blades; but they managed only one away victory—ironically at Hillsborough. They conceded six goals at Huddersfield, five at Sunderland, Derby and Chelsea, and, in mid-November, they fell to a record 10–3 defeat at Middlesbrough. Whether they might have saved themselves had Smith not played in several games with what was finally diagnosed as a broken wrist is debatable. They conceded 101 goals, and the writing was on the wall early in the season.

When the Blades won only one of their first eight games, the Board decided the time had come for drastic action, and in a bid to raise cash to strengthen the team, they elected to sell their biggest asset—Jimmy Dunne. Arsenal manager Herbert Chapman, once a Blades player, had

Jimmy Dunne

Jock Dodds (left) with Harry Gooney, the former 'boy wonder' of Sheffield schools football.

been trying to sign Dunne for at least three years, and his persistence finally paid off when United accepted an £8,500 offer for a man who had cost them £500 from Brighton in 1926. They promptly bought half-back Alec Stacey and full-back Charlie Wilkinson from Leeds, and then paid £2,000 to Clyde for Scottish international centre-forward Billy Boyd.

Whether United would have survived had Dunne stayed is something we shall never know. He failed to make the expected impact at Highbury, and there was always a feeling that leaving Sheffield was a mistake the Irishman regretted. Blades chairman, Albert Platt, insisted the decision to sell was not entirely due to the need for cash: he argued that, after Tunstall's departure, Dunne had never been quite as effective. This was not strictly true, but Platt preferred that line of defence to answering questions on why the Blades failed to find a winger who could provide the crosses to maintain Dunne's scoring rate.

However, there were few complaints about Dunne's successor, for Boyd, who arrived in December, managed 16 goals in his first 22 games and United lost only once in the matches when Boyd scored. The Scot had impressed when playing for Glasgow against Sheffield in an inter-city match at Bramall Lane, and, with 31 goals in his 42 games for United, he could hardly be called a failure. Indeed, he wrote his name into local football folklore by becoming the first man to score a hat-trick in a

Division One derby involving the Sheffield clubs, but United's 5–1 defeat of Wednesday did not halt their slide towards the Second Division.

Once United were down, they replaced trainer Tom Ratcliffe with one of Teddy Davison's best app-ointments: David Steele, the wing-half who had helped Huddersfield win three successive League titles in the mid-1920s. The former Scottish international came to Sheffield after a spell in Denmark. In fact, with United finishing in mid-table in their first year in the lower grade since 1893, Steele did not have immediate success in terms of results; but he was involved in transforming the career of a youngster who was destined to become one of the biggest names in football and a great Blades favourite.

In that same 1934 summer when Steele arrived, United signed a young centre-forward on a free transfer from Huddersfield. He was barely 19, and Davison only gave him a chance because, although Town manager Clem Stephenson had said the boy had a weight and attitude problem, the United boss remembered a comment Tom Sampy had made a few months earlier following a reserve match at Leeds Road. 'Boss,' said Sampy, 'I've seen a future inter-national today—a kid called Jock Dodds.'

Dodds was a well-built Scot who had spent most of his boyhood in Durham, where he had captained the county side. Somehow, he had failed to fulfil his early promise, and, said Jack Smith, he didn't impress anyone when he first went to Bramall Lane. Smith recalled:

David Steele despaired of the lad, and, frankly, Jock looked pretty useless in his early months. But I was present when Steele gave him the lecture which led to a dramatic change. Steele said 'Now, Jock, do you want to make headway in this game?' and when he said yes, he said 'Well, you'll never get anywhere until you're prepared to work, and the first thing you've got to work on is ensuring you can use both feet'. At the time Jock was useless with his left peg, but, having already had a taste of the first team, he insisted he would do anything to ensure he stayed there and made progress.

Steele said 'Right, we'll start straight away', and he roped me in to help. The idea was that Jock had to wear a slipper on his good foot and a boot on his left, and, with me and David crossing balls into the goalmouth, Jock had to meet the ball with his left foot every time. At first, every time he connected, the ball missed the target by a mile.

I think at first he put more balls out of the ground than anywhere near the goal, and he wasn't exactly thrilled when Steele kept him at it for hours at a time every afternoon for weeks. Then, suddenly, he got the knack, so to make it harder, Steele dipped the balls in a bath. They weighed a ton, and it took me all my time to hit them into the goalmouth. Anyway, the point is that it really was blood, sweat and tears for Jock, but he got the reward.

I'll never forget one match when the opposing centre-half, knowing Jock from a previous game, deliberately forced him onto his left foot, thinking he only used it to stand on. He was astonished when he promptly hit a goal with his 'dud' peg . . . and I think Jock finished with four that day for the first time in his career!

Dodds was to score 124 goals in 196 games for United before joining Blackpool for £10,000 in 1939, and he played eight times for Scotland during the war. In seven years at Blackpool he hit over 230 goals, and it was unfortunate that his best days coincided with wartime. He helped Blackpool win the League North War Cup in 1943 when they beat Wednesday in the final (and Jock was involved in the clash that caused Ted Catlin to miss the second leg with an injury that just about ended his playing days!).

Dodds scored 34 League goals in United's second term in the lower grade: this being the year in which they finished third in the table, three points short of promoted Charlton, and also reached Wembley. They paid for a poor start (one win in the first six) and a modest finish (three wins in the last twelve) which devalued a fifteen-match unbeaten League run stretched to 22 games by the FA Cup. That 22-game run, which equalled their 1899–1900 feat in Division One, began with a 7–1 defeat of Hull just before Christmas. Dodds did not score that day but Pickering (3), Barclay (2), Williams and Stacey did. However, Dodds promptly hit fourteen in a seven-match run, and in early February, United topped the table. Alas they could not stay there.

United started on the Wembley trail with a 0–0 draw at Burnley, goals by winger Harold Barton and Barclay saw them through in the replay. Two attempts were required to dispose of Preston at the next stage, and the 2–0 triumph at Bramall Lane was achieved despite the loss of Stacey with damaged ligaments after only twenty minutes.

The fifth-round game with Leeds has passed into the history books largely because a 68,287 crowd smashed the ground attendance record; but many of those present saw little of the game. It was a typically gloomy Sheffield day of the period and the light was getting worse by the minute even before the kick-off. Those spectators on the pavilion side of the ground decided they wanted a better view and suddenly swarmed across the cricket pitch and stood twenty deep along the touchline. Remarkably, the whole episode passed in an atmosphere of good humour, and many who could not watch the game staged their own makeshift matches with tennis balls. In the 'real' game, United won 3–1. Leeds took an early lead through Furness, but Pickering quickly equalised, and the Blades went in front after 57 minutes when Dodds capitalised on some excellent work by Williams. A place in the last eight was confirmed when Pickering scored the third ten minutes before the end.

When United faced Tottenham in the quarter-final, the attendance at Bramall Lane was only 22,295 (Wednesday played Leeds in a League game at Hillsborough on the same day and attracted barely 6,000), owing to dreadful and bitterly cold weather; but the rain, snow and sleet did not prevent the teams from producing a thoroughly entertaining tie. United however, always had the edge after Barclay scored on the half-hour; though Smith made two brilliant saves before Dodds made it 2–0 after 64 minutes and 3–0 ten minutes later. Morrison got a late consolation for Spurs.

1936 FA Cup final — Blades goalkeeper Jack Smith makes a crucial save with Arsenal's Ted Drake poised to pounce.

The feature of United's 2–1 victory in the all-Second Division semi-final with Fulham at Wolverhampton was the quality of the goals, one in each half, which sealed the Blades' triumph. Bill Bird, a winger signed from Derby at Christmas, notched a splendid first within ten minutes of the start. Early in the second half the same man left the field briefly after colliding with an opponent (he had a piece of chewing gum lodged in his throat!), but returned in time to see Jack Pickering dispossess a Fulham defender and proceed to hit a terrific second goal from eighteen yards.

This game marked the FA Cup debut of Albert Cox. The 18-year-old from Treeton had played in only four senior matches, but the big occasion did not trouble him, and he told Charles Clegg he was 'quite pleased' to have helped the team reach Wembley and equal the club's record unbeaten run. By coincidence, it was Fulham whom United met as they attempted to extend the record at Bramall Lane on the following Thursday. Alas they fell to their first home defeat since the season's opening day with a penalty enabling Mike Keeping to give Fulham a 1–0 victory.

Few people gave United much chance in the final, for Arsenal had won the trophy in 1930 and been in the 1932 final; moreover, they had been League Champions four times since 1931. In the event, the Blades pushed them all the way and lost to a solitary goal from Ted Drake fifteen minutes from the end. A few months earlier Drake had scored seven in a game at Aston Villa, but Tom Johnson kept him quiet; though, in truth, Arsenal took a gamble in playing him, for he was recovering from a cartilage operation.

United, who had Wilkinson back in defence and Bert Williams on the wing instead of Bird, were desperately unlucky in that they did not profit from a start in which they dominated their First Division opponents. Soon after Arsenal's goal, Dodds was within a whisker of equalising when he headed against the bar. Dodds once told me that Herbie Roberts, the Gunners' centre-half, nudged him in the back just as his head made contact with the ball 'otherwise I would have scored, I'm sure.' Most people felt Arsenal's greater experience made all the difference, but, as Blades director Bill Parker argued, it was a final won as much with physique as skill. The 1936 Wembley teams were:

Arsenal: *Wilson; Male, Hapgood; Crayston, Roberts, Copping; Hulme, Bowden, Drake, James, Bastin*

United: *Smith; Hooper, Wilkinson; Jackson, Johnson, McPherson; Barton, Barclay, Dodds, Pickering, Williams*

Soon after the 1936 final, David Steele left to become manager at Bradford (Park Avenue), and Teddy Davison recruited another Scot, Dugald Livingstone, as coach. A native of the Vale of Leven, Livingstone had been a full-back with Celtic, Everton and Plymouth, and he arrived in Sheffield, after a spell as trainer at Exeter, with a reputation as a strong disciplinarian. Davison, as he had done with Steele, left everything concerning the day-to-day management of the players to his new man.

United finished seventh in Livingstone's first season. They had an excellent home record, and after losing to Blackburn in their first match at Bramall Lane in 1936–37 they did not fall again before their own supporters, until Chesterfield defeated them in November 1937—a run of 27 games. However, once again they turned in some dismal away displays and managed only two victories on their travels.

There was considerable improvement in United's away form in 1937–38, when they returned with maximum points from seven trips; but, while losing only twice at home, they showed a lack of consistency and their best unbeaten sequence of the season was a seven-match run which ended in late October. They did well in December and January when winning seven out of nine, including a 5–0 defeat of Southampton and a 6–3 win against Barnsley; and they had several spells on top of the table. But the critics insisted the Blades were not good enough to go up.

The two defeats they suffered in their last seven games were the ones that made all the difference, especially the 5–1 setback at Bradford. Yet a point at Southampton in their final fixture would still have seen them up. Alas, they lost, and Manchester United, with a game still to play, made no mistake in beating Bury to pip the Blades to promotion on goal-average.

There was, incidentally, an amusing incident in the January date with Newcastle, which United won 4–0, for the game was played in continuous rain and deep mud, and, in fact, the referee suspended play and took the players off at one stage. After the match resumed, United were awarded a penalty, but nobody could find the spot, even though some of the United lads got down on their hands and knees to look for it!

At last, in 1938–39, United clinched promotion, but it was another close race and the Blades, in pipping Wednesday by a point, were grateful that it was their turn to complete their programme with a home date a week after their rivals—circumstances that made it difficult for them to fail. However, the backbone of their success was a run between 29th October and 4th February when they lost only one game in seventeen; and they finished the season with a nine-match unbeaten sequence which included six victories. Significantly, they won eleven away matches, and the last of these, at Coventry, was as crucial as

Tom Johnson

their final-day home defeat of Tottenham.

With the likes of Tom Johnson, Ernest Jackson, George Jones, Albert Cox and the impressive young back, Joe Carr, United had abundant local talent, but the club made several important signings during the season: including a young inside-forward called Jimmy Hagan, who cost £2,925 from Derby in November; Scottish international winger Bobby Reid, a £6,000 buy from Brentford in February; and George Henson, a centre-forward, bought from Bradford in March. Harold Hampson had arrived from Southport in the summer, and another inside-forward, West Brom veteran Ted Sandford, was acquired just before the transfer deadline.

It all pointed to a great determination at the club to do everything possible to ensure the team would compensate for the disappointment of the previous year. There was some dismay that Dodds moved to Blackpool in March, but he made it plain he wanted to go; and the club, having paid £2,600 for Henson the previous day, were considered to have completed a splendid piece of business in netting £10,000 for the Scot. Of course, supporters might not have forgotten his departure so readily if the Blades had failed to clinch promotion!

All the newcomers contributed to the success, but looked at in the wider context, the signing that proved by far the most significant was Hagan. Few players in the club's history have been so idolised. In truth, he touched a peak in the early post-war era and so merits more attention in a later chapter; but, even though he was not yet 21 when he came, he made an immediate impression, and 10 goals in 28 games ensured he had a key role in helping the Blades back into the First Division.

If United had a major failing in this campaign, it was a tendency to drop home points. They were beaten only three times at Bramall Lane, but drew nine games, and when they shared a goalless draw with leaders Blackburn (watched by 44,282: then a record crowd for an evening game in the city) in late April, the pressure was really on, for the result shattered hopes of a Sheffield promotion double, and the odds were looking in favour of Wednesday being the team to succeed. However, three days later, on the penultimate Saturday of the season, United claimed an unexpected victory at Coventry thanks to goals from Hagan, Hampson and Reid, and even though Wednesday had beaten Spurs 1–0 at home the same afternoon the Owls had completed their programme and the Blades knew they had only to beat Spurs at Bramall Lane on the following Saturday to end a five-season spell in the Second Division.

The first Saturday in May 1939 marked the end of an era in that it was the final Football League programme in the last completed season before the Second World War; and it was a milestone in Sheffield United's history. They got the win they needed in such style that nobody could deny they deserved promotion, crushing Spurs 6–1, with Hagan getting the only Blades hat-trick of the season, Henson scoring twice, and Hampson starting the goal-rush by scoring barely ten seconds after the start of a game watched by 38,460.

United's only ever-presents in 1938–39 were goalkeeper Smith and left-half Alf Settle and, those two apart, only Hampson topped thirty League appearances. Skipper Hooper's run was ended by injury halfway through the season, which meant promotion for young Carr; and Jackson, too, missed the later stages of the campaign. Tom Johnson, whose season had not started until late October owing to an ankle injury, was captain on the run-in: a neat family touch for a man whose father and brother had between them been involved in just about every major triumph the club had enjoyed in its long history.

Pickering, having missed all but one of the previous ten games, returned for that epic last match when Harold Barton dropped out injured. Arthur Eggleston, signed almost two years earlier from Plymouth, retained the right-half spot. United's team against Spurs was:

Smith; Cox, Carr; Eggleston, Johnson, Settle; Pickering, Hampson, Henson, Hagan, Reid.

The top of the Second Division looked like this:

	P	W	D	L	F	A	Pts
1. Blackburn	42	25	5	12	94	60	55
2. Sheff United	42	20	14	8	69	41	54
3. Sheff Wed	42	21	11	10	88	59	53
4. Coventry	42	21	8	13	62	45	50

On the following Monday, United and Wednesday met in the final of the County Cup, but the game produced no goals and, as the Sheffield & Hallamshire FA had decided there would be no replay (and they hadn't heard of penalty shoot-outs!), each club held the trophy for six months—in fact, United held it for more than six years! For, within barely four months the war broke out and the 1939–40 Football League campaign was suspended in early September after the clubs had played only three matches each.

United's 1939 promotion heroes, with skipper Tom Johnson sending a message to Wednesday. Jimmy Hagan is on Johnson's right, and trainer Dug Livingstone is on the extreme right of the front row.

Wednesday in Wartime, 1939–1946

WHEN the Second World War began in September 1939, the Football League and FA Cup competitions were immediately suspended and not revived in their normal format until 1946. In the meantime, the professional game did continue, although because of circumstances, this was in a restricted form and matches were played mainly on a regional basis.

In truth, many of the games in this period were makeshift affairs and the quality of the football tended to vary according to who was available. Clubs often lost their best players, for many served in HM Forces and their appearances were governed by where they were stationed and when they could get leave. Those who went abroad disappeared from the scene for years. Even those who, for various reasons, were not called up had to engage in essential war work, and many a player turned out for his local team having come straight from a long shift in a factory. Clubs were allowed to use guest players who were based in their area, and this was a great profit to some. Aldershot, for example, was an Army town whose team was packed with internationals based at local camps. Other clubs often had to rely on young men who may never have played at top level but for the absence of so many stars.

It does sometimes seem that the playing statistics and records of these years are of little consequence, but it would be wrong to dismiss the games played in this period as unimportant. At the time these matches made a significant contribution to morale and efforts to try to make life on the Home Front as normal as conditions would permit. In a sense, the fixtures were more important than the results, yet the results certainly mattered to those involved; and, by way of illustration, when Wednesday made only modest progress in the early years of the war they did not hesitate to dispense with the services of manager Jimmy McMullan.

Wednesday's record in that wartime phase remained fairly ordinary, and their peak came in 1943 when they reached the League North War Cup final, though the reserves enjoyed a record-breaking season in 1945–46 when they won the Central League title. The best memories of these years were provided by individuals, notably the brilliant and prolific Jackie Robinson, but also players such as Joe Cockroft, Jackie Thompson and, briefly, the amateur Frank Melling. Another bonus was the emergence of several young players who would make their mark in the post-war phase: Hugh Swift, Redfern Froggatt, Charlie Tomlinson, Cyril Turton and Alf Rogers.

However, perhaps the most significant development in the war years was the elevation of Eric Taylor to secretary and later secretary-manager, for he was to emerge as probably the most influential figure in the club's history between 1942 and 1974. He was in charge of team affairs until 1958 and later general manager, and he was the key figure in the ground developments that transformed Hillsborough and made it an automatic choice for FA Cup semi-finals and other big matches.

McMullan always felt himself the victim of harsh circumstances when he lost the manager's job in the spring of 1942. The former Scottish international believed he had done well and would have guided the Owls to promotion within another year but for the outbreak of war. But then the situation changed dramatically overnight. He was forced to take a full-time job in a local factory and Wednesday gave him a temporary contract as part-time boss. He lost some of his best players, and, after three seasons in which the team won 26 of 83 matches, his contract was not renewed.

McMullan, it was said, was not tough or aggressive enough, and found the managerial philosophy that had served him well in peacetime did not pay in the conditions that now prevailed. He never dictated to older players, asking only that they made the best use of their skill and experience; while urging youngsters to follow the lead of their senior colleagues. 'Use your energy to support the old uns,' he would say. 'Remember that the last fifteen minutes of a game are more important than the first fifteen. Take time to size up the opposition, then harry and chase the older players in the other team. Tire them out and let our own older players conserve their energy, and then you'll be able to take

full advantage towards the end of the game.' Alas, that approach brought few rewards in the first two years of wartime football when the Owls won fourteen out of fifty games.

The biggest blow to McMullan was the loss of Charlie Napier, whose influence might have made all the difference. However, the skipper returned to Scotland almost as soon as the war started, and in fact, made only two more appearances in Wednesday's colours. In the first, in 1940, he scored a hat-trick; in the second, in October 1943, he was sent off and suffered a long ban. He had already been in trouble in Scotland, and this was his second substantial suspension. Would things have worked out better for him had there not been a war? Yet, if Napier's absence was McMullan's most serious loss, there were others who went and returned only when it was too late to save the manager.

McMullan's successor was Eric Taylor. In fact, Taylor was not made secretary-manager until June 1945, but, in being appointed secretary in April 1942, he had overall responsibility for all aspects of the club—and that included the recruitment and control of players. Although he had never played the game professionally or even at amateur level after leaving school, he was steeped in football, having been at the club since September 1929 when he was appointed Bob Brown's office boy. Brown's influence was often evident in Taylor's style of management, though the boy from Birley Carr had a touch more flamboyance and knew the value of publicity.

Initially, Taylor did not get too close

to the dressing room, in that he wisely left team talks and tactics to trainers Sam Powell and Tommy Walker and such senior players as Ted Catlin and Walter Millership. It was a formula that paid off, though the new boss was fortunate that, in his first season, several established players became more readily available. They lent the side the experience and consistency that enabled them to go all the way to the final of the League North War Cup. Taylor had a full-time job in Howell's factory, but, putting his bicycle to good use, he made sure he was at the ground more often than not, and this was the period in which he built a reputation as a notable administrator with a flair for organisation. In those years, Hillsborough staged several representative matches, and the experience fired the young man's ambition to make the ground a leading venue for major fixtures once things returned to normal after the war. He already dreamed of converting Wednesday's headquarters into a Wembley of the North, and it marked an important milestone for Taylor as well as the club when, for the first time in 24 years, the ground was chosen as an FA Cup semi-final venue in 1946.

Several factors influenced Wednesday's improved form in 1942–43. For a start, they had been getting the formula right in the previous season, when the consistency of Millership and Joe Cockroft and the immediate success of amateur centre-forward Frank Melling were key features of the side. Now people such as Albert Ashley and Ted Catlin at full-back, Jackie Robinson and Jackie Thompson in the forward line, and, halfway

through the new season, wing-half Dave Russell, all became fixtures in the team again. Moreover, Albert Morton had his best run of appearances in goal, and the problem positions on the wing were filled by Reynolds and Hugh Swift. Reynolds, a guest from Rochdale, was a Sheffield lad who had come home for the duration of the war. Swift, then 21, was a former Burngreave schoolboy who had made his mark as a full-back with a penchant for the sliding tackle, but his terrific speed made him a fair stopgap winger. After the war he gained England 'B' honours in his more familiar role, and his misfortune and Wednesday's was that his career was prematurely ended by injury.

Cockroft had arrived in 1941 after his London home had been blitzed and he decided to return with his family to his native South Yorkshire. He was a Barnsley lad who had started his career at Rotherham and then, after a spell with Gainsborough, really made his mark at West Ham in over 260 games between 1933 and 1939. He had helped the Hammers win the Football League War Cup in 1940, and Wednesday were delighted to obtain his services. His formal transfer was completed as soon as the war ended, and he was Wednesday's first post-war skipper. Later, Cockroft earned a unique place in football records as the oldest man to make his First Division debut—ironically following an unexpected move to Sheffield United, where, unfortunately, he did not enjoy success and soon departed the scene.

The great hero in 1942–43 was Robinson, whose 35 goals included six hat-tricks. 'Wor' Jackie was the player who had everything: terrific

Jackie Robinson

ball control, a superb body swerve, a tremendous burst of speed, and a remarkable talent as a marksman. He had played over 100 times for the Owls before the war and claimed around 30 goals, but in the war years he grabbed over 90 in barely 100 games. To say he was the darling of the Hillsborough fans would be an understatement, yet he owed a great deal to people such as Cockroft, who did much of his leg work and was always there to cover when an attack broke down. It was often said that Robinson played best when he had had a few pints before a game.

Wednesday lost only three of their eighteen League North games between the start of the season and late December, and enjoyed an impressive run at the start of the qualifying stage of the League North War Cup, clinching a place in the competition 'proper' with an 8–2 thrashing of Sheffield United at Hillsborough. Robinson claimed a hat-trick, but a man who played a key role in the triumph was Melling—who was destined to become a Blades director in later years!

Features of Wednesday's run to the final were a 5–1 victory over Nottingham Forest in which Melling scored four, and an exciting 3–2 defeat of Sheffield United after the Blades had led twice on a day when a 37,500 crowd saw Melling get the winner. York were overcome 4–1 on aggregate in the semi-final.

Blackpool, whom Wednesday met in the final, were at that time one of the most successful teams in the north, and their team included the legendary Stanley Matthews (he was then guesting from Stoke) and the former Sheffield United favourite Jock Dodds. The Owls did not enjoy the best of luck in the first leg at Bloomfield Road, for Robinson spent most of the game troubled with an ankle injury, and just after half-time they lost Catlin, with damaged knee ligaments, following a clash with Dodds. Catlin returned to the field for the last 25 minutes, but was so badly handicapped that he might just as well have stayed in the dressing room.

Matthews had set up Blackpool's opening goal, headed by Finan after 35 minutes, but Cockroft made the score 1–1 before half-time from the penalty spot. Despite the problems created by Catlin's injury, Wednesday took the lead when Robinson cashed in on some good work by Thompson, but, in the final seconds, Matthews managed to elude Swift and delivered the cross from which Eddie Burbanks snatched a dramatic equaliser. The teams in that first-leg game were:

Blackpool: *Savage; Pope, Jones; Farrow, Johnston, Powell; Matthews, Dix, Dodds, Finan, Burbanks*

Wednesday: *Morton; Ashley, Catlin; Russell, Millership, Cockroft; Reynolds, Robinson, Melling, Thompson, Swift*

In the second leg on 8th May 1943, when a record 47,657 crowd (receipts £5,965) packed into Hillsborough,

Wednesday, League North Wartime Cup finalists, 1943.
Back row: Eric Taylor (sec-manager), Russell, Ashley, Millership, Morton, Gadsby, Cockroft,
Catlin (missed second leg).
Front row: Reynolds, Robinson, Melling, Thompson, Swift, Sam Powell (trainer).

Ken Gadsby, a Chesterfield product on Leeds United's books, deputised for the injured Catlin; and with Matthews on England duty, Blackpool brought in Tom Gardner, the Burnley and former Aston Villa man. From a Sheffield viewpoint, the game was an anti-climax, for Wednesday never really looked like beating a side that would go on to beat Arsenal in the national final. The turning point came after 24 minutes when Millership fouled Dodds, who hammered the thirty-yard free-kick into the net, the ball taking a deflection as it sped beyond Morton's reach. Gardner made it 2–0 after 76 minutes, and Robinson headed a consolation goal just before the end.

Incidentally, Catlin's knee was never the same again, but before he finally hung up his boots he led the reserves to the Central League title in 1945–46. They collected a record 63 points and enjoyed one unbeaten run of 25 games. Meanwhile, the first team finished fifth in the League North table that season—twelve points behind the champions . . . a certain Sheffield United!

Jack Smith

A Wartime Triumph: United 1939–1946

UNITED lost the use of their Bramall Lane ground for a short spell during the war. On the night of 12th December 1940 about a dozen German bombs destroyed a large section of the John Street stand, shattered the roof of the Shoreham Street stand, and caused extensive damage to the football and cricket pitches. However, after playing some home games at Hillsborough, they were back on familiar soil by the following September.

The high points of the wartime period for United came in the later seasons, for, after Wednesday had reached the final of the League North War Cup in 1943, United made it to the semi-final in 1944. Unfortunately, they lost 6–5 on aggregate to Aston Villa, drawing 2–2 in the home leg after fighting from 3–0 down to lose the first leg by only 4–3. However, they compensated in splendid style in 1945–46 when they romped to the League North Championship in that last wartime campaign.

If you were to ask the average United supporter from this phase what was the most satisfying thing about the Blades, many would suggest it was the pleasure of seeing a side comprising mainly home-grown lads whose spirit was the key to all they achieved. Apart from the occasions when Jimmy Hagan was on duty, there wasn't a star among them, but how hard they worked for each other, and how well they could

perform when they hit their best form. The squad that lifted the League North title in 1946 included eight or nine local wartime discoveries. The exceptions were goalkeeper Jack Smith, wing-half Ernest Jackson, veteran Jack Pickering and the two men signed during the 1938–39 promotion campaign, Hagan and Reid; and of these older favourites only Smith, Jackson and Hagan were to have a lasting impact after the war, while most of the youngsters were to continue to develop and succeed.

Eddie Shimwell

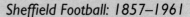

The one youngster who excelled in the later stages of the war but was denied the opportunity of maintaining his progress at the Lane afterwards, was Eddie Shimwell. He had been on the club's books since 1939, and, once he got his chance, formed a very promising back partnership with Fred Furniss. Unfortunately, like Harold Gough in earlier years, Shimwell took a public house (in Derbyshire) and, as it was against club rules, he was transfer-listed and sold to Blackpool, who paid £8,000 for him in December 1946. The Seasiders felt it was money well spent, for Shimwell made 324 appearances and was capped by England; and the player himself never had any regrets, for he played in three FA Cup finals, including the famous 1953 match in which Stanley Matthews inspired an unforgettable triumph over Bolton.

Fred Furniss

Shimwell also had the distinction of being the first full-back to score in a Cup final at Wembley, doing so from the penalty spot against Manchester United. His old Lane colleague, Fred Furniss, was also rather adept at taking penalty-kicks in a career that spanned just over 420 games (including 120 in the war years) for the Blades. A former Sheffield and Yorkshire Boys player, Furniss was the epitome of the local lad who was never happier than when giving his all to his favourite team. One could not imagine him out of the side in the early post-war era, when his regular partner was Albert Cox: but it is intriguing to ponder on what might have happened had Shimwell stayed.

Harry Latham was another local lad who became such a fixture at Bramall Lane that he remained in the club's service for many years after his playing days were over. He played over 200 times during the war and added another 200 appearances later; and while the kid from Carbrook called 'Scodger' was not the most skilful man in the side, he was among the most dependable. It is perhaps out of context to mention it here, but one of the best examples of his ability to mark the most dangerous of centre-forwards out of a game came in the 1952 Sheffield derby at Hillsborough when he hardly allowed Derek Dooley a kick—this being the day when some suggested United would need to take the cricket scoreboard from Bramall Lane to keep count of the goals Dooley was sure to score!

At wing-half United relied mainly on Ernest Jackson, the pre-war favourite, on the right, though Stan Machent proved a very capable deputy. But it was on the left during that run to the League North title that United introduced one of

Ernest Jackson

the most remarkable finds of the war years. This was a red-haired Scot called Alex Forbes, who cost £40 from Dundee North End and arrived in Sheffield in 1944 with his boots wrapped in a brown paper parcel. He was initially used as a centre-forward, however, with the left-half spot causing problems early in the autumn of 1945, Forbes was switched into that role in a game against Everton; and such was the success he enjoyed, he never played in any other position after that. Moreover, he collected his first Scottish cap in 1947 and he was eventually sold for £10,000 to Arsenal, whom he helped to win the League Championship.

It was in the forward line that United had several lads who combined spirit and skill and produced excitement and goals for the fans to savour. Only Reid and Hagan had cost fees, and it says much that they both played in less than half the games in 1945–46. On the flanks there was George Jones, who had made his mark before the war, and Walter Rickett; and though Colin Collindridge was also a winger, he often shared the centre-forward's role with Charlie Thompson. While Hagan or Pickering were the main contenders for the inside-left position, Albert Nightingale made the inside-right shirt his own.

George Jones

Jones had shown a lot of promise pre-war and he missed a lot of the early wartime football in Sheffield because of service in Rochester, but he profited in that spell by guesting with Aldershot, and actually played for them alongside Hagan. The experience of playing with internationals benefited his play.

Rickett, a little man with an enormous heart, was one of the great characters of the team. He arrived on the scene in January 1940 and it was a couple of months later that he made his derby debut against Wednesday at Bramall Lane—and scored with his first kick! After over 200 wartime appearances, he played in fewer than sixty post-war matches before being sold to Blackpool—just in time to contribute in the run to the 1948 FA Cup final.

Albert Nightingale, a product of Thrybergh, scored over 70 goals in some 150 wartimes games, and was leading marksman in 1945–46. He too, made only about 60 peacetime appearances, and only 14 of his 87 Football League goals were for the Blades. He later played with Huddersfield, Leeds and Blackburn.

Colin Collindridge notched over 40 goals in less than 80 outings, and followed up with another 54 in 149 peacetime League and Cup games before moving on to play with Nottingham Forest and Coventry. He was a native of Barnsley and, apart from his speed and scoring touch, the attribute that endeared him to supporters was his readiness to play wherever the team needed him: on the left wing, at centre-forward, and, on at least one famous occasion, in goal as emergency stand-in for Jack Smith.

Charlie Thompson, who came from Bolsover Colliery, was another very popular player who often led the scoring charts in the war years. He was desperately unlucky in breaking his leg in the League North Cup semi-final at Aston Villa in 1944, but, typically, he bounced back.

Among the others who contributed to that 1946 triumph was Harold Brook. He had made his senior debut in 1940 at full-back, but he was to emerge as one of the most notable of United's inside-forwards in the immediate post-war era. He was limited to 29 outings in the war years, but later he hit 97 League and Cup goals. This product of Huntsman's Gardens School had the satisfaction of captaining the Blades in the year they won the Second Division title in 1953, yet, within a year, United allowed him to move to Leeds for a mere £600, where he scored 47 goals in 106 games for the Elland Road club—helping them win promotion in 1956, the year United suffered their second relegation of the post-war era!

The strange thing about United's march to the League North title in 1945–46 was that they kicked off the season with a 6–0 fall at Newcastle. It was some excuse that they made the journey to the North East on a crowded train on which they had to stand. In fact, three of the nine defeats they suffered all season came in the first five matches, and after that their worst experiences were a 5–2 setback at Preston in early December and a 7–2 collapse in the home game with Middlesbrough in January. The latter debacle, however, was the only defeat in a run of 21 games in which they registered 18 wins and bagged 69 goals.

A rundown on appearances will confirm that Smith (41), Nightingale (41), Latham (40), Rickett (39), Furniss (38), Shimwell (34) and Forbes (33) were the most consistent performers, while Nightingale (22), Rickett (15) and Jones (13) were the leading scorers. Pickering, whose wartime record of 74 goals in 180 games was impressive, managed only 11 outings in this term, and in fact, he was to play only once more in the first team. Hagan was limited to 39 games and 18 goals for the Blades

Pickering

in the war years, and 12 of these games (5 goals) came late in the 1945–46 campaign.

There was one young man who made only a single wartime app-earance yet subsequently emerged as one of the great Bramall Lane favourites. His name was Joe Shaw, and it seems fair to suggest that he and Jimmy Hagan are personalities who merit a chapter apiece. Indeed, by virtue of their long service as well as their qualities, their stories offer a significant contribution to the history of United in their time.

The Yo-Yo Years, 1946–1961: A Summary

THE early post-war era was one of the most eventful in Sheffield football history, and, with good reason, these were dubbed the 'Yo-Yo Years'. For in no fewer than ten of the thirteen seasons between 1948–49 and 1960–61 one or other of the city's clubs was either relegated or promoted, and there was one famous occasion when Wednesday went up and United went down in the same year. The football may not always have been of the highest quality, but there was no shortage of excitement! In the fifteen years immediately following the war, the Sheffield clubs spent only two seasons together in the top grade; and while United were relegated twice and promoted twice, Wednesday went up four times and fell back down on three occasions. This was the 'fall and rise' sequence:

A Sheffield United side of 1946 which featured many of the men who first made their mark in the wartime period.

1948–49	United DOWN from Division One
1949–50	Wednesday UP from Division Two
1950–51	Wednesday DOWN from Division One
1951–52	Wednesday UP from Division Two
1952–53	United UP from Division Two
1954–55	Wednesday DOWN from Division One
1955–56	United DOWN from Division One
	Wednesday UP from Division Two
1957–58	Wednesday DOWN from Division One
1958–59	Wednesday UP from Division Two
1960–61	United UP from Division Two

In the light of the chapters that follow, focusing on Jimmy Hagan and Joe Shaw at Sheffield United and Derek Dooley and Redfern Froggatt at Sheffield Wednesday, and also featuring other key figures, it may be useful here to summarise the seasons in question and establish a general picture of the period.

1946–1947

This was the year of the 'Big Freeze' and the season did not end until June. United finished sixth in Division One and also reached the quarter-final of the FA Cup (losing at home to Newcastle), while Wednesday struggled to avoid falling into the Third Division (North). United's biggest wins, 6–1 *v* Brentford and 6–2 *v* Leeds, came in successive matches. Wednesday's best victory was a 5–1 defeat of Spurs in which a teenage centre-forward called Jimmy Dailey notched a hat-trick. United's top scorer was Colin Collindridge (18); Wednesday's was Tommy Ward (18).

1947–1948

United's centre-forward problems continued and they bought Cliff Whitlum (Sunderland) and F.E. Smith (Derby) without success. They finished twelfth and were knocked out of the FA Cup by Third Division Crewe. A highlight was the 2–1 defeat of Manchester United after being a goal down and losing goalkeeper Jack Smith with a knee injury. Wednesday climbed to fourth in Division Two, and Eddie Quigley (destined to hit 52 goals in 78 games over $2\frac{1}{2}$ seasons, including four in the 1947 Boxing Day defeat of West Ham) and Clarrie Jordan arrived from Bury and Doncaster respectively.

Incidentally, in May 1948 a break with tradition was made when United and Wednesday met in Douglas, Isle of Man, and shared a 2–2 draw, with Collindridge and Paddy Sloan (who arrived in the deal that took Forbes to Arsenal) scoring for the Blades and Quigley claiming a double for the Owls.

A Wednesday team group of 1948–49.

1948–1949

United began the season with a victory, but then went fourteen games without a win, and this plus a solitary success in their final nine matches doomed them to the drop. Of several players introduced, four major signings (Alec Blakeman and Joe Cockroft in November, and Andy McLaren and Jack Chisholm in March) all flopped.

The £4,000 capture of Cockroft from Wednesday was the surprise of the season, and the wing-half, who was 37 years and five months, had the distinction of being the oldest man in Football League history to make his First Division debut when he played for the Blades in their 3–2 defeat of Preston. However, he made only twelve senior appearances, and, having seldom missed a penalty in all his years with the Owls, he failed twice for the Blades!

Wednesday, meanwhile, slipped down to eighth. Jordan (14) and Quigley (17) led the scoring charts, but the Owls paid for poor away form. However, they made two notable signings, paying £15,000 for Eire wing-half Eddie Gannon (Notts County) and a record £20,000 for winger Eddie Kilshaw from Bury. Sadly, Kilshaw played only seventeen times before a knee injury ended his career.

1949–1950

This was a famous year in Sheffield football history, for Wednesday pipped United to promotion to the First Division by .008 of a goal after a goalless draw with Tottenham in their final Second Division game of the season. The Blades and the Owls each lost just two home games, but while Wednesday claimed twelve wins United managed only nine. Yet United bagged ten victories on their travels compared with Wednesday's six. In the end it was the one goal fewer conceded by the Owls that made the difference, and their respective records were:

	P	W	D	L	F	A	Pts
Wednesday	42	18	16	8	67	48	52
United	42	19	14	9	68	49	52

Wednesday went up with Spurs, while Southampton, level on points with both Sheffield clubs, stayed down with the Blades. Wednesday's top scorer was Froggatt (14); United's was Brook (17).

United paid for a poor start, for they won only two of their first twelve, and though they later lost only one in thirteen matches it came just too late to enable them to prevent Wednesday from exploiting their games in hand.

The Sheffield derby in September at Hillsborough was notable in that United brought veteran goalkeeper Jack Smith out of retirement to play because of an injury crisis, and the veteran was unlucky to concede the disputed penalty from which Quigley (soon to make a record £26,000 move to Preston) scored the winner. United had their revenge in the return at Bramall Lane in Janauary, when, incidentally, the Owls included ex-Blades favourite, Rickett, signed from Blackpool.

1950–1951

Wednesday, alas, were relegated in their first season back in the First Division . . . and it was not without irony that they went down on goal-average despite winning their last game, at home to Everton, 6–0. They spent most of the campaign in the bottom three places, but their fate was in the balance until the last kick of the last match.

This was the year in which, failing to persuade Hagan to move across the city, Wednesday paid a British record £35,000 for Jackie Sewell, a young inside-forward who had helped Notts County win the Third Division (South) title in 1950.

United finished eighth in Division Two and they never caught up after a start of two wins in the first nine matches, plus a disappointing away record. While Wednesday had some consolation from a poor season in that it at least marked the arrival on the senior scene of two youngsters, Alan Finney and Albert Quixall, destined for big things, United could similarly point to two new signings—wingers Alf Ringstead and Derek

This photograph was actually taken when this trio of veterans were all working together at Rotherham United, but Mark Hooper (left) and Andy Smailes (right) were once players with Sheffield Wednesday, while Reg Freeman (centre) became Sheffield United's manager in 1952 and led them to the Second Division championship in 1953.

Hawksworth—as men who were going to become big favourites at Bramall Lane. Indeed, Ringstead collected his first Eire cap at the end of the season . . . and he had never seen a Football League match until he played in one with the Blades!

1951–1952

This was the season in which United beat Wednesday twice with two of the most famous triumphs in Sheffield derby history, but the Owls took the glory that really mattered by winning the Second Division championship. The Blades, after starting with only two defeats in fifteen games and leading the table by five points,

finished in eleventh place. Manager Teddy Davison was so disappointed he resigned after twenty years!

In September, United hit 24 goals in six games, beating Wednesday (7–3), West Ham (6–1) and Swansea (5–0), and by the end of the month they boasted twice as many points as Wednesday. But then Owls boss Eric Taylor made the change that was to transform the Hillsborough outlook: he introduced the flame-haired Derek Dooley, the raw-boned centre-forward shot to fame with 46 goals in 30 matches. Sewell was the only other man in double figures as the Owls notched a century of goals.

1952–1953

New manager Reg Freeman inspired the Blades to emulate the Owls' feat of the previous season by lifting the Second Division crown. The Blades bagged 97 goals, with Ringstead (22), Brook (17), Browning (17) and Hagan (16) topping the scoring charts. United first went top in October, lost the leadership briefly but regained it in late November with a burst of four wins in which they scored nineteen goals—and, thereafter, their promotion bid never looked seriously threatened. There was perhaps a touch of irony in that on the late April day when United clinched the championship of the lower grade, Wednesday wcrc winning their final home game, at last putting an end to the threat of relegation from Division One. What's more, the Second Division championship trophy was still at Hillsborough!

Wednesday's return to the top grade had turned traumatic when, in February, Dooley broke a leg at Preston and the limb had to be amputated to save his life. After the loss of the big centre-forward, the Owls won only three of their remaining twelve games.

1953–1954

In the First Division, together for the first time since 1934, Wednesday and United both finished in the bottom four: the Owls six points clear of relegation and the Blades safe by three points. United's record included their heaviest home defeat since 1930 when Huddersfield visited the Lane and won 6–3. Both United and Wednesday won only one of their final seven games.

The season was notable in that the Sheffield clubs were paired in the FA Cup for the first time since 1928, and Wednesday, after winning the third-round clash in a bad-tempered Bramall Lane replay in which Owls defender Vin Kenny was sent off, went on to reach the FA Cup semi-final before losing to Preston at Maine Road, Manchester.

Most notable of United's new-comers was winger Colin Grainger. Wednesday's debutants included Jack Shaw, the well-known forward from Rotherham, and young Brian Ryalls, a 20-year-old goalkeeper who made his senior debut in the Sheffield derby at Bramall Lane in September.

1954–1955

It is worthy of note that United and Wednesday spent only two terms together in Division One in the period under review and between them managed 51 wins in 168 games. This was the second of those seasons, and while United finished four points clear of the drop, Wednesday, with only eight wins and 100 goals conceded in 42 games, ended bottom of the table, nine points adrift of relegation companions Leicester. The Owls signed Don McEvoy and promoted two bright youngsters in Tony Kay and Derek Wilkinson.

United, too, made a notable discovery in young goalkeeper Alan Hodgkinson, and wing-half Jim Iley was another of Reg Freeman's notable local captures; but, sadly, the manager was not in good health, and, in the summer of 1955, he had to return home early from a pre-season tour. He died in early August. United were keen to recruit Peter Doherty, the former Irish international who was then boss at Doncaster, but when Blades chairman E. Senior Atkin learned that Joe Mercer was looking to return to football, he visited the old Everton and Arsenal star and set him on . . . without telling his Board colleagues first!

1955–1956

This was the season in which United, under new manager Joe Mercer, were relegated while Wednesday were promoted after winning the Second Division championship at the first attempt yet again. United did not win a game until early September and lost twelve of their first twenty; while Wednesday lost only two of their first seventeen. The Owls clinched the title by conceding only four points in the last ten matches. United finished with only two wins and five defeats in their final eleven.

Newcomers who had arrived prior to Mercer's appointment included Cliff Mason, Bobby Howitt and Des Thompson. He later recruited centre-forward Jack Wilkinson from his former club, Arsenal. Wednesday's signings included Albert Broadbent, from Notts County, and Ron Staniforth and Roy Shiner, both of whom followed McEvoy from Huddersfield: and Shiner, who had spent most of his time at Leeds Road in the reserves, was an instant hit with 33 goals. Other leading marksmen in the promotion success were: Quixall (17), Sewell (13; he moved to Aston Villa in December 1955), and Broadbent (12).

Sheffield United v. Aston Villa
Photo. by Sheffield Telegraph & Star Ltd.

Football League—Division 1.
NEWCASTLE versus UNITED
Kick-off 2.15 p.m.
SATURDAY, 17th DECEMBER, 1955.

1956–1957

While Wednesday finished in mid-table following their third return to the First Division in six years, United's seventh place in the Second Division was hardly the form of promotion contenders. Indeed, Mercer came under fire from the fans.

It was a good year for Alan Hodgkinson, who joined the 'full' international ranks, and Graham Shaw, who was capped at England Under-23 level; but Grainger departed for Sunderland, and Alf Ringstead spent most of the season sidelined by damaged ligaments. There were problems in both the boardroom (which led to E. Senior Atkin resigning) and the dressing room.

Albert Quixall topped Wednesday's scorers, and among the youngsters who were given a taste of life at the top in this term were two future stars, Peter Swan and Gerry Young.

1957–1958

This was the season in which Wednesday began their First Division programme a week late owing to a 'flu epidemic at Hillsborough and never made up the lost ground. They won twelve home games (more than anyone else in the bottom eight) but did not manage a single away victory. Manager Taylor often said that if he had signed goalkeeper Ron Springett from Queen's Park Rangers sooner than March, Wednesday would not have been relegated for the third time in seven years. By the same token United fans always believed that had Joe Mercer captured centre-forward Derek Pace from Aston Villa earlier than Christmas, the Blades might have finished higher than sixth in Division Two—for only four points separated them from promoted Blackburn Rovers.

United's other new faces of note included Gerry Summers, Billy Hodgson, Billy Russell, and Willie Hamilton, and, with young Brian Richardson getting a debut, the feature of this season that had the greatest significance long term (other than Pace's arrival) was the first appearance together of the most famous 'first six' in modern Lane history: Hodgkinson, Coldwell, G. Shaw, Richardson, J. Shaw and Summers.

Pace was not the only future record marksman to step onto the local scene, for Wednesday introduced a Sheffield lad called Johnny Fantham,

destined to top even Redfern Froggatt's post-war haul.

But 1957–58 will always be synonymous with the Munich Air Disaster of 6th February 1958 when the plane carrying Manchester United home from a European Cup tie crashed; and it will not be forgotten that Wednesday were the first visiting team to play at Old Trafford after the tragedy. In a highly-emotional FA Cup fifth-round tie, the Owls were beaten 3–0.

1958–1959

Eric Taylor, in charge of team affairs since 1942, relinquished the duties following relegation in 1958, and Wednesday appointed Harry Catterick, at the time a well-known former centre-forward but not familiar to many Hillsborough fans as a manager. He had served his apprenticeship at Crewe and Rochdale, and would prove one of the outstanding managers in the club's history in what was a comparatively short stay in Sheffield before he was lured back to his old club Everton. Catterick, largely with the players he inherited, guided the Owls to the Second Division title in his first season, with Shiner (28) and skipper Froggatt (26) contributing half the team's tally of 106 goals; but the new boss elected to sell Albert Quixall to Manchester United for a British record £45,000 fee.

United meanwhile missed promotion by only seven points, finishing third in the table in a season best remembered as the one in which Joe Mercer walked out and John Harris came in. Mercer had been linked with the vacancy at Arsenal in the summer, but insisted he was staying and all the speculation was forgotten when George Swindon moved from Peterborough to take the job.

However, when Eric Houghton quit Aston Villa in November, it wasn't long before Mercer, despite his contract at Bramall Lane, applied for the job, and on 23rd December he moved to the Midlands, taking his assistant, Dick Taylor, with him. Archie Clark, chief scout, took over and, in fact, guided the Blades all the way to the FA Cup quarter-finals, where they lost in a famous replay at Norwich after the Third Division side had forced a draw at Bramall Lane, despite having goalkeeper Nethercott playing half the game with a dislocated shoulder.

In March 1959, John Harris, the old Chelsea centre-half, was appointed manager. The bachelor Scot had served his apprenticeship at Chester. Mercer, meanwhile, concluded that season with three regrets: he couldn't save Villa from relegation (someone in Sheffield sent him a telegram: 'Congratulations, Joe, you've done it again!'); United refused to sell him Cec Coldwell; and he wished he had never persuaded Villa to let Derek Pace move to Bramall Lane!

1959–1960

The introduction of Don Megson at left-back and the signing of Bobby Craig, an inside-forward bought from Third Lanark, were features of a season in which Wednesday enjoyed one run in which they lost only three of 27 League and Cup games and finished in the First Division's top five. They reached the FA Cup semifinal before losing to Blackburn Rovers at Maine Road, Manchester. Their Cup run included a famous and somewhat fortuitous victory over United in the quarter-final at Bramall Lane, where a temporary stand was erected on the cricket side to boost the attendance to 59,692.

In the Second Division, meanwhile, United finished eight points adrift of the promotion boat.

1960–1961

This was the year when Wednesday finished First Division runners-up to the all-conquering Tottenham, who claimed the first League and Cup double since 1897; while United came second in the Division Two promotion race, one point behind Ipswich, who, managed by Alf Ramsey, were destined to claim the League Championship within a year.

In many another year, Wednesday's 58 points might have been enough to give them the top prize. The Owls began the season with an unbeaten twelve-match run; in November they were the first team to beat Spurs; and in early December they began a sequence of nineteen League matches without defeat.

United lost only two of their first fifteen games, and had extended their unbeaten home League run to twenty matches spanning nearly a year before falling to Bristol Rovers at the Lane in early December. In fact, this marked a spell when the Blades went six games without a win; but they concluded the season with only three defeats in seventeen and were six points clear of third-placed Liverpool.

This season is remembered at Bramall Lane for a number of notable and timely signings made by manager Harris: Len Allchurch's, a £12,500 buy from Swansea, was especially astute, and there was also Barry Hartle (Watford), Keith Kettleborough (Rotherham) and John Docherty (Brentford).

United also reached the FA Cup semi-final and only fell at the end of a three-game marathon with Leicester City. United's top League marksmen were: Pace (26), Russell (18), and Simpson (11); Wednesday's were Fantham (20), Keith Ellis (14), and Bobby Craig (12).

A Hero Called Hagan

IN the early post-war era it was a constant source of dismay to Sheffield United supporters that the genius of Jimmy Hagan was ignored by the England selectors. Many people in the game frequently expressed surprise that one of the finest inside-forwards of his generation, having collected sixteen unofficial caps between 1941 and 1946, was limited to a single international appearance after the war.

Hagan was, perhaps, unfortunate that the peak of his Blades career coincided with the Yo-Yo phase, and no doubt it was to his disadvantage that over half his League games came in the Second Division. Promotion in 1939 and the Second Division championship in 1953 were his only club honours, and, of course, United were twice relegated in his time at Bramall Lane. It didn't help his cause, either, that there was such an abundance of inside-forward talent, and most of his rivals were fixtures in the First Division. Yet few players in United's entire history, and probably none in the past half-century, have been more idolised by supporters: so, if he was around in times low on triumph and glory, he certainly lent a unique touch of class and colour to the scene, and thousands still treasure the memory of his many magical moments. Former team-mates invariably enthuse about the brilliance of the man who made some 450 appearances and scored around 150 goals for the Blades.

Joe Shaw said: 'It was a privilege to have played with Jimmy. He was a wonderful footballer, one of the best I ever saw. His ball control was extraordinary. He could beat two or three players on a sixpence, and had such vision that, with a short or long pass, he opened a defence as if by magic. Honest, some of his passing was unbelieveable, and many of the goals he scored were fabulous, so stunning they took your breath away'.

Hagan was already rather special when, not yet 21, he arrived at Bramall Lane from Derby for £2,925 in November 1938 and immediately contributed ten goals to United's successful promotion push. It was one of the best bargains Teddy Davison ever made, the mystery was why Derby, for whom he had made 31 appearances, let him go. It has been suggested that County manager, George Jobey, found his fellow Geordie as strong-willed as himself and decided there wasn't room at the Baseball Ground for them both.

Hagan always had a mind of his own. The slightly-built schoolboy international from Washington, County Durham, joined Derby at 15 and Jobey wanted him to take an apprenticeship as a motor mechanic; but one day at the factory was enough for Jimmy. 'I don't want to work, I want to play football,' he insisted. 'You work or go home,' Jobey replied; the lad promptly packed his bag and returned to Durham. It was the manager who had

Jimmy Hagan, taken shortly before he joined United in 1938.

to compromise before Hagan went back to Derby!

If Hagan, like so many of his contemporaries, lost some good years to the war, his consolation was that his time in the Army hastened his development and opened up horizons that might otherwise have been denied him. Service in the Army Physical Training Corps at Aldershot enabled him to play alongside many of the biggest stars in English football. Not just in guesting with Aldershot Town but in the Army XI and in England teams that figured in some of the most memorable matches of that era. Not least of these that famous 8–0 defeat of Scotland at Maine Road in October 1943 which is still remembered as one of the greatest displays of the period.

Whilst he scored 76 goals in 92 games for Aldershot and 12 in 16 matches for England, Hagan was limited to 39 wartime outings for the Blades. There was a certain novelty in the way he returned to Bramall Lane during that League North Championship campaign of 1945–46, as a star recalled to a side whose strength was in having no stars but terrific team effort and spirit. Some feared Hagan's return might not be entirely beneficial and his individualism could hinder the 'one for all, all for one' formula: but though the Blades lost two of their last four games they lifted the title with five points to spare.

Hagan did, however, refuse to re-sign at the start of the 1946–47 season in which United made their belated bow in the First Division and went on to finish in the top six. He said he was worried about his long-term future and missed the first four matches before it was resolved that he would become a part-timer and study to be a chartered surveyor. In fact, when his playing days did end, he stayed in football and managed Peterborough, West Brom, Benfica, Sporting Lisbon and Oporto and never needed to turn to any other profession right up to his retirement in the late 1970s. However, his stance was the first evidence not only of his determination to provide for the future but of how the war years had strengthened an independent attitude which often made him seem a man apart, not only in terms of ability but philosophy.

Those early post-war years witnessed many golden moments from Hagan, but there were disappointments too, as the maestro, despite missing only two games in 1948–49, was unable to save the Blades from relegation. His lone England call-up, against Denmark in Copenhagen in September 1948, was an anticlimax. The following season, 1949–50, was even more frustrating, for United were pipped to promotion by Wednesday on goal-average. Hagan suffered the indignity of being dropped early in the campaign, then suffered an injury that sidelined him for twelve weeks—not that his absence from January to early April explained the Blades' failure to make it back to the top grade at the first attempt. In truth, they never compensated for a poor start to a campaign blighted in those early months by internal strife.

They won only two of their first twelve games. Hagan asked to be relieved of the captaincy—this passed to Harry Latham, but as he was subsequently one of several injury victims the job was also done by Jack Chisholm and Harold Brook. Then, in

October, Hagan was axed for three games. All this coincided with added evidence of problems behind the scenes with the sudden departure of Dugald Livingstone after sixteen years as coach. There was some improvement in results when Reg Wright was promoted to the first-team job, but not enough to prevent Wednesday pipping the Blades into second place in the table.

Ironically, Wednesday's success and then subsequent struggle in the top grade in 1950–51 inspired an unexpected twist in the Hagan story. A remarkable footnote was added to local sporting folklore when United agreed to sell their greatest hero to their city rivals for £32,250. The most sensational transfer in Sheffield football history only collapsed because Hagan refused to move— which prompted the Owls to pay a record £35,000 for a young inside-forward called Jackie Sewell from Notts County soon afterwards, in March 1951. It was remarkable that the Blades' board should have voted to sell their most popular player to their biggest rivals, but almost as surprising that Hagan stayed. However, he was scheduled to join the FA's tour of Australia in May, and, as he told Wednesday secretary-manager Eric Taylor, he was in the meantime scheduled to undergo an operation on his thumb and would miss the last half-dozen games of the season—a situation that would hardly have enabled him to make more than a token contribution to the Owls' fight against relegation. It was a fight they lost.

Not that the 1950–51 campaign was exactly successful for United. It was a season that never took off, and they finished eighth, but they had consolations, not least in the arrival of a young Irish winger who would profit from Hagan's influence. Alf Ringstead, who had once been an Everton amateur, reached Bramall Lane via Ellesmere Port and Northwich Victoria. He cost £2,500 and was destined to score 106 goals for the Blades in 261 games between 1950 and 1959. He collected 20 Eire caps—the first of which came at the end of a first term with United in which his 10 goals in 24 games included one with his head on his December debut against Coventry. Ringstead had his best scoring season with 27 in League and Cup in 1951–52 including doubles in the two famous victories over Wednesday, but that was the year when United's promotion bid collapsed after an excellent start and, ironically, it was the Owls who romped to the Second Division title after a modest beginning.

United were top of the table when they beat Wednesday 7–3 in September, but two wins in twelve games had caused them to lose ground before the Hillsborough return in which they caused a major surprise by winning 3–1. Hagan, however, missed the second derby, and his absence with a knee injury from November to February contributed to the run of ten defeats in sixteen games that shattered United's promotion hopes and led to Davison's departure.

What a different story it was for both Hagan and United in 1952–53 when the Blades, under new manager Reg Freeman, captured the Second Division championship and their great idol enjoyed one of the most memorable campaigns of his career. Hagan missed only five games, his sixteen goals included his first hat-trick (against Southampton) since 1939 and took his League total past

Sheffield United 1952.
Back row: Joe Shaw, Fred Furniss, Ted Burgin, Howard Johnson, Colin Rawson, Graham Shaw.
Front row: Alf Ringstead, Jimmy Hagan, Len Browning, Harold Brook, Derek Hawksworth.

the century mark. Some of his performances were truly unforgettable.

One display, against Notts County in April, had R.A. Sparling of the *Sheffield Telegraph* describing him as the best inside-right in the country. However, rather than impressing the Football Association, Hagan got the wrong side of them in December when he was severely censured after being sent off five minutes from the end of the Blades' 7–1 defeat of Swansea at Bramall Lane. This was another of those occasions when he totally dominated proceedings but so tantalised the opposition that his marker, Billy Lucas, decided the only way to stop him was to clatter him on the ankles at every opportunity. Hagan, never the type to turn the other cheek, took the punishment for 85 minutes before his patience snapped and he retaliated. He was not entirely surprised when referee Burgess ordered an early bath.

By coincidence, Hagan was involved in another sending-off incident a year later when United met Wednesday in an FA Cup third-round replay at Bramall Lane, although on this occasion it was Owls defender 'Mick' Kenny who was dismissed for a foul on 'Sir Jimmy'. For the record, Kenny, even to this day, has always insisted: 'I was innocent, I never touched him.'

The background to this match is that, earlier in that 1953–54 season, United had beaten Wednesday 2–0 at Bramall Lane and Hagan had been in brilliant form, scoring the first goal after 21 minutes and setting up the second for Derek Hawksworth nine minutes later. When the clubs were paired in the knockout competition, Wednesday were keen to subdue the Hagan threat. In the first game at Hillsborough, however, he was the man who created the opening goal for Bill Toner, and the Owls were grateful to take the tie to a replay thanks to Jack Shaw's equaliser. United went into the replay without skipper Harold Brook, but still remained favourites, for, wartime matches excepted, Wednesday had not won at Bramall Lane since 1933. The way the first half went, the odds looked very much in favour of the Blades. They had the wind behind them, and despite wasting several chances and missing a penalty, claimed the lead when young Brian Ryalls in the Wednesday goal allowed a harmless-looking 25-yard effort from Derek Hawksworth (one of six the former Bradford winger scored in seventeen Cup games) to reach the net.

All the fireworks followed Alan Finney's equaliser for Wednesday seven minutes after the interval. Referee Jack Clough called rival captains Joe Shaw and Jack Sewell together and issued a warning about rough play; but, within barely five minutes, Kenny was sent off after a clash with Hagan. Remarkably, it was when they were reduced to ten men that Wednesday struck their best form, and goals from George Davies and Sewell sealed a famous victory. The teams in that game were:

United: *Ted Burgin; Cec Coldwell, Roy Ridge; Joe Shaw, Howard Johnson, Colin Rawson; Alf Ringstead, Jimmy Hagan, Bill Toner, Peter Wragg, Derek Hawksworth*

Wednesday: *Brian Ryalls; 'Mick' Kenny, Ivor Seemley; Eddie Gannon, Barry Butler, George Davies; Alan Finney, Albert Quixall, Jack Shaw, Jack Sewell, Dennis Woodhead*

Sheffield United v. Bristol Rovers   *Photo. Sheffield Telegraph*

United finished three points clear of relegation in 1953–54, a season that marked the end of the line for Hagan's pal, Harold Brook. Brook was allowed to join Leeds for a mere £600 and went on to score 47 goals in 106 games for the Elland Road club, helping them to promotion in 1956—the year the Blades went down again! Brook, who scored 97 League and Cup goals for United, had been captain in the Second Division title-winning term and his departure was subsequently recognised as a bad error of judgement. He and Hagan, incidentally, were business partners for some years and owned a sports outfitter's shop, later Brook enjoyed outstanding success as a newsagent.

United again struggled in 1954–55, finishing thirteenth but only four points clear of the relegation fate that

claimed Wednesday. While it was another term in which Hagan enjoyed some memorable afternoons (notably in a 3–0 defeat of Manchester United in November and a 6–2 triumph over Newcastle on New Year's Day when United scored four times in the first eight minutes), he was limited to 28 outings. This was Freeman's last term as manager, for he fell seriously ill in the summer and died in August 1955 at the age of 61 after returning home early from a pre-season tour of Germany and Holland. Freeman will be remembered as one of South Yorkshire football's most popular figures, for he gave excellent service to Rotherham from 1930 to 1952, and when he led the Blades to the Second Division championship in 1953 it completed a hat-trick of titles. As a player he had helped Middlesbrough top the Second Division and as a manager had guided the Millers out of the old Third Division (North).

Freeman's successor was Joe Mercer, the former Everton, Arsenal and England wing-half, and it was an appointment that Hagan could appreciate, for he and the new boss were old pals, having played together a dozen times for England during the war. In fact, few people had a better insight into Hagan's development, as Mercer had been in the opposing Everton side on the day in December 1935 when Hagan, then 17, made his Football League debut with Derby. Mercer had captained Arsenal to an FA Cup triumph in 1950 (when he was Footballer of the Year) and twice helped them win the League title, in 1948 and 1953, but when his playing days were ended by injury he had returned to his native Ellesmere Port and gone into the grocery business.

He was in his shop two days before the start of the 1955–56 campaign when he learned E. Senior Atkin, the autocratic bowler-hatted Sheffield United chairman wanted to talk to him about the vacancy at Bramall Lane.

It was always said that Atkin, a local silversmith, took it entirely upon himself to approach and appoint Mercer, and this was the action that set in train the events leading to a boardroom rebellion and the chairman's resignation in 1957. Mercer often told the story of how he was called into the boardroom on that August day in 1955 to be told by Atkin: 'You've got the job. You're a manager, and I hope you *are* going to manage because I know damn all about this game, and [he indicated the other directors] they know a damn sight less!'

Unfortunately, the Mercer era proved less than memorable, and in his first season the Blades were relegated. They finished seventh and sixth in each of the next two seasons and never really had the look of genuine promotion contenders. Halfway through his fourth term at the helm, Mercer walked out on the Blades to become manager of Aston Villa. He went, he said, because the job offered him more scope, but his first season at Villa Park ended in relegation.

Hagan was to make barely 50 League appearances under Mercer's management before he retired, the new manager making few demands on his old pal, allowing him a free rein in terms of keeping himself fit and, naturally, declining to tell the veteran what was expected of him on the field. In Mercer's first term, Hagan was limited to 22 games, and

the fact that he made only six appearances between October and March severely handicapped United's bid to beat the threat of relegation. Hagan returned to produce a memorable display at Everton, where he set up all United's goals in a 4–1 victory, including a hat-trick for newcomer Jack Wilkinson; but the Blades won only one of their next eight games and their fall from the top grade also marked the end of Hagan's career as a First Division player.

United's only real consolation was the rapid improvement in the form of outside-left Colin Grainger, who had been signed by Reg Freeman from Wrexham in 1953. Despite the slide to relegation, Grainger made such a big impression that, in May 1956, he was capped by England against Brazil at Wembley and stayed in for the tour games in Sweden, Finland and Germany. He went on to collect seven caps, but, significantly perhaps, the last, in April 1957, came two months after he had been sold to Sunderland for £17,000.

If United's first season back in the lower grade was notable for Grainger, it was painful for Ringstead, who missed most of the campaign with damaged ligaments. The loss of the Irishman was crucial, and Mercer was often under fire from the fans for his team selections. Hagan, as always, provided the occasional golden moment. His display at Huddersfield in November 1956, when he inspired a 4–1 Blades' victory, was described as fantastic by the critics, and that defeat incidentally, prompted Town boss Andy Beattie to resign and make way for a certain Bill Shankly—a man destined for managerial greatness in later years at Anfield.

By coincidence, it was when United visited Liverpool in the following April that Hagan, back after a three-month injury lay-off, produced his last supreme performance in a United shirt. All the old magic was there as he strolled through a glorious afternoon when everything he tried came off. He set up a goal for Bobby Howitt and the one he scored himself in the 3–0 triumph was really special—it was Hagan's last for the Blades.

Hagan made only four appearances in his final term with United. His last League outing at Bramall Lane came on 2nd September *v* Charlton and, symbolically perhaps, he bowed from the senior scene after the game at Derby later in the same month. The following March he was given a testimonial match which, ironically, was staged on the coldest night of the year. But 29,166 fans braved the elements to pay homage to a hero they would never forget.

Hagan went off to the United States and Australia that summer as a guest of Blackpool, and, in the meantime, there was speculation about Mercer's future. The United boss was linked with the vacant job at Arsenal, but insisted he was staying to honour his contract at the Lane. He did stay, for George Swindon, the one-time Gunners goalkeeper, was appointed to the Highbury post. Swindon thus created a vacancy at Peterborough United of the Midland League; and the man who filled it and so got his start in management was none other than—Jimmy Hagan.

Hagan, who led Peterborough into the Football League in 1960, had an eventful and often controversial career in management, his greatest successes came in Portugal. His methods did not make him the most popular of team bosses in English football, though you could never deny that, to the end, he always insisted the game was all about entertainment—as you might expect from someone who was one of the greatest entertainers to wear the famous Blades stripes.

The Joe Shaw Era

JOE SHAW would be assured of a unique place in Sheffield United's Hall of Fame on statistical evidence alone. Between August 1948 and February 1966, his 631 Football League appearances established a club record that may never be equalled; and his full tally of games for the Blades far exceeds 700 if County Cup and friendly fixtures are added to the 58 matches he played in the FA Cup and League Cup.

The figures, of course, serve to emphasise Shaw's consistency and durability, but quality was his keynote. His talent was not only his ability to win and use the ball, but, especially in his peak years, a remarkable positional sense and excellent anticipation and awareness that enabled him to make it all look so easy. Joe Mercer, United's manager from August 1955 to December 1958, did not give praise lightly, but once said that Shaw's class was evident in the way he always seemed to have enough time to take the lace out of the ball! In truth, there was some irony in Mercer's appreciation, for in his early days at Bramall Lane he felt Shaw's lack of height a handicap and believed the lad did not relish facing big, physical centre-forwards. Manager Joe preferred player Joe at right-half, and even in that role there was one spell when Shaw was dropped and the boss handed the captaincy to Cliff Mason.

Shaw has passed into local sporting folklore as the best uncapped centre-half of his day, greatly respected by his peers and admired by spectators but overlooked by the international committee; regarded by Blades fans as yet another victim, like Hagan, of United's unfashionable image. Chosen as reserve for England's game with Scotland at Wembley in April 1955, he was ignored when a vacancy

SOUVENIR **6**D. PROGRAMME

ON MONDAY, 29th MARCH, 1965.   KICK-OFF 7.30 P.M.

JOE SHAW
TESTIMONIAL MATCH

SHEFFIELD UNITED
versus
ALL STAR XI

BRAMALL LANE GROUND, SHEFFIELD

Joe Shaw testimonial programme

occurred in his old wing-half position after the withdrawal of Bill McGarry and Len Phillips through injuries. To the dismay of every Sheffield supporter, Chelsea's Ken Armstrong was called up. So two 'caps' collected on the FA Tour of Australia in 1951 (he went with colleagues Hagan and Ted Burgin and Wednesday's Sewell) and two appearances in the Football League XI were his only representative honours.

The prizes proved elusive at club level too, though he helped United win the Second Division title in 1953 and was an ever-present in the 1960–61 side that climbed back to the First Division and reached the FA Cup semi-final for the first time since 1936 in John Harris's second full term as boss. The latter campaign was the one in which Harris recruited the likes of Barry Hartle (£2,750 from Watford) and John Docherty (£6,000 from Brentford) but, more notably, Keith Kettleborough (£15,000 from Rotherham) and Len Allchurch (£12,500 from Swansea) in the push that clinched promotion one point behind Alf Ramsey's Ipswich.

It was the year when it took three games to settle the semi-final with Leicester, who won with a double strike at Birmingham after goalless draws at Leeds and Nottingham. The Blades had reached the sixth round the previous year and lost to a Wednesday side that had all the luck going, and they felt sure 1961 was going to bring their moment of Wembley glory.

A product of Murton, County Durham, and a Sunderland fan whose boyhood idol was Raich Carter, Shaw arrived in South Yorkshire as an 11-year-old when a job in a local pit

brought his father to the area. It was while playing in an Upton Colliery side defeated 1–0 by Sheffield United's reserves at Bramall Lane that he was spotted by manager Teddy Davison—though one suspects coach Dugald Livingstone may have been the man whose eye the 16-year-old caught. Certainly Livingstone was a key figure later when, after Shaw became a professional, he habitually kept the lad behind after training for extra work aimed at improving weaknesses in his game.

Shaw was invited to have a trial in a League North wartime fixture with Huddersfield in April 1945, and he made an immediate impression. Unfortunately, in order to play he had taken time off from his job as a locomotive fireman without permission, and he faced the sack! As it happened, within a few months (he was 17 in late June) United offered him a contract. It was only £1 a match at the outset, but it was a beginning, and when he signed full-time to begin a 22-year career with the Blades he was paid £11 10s (£11.50) a week. Such riches!

He was left with painful memories of his Football League debut in the home First Division game with Liverpool on 30th August 1948, for he broke his nose and United lost. Indeed, it was not the happiest of seasons as the Blades were relegated. However, switching to wing-half, initially on the left but later on the right, from inside-right, he soon began to make his mark. In fact, it was Jimmy Hagan who urged his move to wing-half, and Shaw often looked back on that spell, during which Hagan talked him through matches and taught him some invaluable touches, as one of the most satisfying of his career. Hagan, Ernest Jackson and Harry Latham were colleagues who proved major influences on Shaw's early career.

At just fractionally over 5ft 8in tall, Shaw was not physically built in a way that automatically suggested the centre-half position might suit him, but circumstances pushed him into the role on several occasions before he began the run in which he made the number 5 shirt his own. It is probably relevant to note that the centre-half position seemed to cause concern with some frequency in the early post-war era. Harry Latham was the most dependable of defenders, but he had Dick Young as his first serious rival, and in March 1949 United paid £15,000 for the bearded Jack Chisholm from Brentford. In the event, Chisholm made only 21 appearances before he left to begin a successful time at Plymouth. Subsequently, Bill Toner, signed on a free after being released by Celtic, Howard Johnson, formerly with Norton Woodseats, and ex-Marine commando Harry Hitchen, from New Brighton, filled the role; and it is worth mentioning that Cec Coldwell, although he came to prominence as a back, arrived from Norton Woodseats as a centre-half.

It would have been so easy for Shaw's career to have gone in another direction. His debut as pivot came at West Ham in September 1950 when United won a remarkable game 5–3, with Fred Furniss scoring twice from the penalty spot, Hammers defender Ernest Devlin conceding two own-goals, and Hagan finding the net with a rare header. Latham and his deputy George Underwood were injured.

Shaw retained the role the following week and excelled when facing the legendary Tommy Lawton: unfortunately, though the former England centre-forward was kept quiet, a young inside-forward called Jackie Sewell was allowed to score the goals that gave Notts County the points!

It was in another game with West Ham, an FA Cup fourth-round tie in February 1952, that Shaw switched to centre-half again after Latham was injured in the first match; and he stayed there in the Bramall Lane replay, which United won 4–2 on a day remembered because a white ball was used throughout a game for the first time in Sheffield.

However, the real turning point came in the second match of the 1954–55 season when United went to Maine Road and, in the first half, endured a torrid time facing Manchester City's innovative use of Don Revie as a deep-lying centre-forward (as exploited by the Hungarians in that famous 1953 defeat of England at Wembley). At half-time, manager Reg Freeman told nominal number 5 Howard Johnson to follow Revie wherever he went, while Shaw was instructed to fill the gap at the heart of defence. The Blades still lost 5–2, but City's goal-rush had been halted. Shaw seldom played in any other position after that. As part of the subsequent tightening of the defence, a very promising young goalkeeper called Alan Hodgkinson was given his debut in place of Ted Burgin.

It would be wrong to suggest that Joe Shaw's career was untroubled from this point, for, in September 1956, with the Blades back in the

Second Division, Joe Mercer recruited
a new centre-half, 6ft veteran Malcolm
Barrass from Bolton. It was one of
several changes that did not impress
supporters critical of some of
Mercer's selections—not least using
full-back Graham Shaw on the right
wing and, in a desperate bid to solve
the problems at centre-forward,
playing Howard Johnson in attack.

Mercer made it plain to Joe Shaw
that he did not fancy him at the heart
of the defence and, with Tommy
Hoyland and Jim Iley then established
at wing-half, the manager said he
would have to fight if he hoped to get
back into the side in his former role.
For the only time in his long years as a
United player, Shaw began to feel his
future might lie elsewhere. In the
event, Barrass, who was also installed
as captain, enjoyed a run of only 18
League games during which United
conceded 42 goals, including seven in
a home match with Rotherham and
five at Liverpool, Leicester and Bristol
City.

The setback at Bristol, where big
John Atyeo exposed Barrass's lack of
mobility, prompted Mercer to admit
he had been wrong to dispense with
Shaw, and at least he was honest
enough to apologise to him. Shaw's
recall however, was only one
significant decision the manager
made: he also announced that
forthwith Hodgkinson would be the
first-choice goalkeeper. Hodgy, who
was nearing the end of his National
Service, had already been picked in
the England Under-23s and before the
end of the season had collected the
first of his five senior caps. It was a
remarkable turnabout for a lad who
had begun the campaign in the
Yorkshire League side. Mind you,

Alan Hodgkinson

Burgin did get an unexpected recall
just 24 hours after Hodgkinson was
installed as the new number 1, for the
youngster was injured against Lincoln,
and the man he replaced had to be
called from his sick bed to play in the
Boxing Day return.

Hodgkinson was not the only
United man to gain international
recognition in 1956–57, for Graham
Shaw was capped at England Under-
23 level and he would gain a full cap
by late 1958. The departure of Iley to

Spurs, the arrival of Gerry Summers from West Brom, and the promotion of local product Brian Richardson created the circumstances that, early in the 1957–58 campaign, saw the following names appear together on the Blades' team-sheet for the first time:

Hodgkinson

Coldwell   G. Shaw

Richardson   J. Shaw   Summers

they made for the Blades in their careers at Bramall Lane, for it serves to emphasise their contribution.

	Lge	FAC	LC	Total
Hodgkinson	576	52	24	652
Coldwell	410	41	10	461
G. Shaw	442	37	9	488
Richardson	291	28	10	329
J. Shaw	631	51	7	689
Summers	260	32	6	298
	2610	241	66	2917

Mercer did not manage to take United back to the First Division before he chose to walk out and join Aston Villa in December 1958, but he did make one signing for which his successor, John Harris, was grateful. In fact, it would be fair to say many of his Sheffield critics forgave him his other failings simply because he brought centre-forward Derek Pace to Bramall Lane.

Cec Coldwell

Those six remained an integral part of the United team as a group right through to 1963, and it might be appropriate to list the appearances

Derek Pace

When Mercer paid Aston Villa £12,000 for Pace, who made his

Archie Clark

Blades debut on Boxing Day 1957 (and scored within eight minutes), it was a Christmas present that profited the club for years. He had notched 42 goals in 106 games for Villa, but he wrote his name into United's record books with 163 goals in 294 matches before leaving in 1964 and ending his career at Notts County and Walsall. Few players have been so popular with colleagues and supporters alike: he was a man who gave everything, and he was quickly hailed as the best centre-forward to play for United since the war. It was widely acknowledged that, had he been signed a few months earlier, United might well have been promoted in 1957–58.

Not surprisingly, when Mercer became Villa's manager, he admitted he wished he had left Pace in the Midlands. Pace, who had been nicknamed 'Doc' since serving in the

Medical Corps during National Service, would surely have cured all Joe's ills! Mercer had the sense to know United would not sell their new scoring hero, but he did try to buy skipper Cec Coldwell, and, naturally, was politely told where to go by Football Committee chairman, H. Blacow Yates, who tended to be a little more subtle in his choice of words than his predecessor, Senior Atkin!

There was another Mercer recruit for whom United were especially grateful: chief scout Archie Clark, who arrived in September 1958 and remained until his sudden death at the age of 64 in January 1967. A former Arsenal and Everton player, Clark was a wonderful character, a strong disciplinarian and a very knowledgeable football man; there were many who felt he was desperately unlucky not to be named as Mercer's successor. For, when he stood in during the months before John Harris took over, Clark generated a terrific spirit and things went very well. This was the year when they achieved a famous victory over Arsenal, in a fifth-round replay after a memorable duel at Highbury in the first game; but then fell to Third Division Norwich by a 3–2 margin at Carrow Road after the East Anglians had battled to earn a 1–1 draw at Bramall Lane, despite goalkeeper Ken Nethercott playing with a dislocated shoulder for more than half the match.

It was on 13th March 1959 that United confirmed Harris as their new manager. If Clark was disappointed, he never made his feelings public, and in the next eight years, nobody was more grateful for his support than

John Harris speaking to the Press.

Harris. Clark continued to answer the telephone in the manager's office, not with the number, but with the words that were a mixture of truth and wit typical of the man: 'Best club in England!' He was the key to the recruitment and development of a succession of talented youngsters such as Len Badger, Bernard Shaw, Tony and Barry Wagstaff, Ken Mallender, Mick Jones, Alan Birchenall, David Munks, Frank Barlow and Alan Woodward; and, with Harris having an astonishing knack for finding bargains in the transfer market, the Harris-Clark partnership was extremely profitable to the Blades.

Harris must rank as one of the best managers United have ever had: he had ideal credentials for the challenge of guiding the Blades back into Division One and keeping them there, despite limited resources, in a phase in football history when removal of the maximum wage (in 1961) made the task harder than ever. The new manager, then 41, was

steeped in football. At the time of his birth in Glasgow in 1917, his father, Neil, had been Partick Thistle's centre-forward, but in the following years he served Newcastle, Notts County and Oldham and was capped by Scotland. Later, Neil managed Burton Town and Distillery, before joining Swansea Town, where John, by then a teenager, worked in the office. It wasn't long before Swansea's directors urged Neil to offer John, a promising inside-forward or wing-half, professional terms, and the lad made his League debut in April 1935. His playing career spanned some 400 League and Cup games in peacetime.

In 1939 John was sold by his father to Spurs, but it was a free transfer to Wolves that marked a turning point, for Molineux boss, Major Frank Buckley, converted him to centre-half, the role in which he excelled as a wartime guest with Southampton and Chelsea and was capped by Scotland. He captained Chelsea in two wartime cup finals at Wembley, and formally transferred to them for £8,000 in

1945, he was a big favourite at Stamford Bridge and figured in the 1955 League Championship-winning side. It was in April 1956 that he began his managerial apprenticeship at Chester—though, as he admitted years later, he never really wanted to be a manager.

> I'd have been happy as a coach. I had seen my father have some hard times as a manager. He once said he'd rather endure five years' hard labour as a player than be a manager for one year. I never fancied inheriting the kind of worry and problems which sent him to an early grave, but, when the opportunity came to have a go at the job at Chester, my mother said I really ought to accept the challenge, if only for the sake of my father's memory.

Harris, who remained a bachelor to the end of his life, had a reputation as a man of few words, but this was a false image. He could talk about football with great fluency, but was not a media man and belonged to that breed of managers reluctant to speak in public. He would not have been happy in the modern era of post-match press conferences, yet he was the sort of man who, in the right company, would discuss a subject in detail and with remarkable openness.

What really mattered was that he had a great depth of knowledge of the game and its tactics, and while he inherited a good team, he proved his credentials in the way he led the Blades to promotion and the FA Cup semi final in his second full season at the helm. It was a measure of his abilities that he made exactly the right signings to swing the balance on that push towards the First Division in 1960–61. Significantly, the Blades lost only one of their last nine League games (the defeat actually came after promotion had been clinched) and the purchase of Len Allchurch from Swansea in March was the step that proved the masterstroke—the final piece in the jigsaw to follow earlier moves.

Harris sold Kevin Lewis to Liverpool and used the money to bring in Barry Hartle from Watford and then Keith Kettleborough from Rotherham. Kettleborough, who cost around £15,000 when he arrived in December 1960, proved a very useful acquisition; but he did not remember his debut with much affection. On a dreadful, wet and muddy day, United led Bristol Rovers 2–0 but ended up losing 3–2; a defeat that shattered an unbeaten home run of 20 League games.

United won their first ten home games that season and a run of eight straight League wins in September and October was only marred by defeat in the club's first Football League Cup tie (at Bury). The setback the Blades suffered on Kettleborough's debut came early in a spell when they picked up only two points from six games, but that was the only time they wobbled on the promotion road. In a sense, that slight hitch was beneficial, for it persuaded the Blades' board to back a Harris plan that prompted the sale of Willie Hamilton to Middlesbrough in February and the acquisition of John Docherty (£6,000 from Brentford) and Allchurch, a bargain at £12,500. Winger Allchurch was an immediate success and contributed six vital goals in eight games. In his time at Bramall Lane, the Welsh international, brother of the legendary Ivor, notched 32 goals in 123 League matches, but none proved more welcome than those that helped seal promotion in 1961.

United finished with the following record:

	P	W	D	L	F	A
Home	21	16	2	3	49	22
Away	21	10	4	7	32	29

The top of the Second Division looked like this:

	P	W	D	L	F	A	Pts
1. Ipswich	42	26	7	9	100	55	59
2. Sheff. Utd	42	26	6	10	81	51	58
3. Liverpool	42	21	10	11	87	58	52

Ipswich clinched the title by virtue of one more away win and one less defeat than United, who actually had a better home record than the East Anglian side managed by Alf Ramsey —a man who was destined to stun the football world by leading Ipswich to the First Division championship within a year.

Of course, the scoring heroes of 1960–61 were Derek Pace (26) and

Billy Russell (18). Russell, the former Rhyl forward who had helped Bishop Auckland win the FA Amateur Cup before joining United in 1957, believed at one stage that he was going to figure in a famous promotion and FA Cup double with the Blades. He scored the goal that gave United a 1–0 win at Everton in the third round, claimed two in the 3–1 defeat of Lincoln at the next stage, and he and Bill Hodgson were on target when the Blades beat Blackburn in the fifth round. Amateur international Russell scored some 70 goals in 170 games for the Blades between 1957 and 1963, but his most memorable day was almost certainly that afternoon in 1961 when he grabbed three goals in the first eighteen minutes of United's FA Cup sixth-round tie at Newcastle to set up a famous victory—as unforgettable as the one in 1958 when Russell had helped in a great triumph at Tottenham.

Sheffield United 1960–61.

Alas, the semi-final with Leicester City proved an anti-climax, for it turned into a dour marathon in which, after goalless draws at Leeds and Nottingham, United lost 2–0 at Birmingham in a duel remembered for an Alan Hodgkinson penalty save, a missed spot kick by Graham Shaw, and a Leicester strike that ended the goal famine after an incredible four hours and seventeen minutes. With Wednesday having finished runners-up to Spurs in the title race, United would have made it a novel Sheffield double, if they could have been the side seeking to deny the North Londoners a Cup triumph at Wembley, to top up their Championship success. But it wasn't to be. The consolation was that the Sheffield clubs had kicked off the 1960s in style, were back together in the top grade, and all set for an eventful decade of drama and change.

Joe Shaw

For the record, Joe Shaw played on in the senior side until February 1966. The following summer saw him join the training staff, where he might have remained for many years. However, in late 1967 he elected to apply for, and got, the manager's job at York; but he quit the post in the following August. Though he later managed Chesterfield, from September 1973 to October 1976, he was ultimately lost to football.

36

Redfern Froggatt

EDFERN FROGGATT was the
only man to play for Wednesday in
every season of Eric Taylor's sixteen-
year spell as team boss. In fact, he
played on in the senior side for
another two years after Taylor had
handed the reins to Harry Catterick.
Thus he ended up with some 540
appearances and 160 goals between
February 1943 and April 1960, and his
140 League goals in 434 matches was
a club post-war aggregate scoring
record, until Johnny Fantham topped
it in 1968.

Froggatt had the distinction of
sharing in four promotion successes
(1950, 1952, 1956 and 1959) and,
when collecting his third Second
Division championship medal in
1959, had the distinction of emulating
father Frank's 1926 feat of captaining
the Owls to a title triumph. Moreover,
his 26 goals made it the best scoring
year of his career, being nearly twice
his previous highest tally in a season.

The Owls may have had bigger and
costlier stars in the 1950s and some
were probably greater favourites, but
it is doubtful whether the club had a
more loyal or consistent player in this
period. His quality was confirmed by
the four England caps he collected
between November 1952 and June
1953, though, in truth, he feels he
was a much more accomplished
inside-forward (and got more ful-
filment from his football) in the later
stages of his career.

Like Joe Shaw across at Bramall

Lane, Froggatt was the essential one-
club man, and in his time rejected the
chances to join Arsenal and Spurs. He
even said no to an offer from Italy.
There was only one spell when he
gave any serious thought to leaving
Hillsborough, and this was around
1953–54 when, with Jackie Sewell and
Albert Quixall keeping him out of the
side, he sought a transfer. There was
a strong hint that he might sign for
Sheffield United, but it never got
beyond the speculative stage, and
Froggatt was still at Hillsborough long
after Sewell and Quixall had gone. A
joke often told about his failure to
join United suggested that the Blades
had got Cross (a centre-forward from
Northampton called Jack) because
they couldn't have Froggatt!

Although his scoring record
ensures Froggatt's name will always
be synonymous with goals, he did not
really start out as a marksman, and to
judge him solely as such is mis-
leading. He had several spells on
the wing, and was more often the
provider than the finisher, and in fact,
was seldom prolific. In his first
peacetime season, the 1946–47
campaign in which Wednesday
narrowly escaped falling into the old
Third Division (North), he found the
net only once.

However, he scored ten in each of
the next two seasons as the Owls
finished fourth and then eighth in the
table. Despite missing a dozen games
in 1949–50, he led the charts with

fourteen as promotion was finally clinched and Wednesday pipped Sheffield United and Southampton thanks to a 0–0 draw in their last match, at home to champions Spurs. On that May day in 1950, a 50,883 crowd saw the Owls gain the only result other than a victory that could see them up. They were promoted with a .008 superior goal-average, and had they drawn 1–1 would have faced a play-off with the Blades!

By coincidence, they did play United the following week in a County Cup final in which goals from Hugh McJarrow (a recent buy from Chesterfield) and Charlie Tomlinson gave them a 2–1 victory before a crowd of 31,861, which would certainly have been nearer 60,000 had a place in the First Division been at stake.

Reference to the County Cup and the 1949–50 season brings to mind Eddie Quigley, who left Wednesday midway through that promotion campaign—sold to Preston for a British record fee of £26,000, more than double the amount the Owls had paid for him when he arrived from Bury in October 1947. With 52 goals in 78 League and Cup games, Quigley gave Wednesday good value, but many felt he had lost some of his effectiveness and wanted a new challenge by the time of his de-parture. In fact, in the early weeks of his final term he had scored ten in ten games, but it was after he was sidelined that Wednesday began the thirteen-match unbeaten run that set them on course for a serious push towards promotion, and Eric Taylor did not hesitate to accept Preston's offer. Quigley was popular, for though he was one of those players who always seemed slightly overweight and somewhat reluctant to appear especially energetic, he had great positional sense and terrific reactions when a chance was offered. Remarkably, a year before he came to Sheffield he had been a full-back, but switched into attack in an emergency when Bury met Millwall, he promptly scored five goals and never returned to defence. He twice scored four in a match for the Owls (against West Ham and Chesterfield), and twice notched two in a couple of memorable matches against Sheffield United.

The first double came in the unique friendly staged at Douglas, Isle of Man, in May 1948, and the second in

Eddie Quigley

the County Cup semi-final at Hillsborough in February 1949, when a staggering crowd of 49,980 turned up on a blustery day, remembered as the occasion when Quigley followed an Owls tradition and paid for ignoring the elements. Winning the toss, he chose to attack the Leppings Lane end in the first half, giving United the advantage of a strong wind which they exploited so well that they were four goals up at the interval. Quigley's second-half double was not enough to spare his blushes. Someone had told him Wednesday always did well when they kicked downhill towards the Kop after half-time!

Within a year of reaching Division One for the first time since 1937 on goal-average, Wednesday were relegated in similar circumstances, going down despite a six-goal victory on the season's final day. Froggatt (14) was joint leading scorer with Hugh McJarrow and Dennis Woodhead, but while the Owls scored more goals than ten of their First Division rivals, they conceded 83, and only two other clubs had a worse defensive record. It was a year when they never made up for a poor start and reached the last day of the season knowing the odds against them surviving were very slim. Chelsea and Wednesday had 30 points and Everton, the Owls' opponents at Hillsborough, had 32. If Everton got anything they would stay up, but if they didn't and Chelsea and Wednesday both won it would all be down to goal-average. Wednesday felt a 6–0 victory would be enough, and remarkably, that is what they got . . . but Chelsea's 4–0 defeat of Bolton sent the Owls down by .044 of a goal!

All the drama in this season was not confined to the field, for in February Eric Taylor attempted to pull off what would have been the most sensational transfer in Sheffield football history: he tried to sign Blades idol Jimmy Hagan, and United's board actually accepted the £32,250 offer on a majority vote. However, Hagan himself quashed the deal because he was scheduled for a thumb operation he wanted to have before the end of the season in order to be fit to join the FA's Australian tour. It was always something of a surprise that a player of Hagan's calibre remained at Bramall Lane so long, but this was the age of the maximum wage and as he had business interests and an arrangement that suited him he was not looking to move. Had he wanted to go, he would never have had a better excuse than when he had been dropped in 1949. Even so, most Unitedites would not have welcomed him joining Wednesday; but this really was a distinct possibility stemming from a conversation between Blades chairman G.E. Marlow and Owls vice-chairman James Longden when they chanced to meet on the Sheffield–London train.

Eric Taylor was seldom a man put down for long, and within barely a month of Hagan's rejection the Wednesday manager signed Notts County's 24-year-old inside-forward Jackie Sewell for a British record fee of £35,000. He had hoped to take his spending on that March day in 1951 to £52,525 by buying Jessie Pye, the Wolves centre-forward; but though Pye was a native of Treeton, his wife declined to move to Sheffield.

Sewell, a product of Cumberland, had been at Meadow Lane for seven years, and in barely four seasons as a first-team regular had scored 97 League goals, his development being enhanced by playing alongside the former England legend, Tommy Lawton. Sewell recalled some years later:

> I was very happy at Notts County and made it plain to Mr Taylor that I had no thoughts of leaving. When it was obvious the Notts directors were keen to get their hands on some money, I remember telling Mr Taylor that I hoped he knew what he was doing. It wasn't until I read the papers the next day that I learned the size of the fee, and I can tell you I was petrified. I told Tommy Lawton I feared I would never justify that kind of money, but he said I'd be okay so long as I kept working at my game and had faith in my ability.

Sewell was unable to help Wednesday beat the drop, but 92 goals in 175 games in under five years was evidence of his merit. Ironically, at the end of his first season he went to Australia in the same FA party as

Redfern Froggatt (centre) 'interviews' Dooley, while Tommy McAnearney looks on.

Jimmy Hagan. He won his first cap within nine months of joining the Owls and played six times for England—his last appearances, in November 1953 and May 1954, being in those famous games in which Hungary won 6–3 at Wembley and 7–1 in Budapest to shatter many illusions about the superiority of English football.

When Wednesday bounced back to Division One at the first attempt, as Second Division champions in 1951–52, Sewell contributed 23 goals but the great hero was Derek Dooley (of whom more in the next chapter). Meanwhile, Froggatt had one of his leanest seasons. He did not get into the team until late November, and 13 of his 23 outings were in the number 7 shirt. At least he was on the losing side only four times; and the following autumn, he was capped twice in the space of a fortnight and went on to play against Scotland at Wembley in April 1953 and against the United States in the summer.

Yet Wednesday's second term back at the top, 1953–54, brought a dramatic turnabout in Froggatt's fortunes, for while he began the season with his place looking secure, all the more so as Albert Quixall was away on National Service, he suddenly fell out of favour. In fact, Quixall's spell in the army was boosting rather than handicapping his progress. The youngster was called into the Football League XI in September and played for England in October and November. Sewell, too, was very much in the eye of the international selectors. The upshot was that, between October and March, Froggatt made only six appearances for the Owls, four at centre-forward, and he

never got a look-in during the run
to the FA Cup semi-final in which
Wednesday lost to Preston at Maine
Road. Yet Froggatt's bid for a transfer
came to naught, even though his
frustrations continued into the 1954–
55 campaign in which Wednesday
might be said to have romped
towards the relegation precipice.
They won only eight games all season,
and three of those victories came
after their fate had been decided.
They became the first club since
Grimsby in 1947–48 to concede a
century of goals in the First Division.
Froggatt made only 21 appearances,
12 of them at outside-left.

Fortunately, things took a turn for
the better for Froggatt and the team

in 1955–56, when they again won the
Second Division title. He again began
the season on the wing, but returned
to his customary position in mid-term
following Sewell's transfer to Aston
Villa. Froggatt, in fact, missed only
one League fixture and contributed
fourteen goals. However, the surprise
package of the season was new
centre-forward Roy Shiner, a summer
buy from Huddersfield in the deal
that also brought former England
back Ron Staniforth to Hillsborough.
The captain, by the way, was another
ex-Huddersfield man, Don McEvoy.

For a change, Wednesday did not
have to struggle to avoid a prompt
drop into the Second Division in
1956–57, despite one run between

Wednesday, Second Division champions 1955–56.
Back row: Froggatt, O'Donnell, Broadbent, McIntosh, Tom McAnearney, Staniforth, Bingley.
Front row: Jack Marshall (trainer-coach), Martin, Shiner, McEvoy, Curtis, Finney, Quixall,
E.W. Taylor (sec-manager).

early February and mid-April when they won only two of thirteen matches; but they were on the slide again in 1957–58 when a 'flu epidemic caused postponement of their first two matches and they kicked off the campaign a week late. They never made up the lost ground, and Froggatt, having played in only one of the first twelve games, was limited to 25 outings. However, he did play on the day in February when Fantham, a local teenager destined to become the club's most prolific post-war marksman, made his debut in the home game with Tottenham. Froggatt was also on duty in the famous FA Cup fifth-round tie at Old Trafford when Manchester United played their first game after the Munich air crash—but more of that when Quixall's story is told in a later chapter.

Wednesday's relegation in 1958 prompted Taylor to relinquish team duties, and the vacancy was advertised. There were applications from many more famous figures than Harry Catterick, but it was the former Everton centre-forward who was given the job. He had spent five years at Rochdale after an earlier spell as player-manager at Crewe, and he proved an inspired choice; though unfortunately, his stay at Hillsborough was shorter than some might have hoped.

It was largely a Taylor-made team with which Catterick piloted the Owls to their third Second Division title in eight seasons in 1958–59, and after the shock departure of Quixall, who was sold to Manchester United within days of the new manager's arrival, Froggatt, the longest-serving Taylor man of them all, took on the captaincy. In fact, it was in the match

that marked Quixall's farewell, a 6–0 defeat of Sunderland, in which Froggatt bagged a hat-trick. This was the high point of a run during which he claimed 17 goals in 13 games and showed he was still, at 34, one of the best inside-forwards around. Only Shiner, with 28 goals, bettered the Owls' veteran's tally of 26.

Froggatt was limited to eighteen matches after the return to the First Division, but has often said that the opening game of that 1959–60 season was one he always savoured because not only did the Owls win 1–0 at Arsenal, they played as if they were really in the top grade to stay this time. After years of being too good for the Second Division and not quite good enough for the First, they were a match for the best. Alas, the arrival of Bobby Craig from Third Lanark for £6,500 in November 1959 meant there was little chance that the old hero would be sharing in that bright-looking future. It was the end of an era in many ways, not least in that the lifting of the maximum wage was coming and the future Froggatts would go out of the game with a lot more financial security. All he took were a lot of great memories.

Of Froggatt's many colleagues in his time at Hillsborough, the one with whom he tended to be most often associated was defender Hugh Swift, they were inseparable in their time together with the Owls; both were local lads with no wish to play for any other club. Like Froggatt, Swift, a former Burngreave schoolboy, was a wartime product, and he came to the fore during the Owls's run to the League North War Cup—indeed, that was the season in which he made the switch, to back from outside-left, after deputising for the injured Ted Catlin.

Swift made 136 appearances during the war and another 195 afterwards, and he and Frank Westlake enjoyed one run of over 120 consecutive appearances as Wednesday's backs. Swift, along with Owls colleagues Froggatt and Walter Rickett (who had returned to Sheffield from Blackpool in 1949), played for England 'B' against Switzerland at Hillsborough in January 1950, and looked set for further honours until he suffered a fractured jaw at Coventry in February 1950. Although he recovered and got back into the side, that injury led to him having to quit professional football on medical advice, and a player who had much skill and, incidentally, was a master of the sliding tackle, was lost to the game.

Swift's misfortune presented an opportunity that Norman Curtis, a signing from Gainsborough Trinity, took with both hands, and Curtis went on to make 324 League and Cup appearances and share in the Second Division title successes of 1952, 1956 and 1959. Curtis scored 21 goals, 19 of them from the penalty spot; and the manner in which he took a long run and hammered his kicks so hard that the ball would decapitate anyone who got in the way, earned him the nickname 'Cannonball'. He was one of the great characters in the team in the 1950s, taking upon himself the role of emergency goalkeeper; there was one occasion at Preston when Dave McIntosh went off injured and Curtis had the distinction of saving two penalties.

McIntosh, too, was involved in helping Wednesday reach the First Division on three separate occasions, and the Scot from Girvan made over 300 appearances between 1948 and 1957. He was one of the bravest of goalkeepers, and after being an ever-present in the team that captured the Second Division title in 1952 he endured an unfortunate run of injuries, breaking an arm twice in the space of a year.

Wednesday had some splendid characters among their defenders in the 1950s, and chief among these were 'Mick' Kenny, Cyril Turton, Edgar Packard and Ralph O'Donnell—all very different in personality but similarly uncompromising players. Turton was a wartime find who made around 150 appearances at centre-half and had a spell as skipper. It was often suggested that he could run backwards as fast he he could run forwards! His great rival was Packard, who joined the club in 1936 but did not make his League debut until ten years later. There was a famous occasion at Hillsborough in December 1949 when Packard was allowed to gather a ball in his own penalty area and run the length of the field into the other box unchallenged. The West Ham defence kept expecting him to release the ball: eventually he did—firing it into the net for the only League goal of a career that spanned 126 games for the Owls!

The earlier reference to Swift's career being ended prematurely by injury, serves as a reminder that, over the years, Wednesday have lost the services of a number of notable players in this way. One example was Alf Rogers, a very dependable inside-forward in Froggatt's era, and a more famous instance was provided by Eddie Kilshaw. When he was signed from Bury in December 1948 he cost

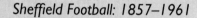
£20,000, which at the time was a record for a winger and only £20 short of the record for a player in any position. Alas, after only nineteen League and Cup appearances Kilshaw's career was ended when he suffered a dislocated knee in a game with Leicester at Hillsborough.

Of course, the best-known case of a Wednesday man's career being shattered by injury was that of Derek Dooley. His story, however, is a special chapter in itself . . .

37

Derek Dooley:
The Goal Kid

DEREK DOOLEY is one of the most remarkable figures in Sheffield football history. In a unique link with the professional game in his native city; spanning almost half a century, he followed 26 years at Hillsborough with more than 20 years at Bramall Lane and has enjoyed the rare privilege of being a favourite in both camps.

His place in local sporting folklore was sealed as a prolific centre-forward who scored 180 goals in 168 games at all levels for the Owls, before his playing days were ended at the age of 23 in February 1953 in circumstances that almost cost him his life. After breaking his right leg in a First Division match at Preston, a scratch on the back of his leg became infected and the limb had to be amputated. He had hit 63 goals in 63 League and Cup matches, including a record 46 in the 1951–52 Second Division championship campaign; there was no more talked-about marksman in English football.

Later, after a long spell in the club's development office, he was Wednesday's team-manager for three years, but was sacked in 1973—on Christmas Eve! The pain of that experience was such that it was nearly twenty years before he could bring himself to go back to Hillsborough to see Wednesday play—and ironically, he did so for a famous derby duel in which United beat their old rivals.

He returned to the game in 1974 as United's commercial manager, and, ten years later, emerged as the city's first paid football director, rising to managing director in 1986. He should have retired in the early 1990s, but was called back to serve as chief executive when Reg Brealey re-claimed ownership of the Bramall Lane club.

It is intriguing to speculate on what pattern Dooley's career might have followed but for the unusual cir-cumstances that prevailed at the end of the 1946–47 campaign. Dooley had then already played for Lincoln City in a Third Division (North) match, and they had invited him to become a part-time professional. However, he wanted to stay an amateur long enough to help the Sheffield & Hallamshire CFA win the Northern Counties Championship, and it was when they reached the final and met Doncaster in June that he learned Wednesday were keen to sign him.

A Pitsmoor product and former Owler Lane schoolboy, Dooley had first attracted attention in junior football as a free-scoring 15-year-old playing with Sheffield YMCA. 'Pop' Bennett, who ran the team, tried to use him as a centre-half, but there was only one position the flame-haired giant was prepared to fill, and he put the ball between the sticks with such frequency and created such havoc in opposing goalmouths that it was no surprise when Lincoln offered him a trial.

The winter of 1946–47 was one of the worst there has ever been, and it caused the football season to be extended. In the meantime, Dooley's registration with Lincoln lapsed. So when, after helping Sheffield beat Doncaster, the lad was approached by Owls trainer Tommy Walker, he was free to accept the offer to meet Eric Taylor. He had been alerted to Dooley's talents by Walter Millership. The former Wednesday defender,

Dooley

after facing the youngster in a Midland League match, said: 'He's the most awkward young devil I've ever played against. He's just like a ruddy tank!' He was not the first, nor would he be the last, to express such sentiments!

In the next four seasons, under the stern eye of Johnny Logan, Dooley scored 55 goals in 38 games in Wednesday's Yorkshire League side (including eight in one match) and 37 in 49 Central League outings. Unfortunately, on the two occasions when he was given a chance in the first team—against Preston in March 1950 and at Charlton the following January—he flopped. However, opportunity knocked a third time.

After relegation in 1951, Wednesday were confident of bouncing straight back into the top grade, but nine points and only three wins from their first eleven games was hardly promotion form. It didn't help that the Blades were sitting atop of the table. With Clarrie Jordan again sidelined, and McJarrow and wingers Rickett and Woodhead tried in the number 9 shirt with mixed success, the fact that Dooley had scored thirteen goals in nine Central League fixtures, prompted Taylor to give him another chance in the home game with Barnsley on 6th October 1951—a red-letter day for the club and the player.

Things did not look promising when Barnsley scored with a tenth-minute penalty, but five minutes after half-time the situation changed when Dooley scored; and on 77 minutes the lad got another. 'He'll Dooley all right!' proclaimed the front-page headline in that evening's *Green Un*: they didn't know how accurate the

Dooley headline

prediction was. Dooley went on to score 46 times in 30 League outings; and in one run, between 27th October and 22nd December, he hit 22 in nine matches, including five against Notts County, four against Everton and three at West Ham. He later put four past Hull and got three at Brentford, waltzing past the 37-goal record that Jimmy Trotter had held for 25 years.

There was an amusing sideline to his five-goal feat against Notts County on a wet afternoon in November. As the visitors travelled to the game, someone asked goalkeeper Roy Smith, a former Wednesday player, what Dooley was like. 'He's a big, awkward lad, a bit useless, really,' said Smith, who was still smiling at half-time but changed his tune later when Dooley beat him five times in 32 minutes. It says much for the way things were in those days that, after the game, Dooley went home to Firth Park on a Sheffield Corporation bus.

On this particular journey he witnessed a humorous incident he never forgot. A supporter who got on at the stop after Dooley was absolutely drenched, and the bus conductor asked him how he had got into such a state. 'I've been on t'Kop at t'match,' he said, 'and when it rained heavy I were coming out, but every time I got to top o' t'Kop, that bugger Dooley scored, so I went back!'

Dooley's goals made all the difference in that promotion run, but he has always been the first to agree that other changes contributed to the transformation of the Owls from also-rans to title-contenders. Significant of these changes were the recall of Keith Bannister (who took on the captaincy), Mick Kenny, George Davies, Alan Finney, Albert Quixall and Walter Rickett also the return of Doug Witcomb and Cyril Turton late in the season. Sewell, incidentally, scored 23 goals and was a constant source of encouragement to Dooley.

PROGRAMME   THREEPENCE

SHEFFIELD WEDNESDAY

F O O T B A L L   C L U B

SECOND DIVISION

1951 -52

CHAMPIONS

In the event, this was another of those Sheffield derbies that defied the form book. Graham Shaw, aged 17, made his Blades debut, and a 65,384 crowd saw Alf Ringstead (2) and George Hutchinson score in a 3–1 triumph. Froggatt had a penalty saved by Ted Burgin, and Dooley, though he escaped the close attentions of the wily Harry Latham once to score, had a torrid afternoon.

It was, as they say, a different ball game when Wednesday reached the First Division, Dooley struggled desperately to find his touch in the opening weeks of the 1952–53 campaign. The big boys were waiting and succeeded in making him look more awkward than ever. After four games he was dropped. Eric Taylor explained: 'We're doing it to give him a chance. We don't think he's had fair treatment, and we don't want to break his heart.' Taylor planned to make Dooley twelfth man for the home game with Charlton, but the player argued that sitting on the sidelines wouldn't help him rediscover his scoring flair, and it was agreed he could play for the reserves who, by coincidence, were visiting Bramall Lane. News of Dooley's appearance raised the attendance to 8,531, and those who went saw him score twice as the Owls hit back to beat United's reserves 3–1. Dooley revealed the secret of his success: he had cast aside the new boots with which he had started the season and gone back to the old pair which had served him so well!

Dooley finished on the losing side only five times, and the most notable defeat came when Sheffield United won at Hillsborough in early January. At the time the fortunes of the two clubs had changed so dramatically that the Owls were odds-on favourites to win, and Harry Heap's cartoon in *The Star* summed up the general feeling when his famous character Alf said United had better take the cricket scoreboard from Bramall lane to keep count of the goals Dooley was certain to score. The Blades had won only two of their previous twelve matches.

Dooley scoring against Cardiff at Hillsborough in January 1953 — the last match in which he found the net at Hillsborough before his accident at Preston in the following month.

Dooley returned to the first team for the home game with Spurs, and, though he didn't score, Wednesday registered their first win of the season. Four days later the goal the whole of Sheffield had been waiting for finally arrived when Dooley found the net in the 70th minute of the match with Middlesbrough. The 41,456 spectators at Hillsborough that evening went wild with delight: hats and caps flew into the air and the cheering lasted several minutes as every man in the Owls team ran to shake the centre-forward's hand. It was one of those moments which everyone who was present will never forget.

Dooley went on to score 16 goals in 24 games. His confidence grew and his game began to acquire a little more polish; but he remained the dashing, fearless forward whose presence in a penalty area spelt chaos for defenders. He was, of course, a marked man subjected to rough

handling, but he took the knocks— and gave plenty back! There was one instance, in the home game with Derby in October, when fouls on Dooley gained Wednesday two penalties, both of which Norman Curtis converted; but there were other times when referees ignored the treatment afforded the Owls hero.

Wherever he went he tended to inspire strong emotions in opposing supporters, and at Tottenham in January a spectator was only prevented from striking him by virtue of a policeman's flying tackle. However, amid the anger and controversy provoked by his presence, there were many ready to defend him. Alan Hoby, a highly-respected critic, wrote: 'There are some people who think Dooley is a dirty player. All I can say is they must be blind or crazy.' Jimmy Seed, the Charlton manager and former Owls idol, said: 'I'd rather have Dooley on my side than against me. He's one of the most dangerous centre-forwards in the country, and he'll get better.' Tottenham manager Arthur Rowe commented after the incident at White Hart Lane: 'Dooley used his weight pretty freely, but I don't think there was anything vicious about his play. He is the sort of player who never gives up, and his persistence is always likely to lead him into situations not encountered by a less tenacious player.'

It was at Tottenham that Dooley scored the last goal of his career in a 2–1 defeat, and three weeks later he suffered the accident that ended his playing days. The fateful day was Saturday 14th February 1953, Wednesday were playing at Preston, where the team announced by Eric Taylor included: young Scot Tommy McAnearney, promoted for only his third senior outing; Dave McIntosh, back after missing 23 games with a broken arm; Bill Shadbolt, a winger from Oswestry, making his League debut; and Albert Quixall, who had managed to get leave from the Army.

Wednesday had travelled from Sheffield two days before the match and stayed at Blackpool, but, with a lot of snow and ice in the area, they feared their preparations would be in vain. On the way to Deepdale the weather conditions did not suggest the pitch would be fit for football, but in fact, the groundstaff had been working on it all morning and the Sheffield party arrived to find that referee Arthur Ellis was in no doubt the game could go ahead.

At half-time there was still no score, Alan Brown, the Owls coach, said he felt they could beat Preston's offside trap and get a result if they exploited Dooley's speed. Quixall was told

to hit quick through balls for the centre-forward to chase, and in the fourteenth minute of the second half, it was such a pass that set up the dash that led to Dooley's unfortunate collision with home goalkeeper George Thompson. It was a straight race between Dooley and Thompson, the ball was just outside the penalty area when the goalkeeper got his feet to it a fraction before the inrushing centre-forward, who deflected it towards the goal. Dooley watched the ball roll agonisingly the wrong side of a post and, in the same moment, he and Thompson collided. Both knew instantly that Dooley's leg was broken: the crowd was in no doubt either, for the crack was heard all round the ground.

Dooley spent the weekend in Preston Infirmary, where an x-ray revealed a double fracture, and he expected to be discharged on the following Monday. Alas, it was while he was making plans for his departure that the discovery was made that shattered his world. He asked a nurse to sign the pot on his leg, and when she caught his toes accidentally but noticed he had shown no reaction, she said the pot might be too tight. A doctor was called, and it was found that a gangrenous infection had developed. At the time of the injury, it was felt, Dooley must have got some dirt or substance from the pitch in a small scratch at the back of the leg. It was fortunate the problem had been spotted, for the infection was spreading fast, and the fight was on to save Dooley's life. The surgeon had no option but to amputate.

At a distance of over forty years it is impossible to recapture the shock with which the news was received in Sheffield. A shilling fund was launched in the city and raised £15,000. Later, in March 1955, a testimonial match was staged to coincide with the opening of the Hillsborough floodlights, and it attracted a 55,000 crowd. Dooley came to terms with his new circumstances, and after a spell working for the firm owned by director Dick Gunstone, he took charge of the club's new development fund when it was launched in 1962. Meanwhile, he remained involved helping the Owls juniors.

After the loss of Dooley in that 1952–53 campaign, Wednesday won only three of their remaining twelve games, and were grateful for a Sewell hat-trick which helped them to a 4–0 victory on the final day of the season removing the threat of relegation. It was a long time before the Owls adequately replaced Dooley, and in truth the problem at centre-forward was not properly solved until Roy Shiner was signed from Huddersfield in the summer of 1955. Ronnie Codd, a Sheffield product, was signed from Bolton but played only twice. Jack Shaw, signed for £10,000 from Rotherham, was to score 27 goals in 65 games, there was much about him to admire, but he had been at his peak in giving outstanding service at Millmoor; and it was always unfair to think that because ex-Sheffield Boys favourite Arthur Hukin was tall and had red hair, he might prove the new Dooley. Hukin scored three goals in six games. Though Keith Ellis made the side in 1955, it was later that he reached his peak in scoring 60 goals in 118 games.

Shiner was no Dooley in build or style, but he was a never-say-die

Jack Shaw

player, and it was a typical 100 per cent display in a Central League match for Huddersfield Reserves at Hillsborough that caught the eye of Eric Taylor. Shiner, who was top scorer in the title triumphs of 1956 and 1959 and claimed 96 goals in 160 games, was a product of the Isle of Wight. After joining Huddersfield from Cheltenham in 1951, he had been limited to 21 senior outings, but his career took off following his move to Sheffield.

It is worthy of note that Clarrie Jordan, who had joined Wednesday from Doncaster Rovers for £6,000 plus Arnold Lowes in February 1948, continued to fight the knee trouble that had dogged his career from around 1950; and, though many had suggested his playing days were over, he returned to the side after the Dooley blow and did not retire until 1955. Jordan, a former miner who had been the scoring sensation of Doncaster's Third Division (North) championship triumph of 1946–47, was one of the most cheerful and courageous footballers of his generation. Many of those who played with him have said he was the ideal centre-forward in that he could not only score goals but led his line well and was very adept at feeding his wingers. It was Wednesday's misfortune as well as his that he was forced to spend so much time on the sidelines. Yet, had the fates been kinder to him, Dooley might never have got his chance. Incidentally,

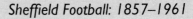
Jordan had to have *both* legs amputated late in life.

Finally, it might be fitting to refer to Dennis Woodhead, who was really an outside-left but spent much time serving as an emergency centre-forward. The grandson of old-time hero, Billy Betts, Woodhead scored 76 goals in 226 games for the Owls between 1946 and 1955, and later played with Chesterfield and Derby. When Dooley was called from the development office in 1971 to take on the team-manager's job, it was Woodhead who succeeded him and remained in the post until June 1987.

Albert Quixall

ALBERT Quixall is remembered as perhaps the first golden boy of English football in the early post-war era. Familiar to a generation of Wednesday supporters as the blond-haired inside-forward with the boyish looks and excessively short shorts who was such an outstanding favourite at Hillsborough in the 1950s. He was the local hero who helped the Owls win the Second Division title in 1952 and 1956 and then, not long after the club's third relegation in eight seasons, joined Manchester United for a British record £45,000 fee in September 1958.

Quixall, brought up little more than a stone's throw from Wednesday's headquarters, was a star long before he signed for the Owls. The kid from Meynell Road was probably Sheffield's best-known schoolboy footballer, and few doubted that he had a big future in the game—though a classmate who also played for England Boys and looked as good a bet was to fail.

There are those who felt Quixall did not achieve as much with

Albert Quixall (third from left on front row) in the inside-right position in the Sheffield Boys team of 1948. On the back row, fourth from the left, is Jerold Bronks, secretary of the Sheffield Schools FA.

Wednesday as he might, but five England caps bear testimony to his talents. Moreover, that Matt Busby saw him as a cornerstone of his team rebuilding at Old Trafford after the Munich air crash, and was prepared to pay so much, serves to emphasise the quality of a player wiser in the arts of the game than his youthful looks might suggest. He did well in Manchester, though an FA Cup winner's medal in 1963 was his only major honour.

Quixall was 17 when he made his senior debut in a friendly at Leicester in January 1951. Two weeks later he helped Wednesday beat United in a County Cup semi-final, and, on 24th February 1951, less than a month before the relegation-threatened Owls paid a record £35,000 for Jackie Sewell. He made his League debut in the home game with Chelsea, scoring in a 2–2 draw against a defence that included John Harris—the man destined to return to Sheffield eight years later as the new manager at Bramall Lane.

Wednesday failed to avoid the drop in that season when Quixall had his first taste of senior football with two outings (the second was against Manchester United), but they bounced back in style the following season. While the recall of Derek Dooley in early October is invariably remembered as the step that inspired a revival of the Owls' fortunes, the day when the big centre-forward launched his stunning goal-scoring sequence also coincided with the start of Quixall's first extended run in the team.

Quixall missed only five of the remaining matches, but there was another game he nearly failed to make—at Brentford in April when a Dooley hat-trick sealed a 3–2 victory. When the team bus arrived at Griffin Park, Quixall stayed outside to distribute tickets to friends who had travelled down from Sheffield, and when he tried to reach the dressing rooms the steward on the players' entrance wouldn't let him through. 'Nay, lad, you're too young to be a player,' said the official, who was only persuaded otherwise when Dooley came in search of his team-mate.

It is generally accepted that Quixall's career touched its first peak in the 1953–54 campaign, which, ironically, coincided with his second year as a National Serviceman based in a camp at Catterick. Soldiering has its drawbacks, but in those days the Army also had advantages for professional footballers. Quixall missed twelve League matches, but excellent form in the First Division and in Army representative games prompted his selection to play for the Football League against the Irish League in Belfast in September, and in October and November he collected three England caps in the games against Wales, a FIFA XI and Northern Ireland.

Quixall's form, which meant there was no place for Froggatt, really caught the headlines during Wednesday's 1954 run to the FA Cup semi-finals. The third round paired the Sheffield clubs for the the first time since 1928, and it was after Jack Shaw's equaliser salvaged a draw for the Owls in the Hillsborough meeting that Taylor's men went on to claim their first triumph at Bramall Lane for 21 years. They won 3–1, despite having defender Mick Kenny sent off for allegedly fouling Jimmy Hagan.

Wednesday met Chesterfield, then in the Third Division (North), at home in the fourth round and a 46,000 crowd saw them held to a goalless draw. The Saltergate replay has passed into the records as 'Quixall's match', for the young forward, along with his wing partner Alan Finney, produced a memorable performance—just when the Owls needed it. Although Shaw gave Wednesday an early lead, they let the advantage slip and were 2–1 down early in the second half. However, in the last twenty minutes Quixall and Finney turned on the style and after they had set up an equaliser for Shaw further goals from Sewell and Woodhead sealed a dramatic victory.

It was again late goals from Sewell and Woodhead that saw Wednesday through at the first attempt when Everton went to Hillsborough in the fifth round; but two games were required to dispose of Bolton in the quarter-final, and when the Owls triumphed 2–0 in the Burnden Park replay, it was Gannon rather than Quixall who took the man-of-the-match award.

Wednesday reserved their most disappointing display of the entire Cup run for the semi-final against Preston at Maine Road, and it was a dash of class from the legendary Tom Finney that set up the goals with which Charlie Wayman and Jimmy Baxter shattered Sheffield dreams of a trip to Wembley. However, a vital key to North End's success was the way the sheer aggression of Willy Forbes and Tommy Docherty subdued Sewell

Wednesday match programme for the Everton FA Cup tie in 1954 when Quixall helped the Owls reach the semi-final.

and Quixall. In the second half Sewell was off the field for ten minutes having treatement and spent the rest of the game a passenger; while somehow Quixall emerged from one Docherty challenge with his shirt ripped.

The season after their run to the semi-final, Wednesday went down again, and, once more, they promptly won the Second Division title and shot back into the top grade. A feature of the 1955–56 promotion run was the way Quixall suddenly emerged as a marksman. His tally of seventeen goals was half a dozen more than he had scored in all the the five previous seasons put together. Moreover, he continued in the same vein in 1956–57 when he notched 22 in the First Division plus two in the FA Cup. That made it 41 in 84 matches compared with 11 in in the previous 132!

Unfortunately, in 1957–58 the Owls were on the slide again in a campaign that they kicked off a week late because of a 'flu epidemic at the club. Wednesday had hoped to mark their 90th anniversary in September 1957 in happier circumstances, but two wins in their first eight matches did not bode well for their prospects. In the season as a whole they were seldom free of injuries, and significantly, only winger Finney was an ever-present, and Quixall, who missed five matches, was one of only two other players to top 30 appearances. Finney, by the way, was to make over 500 appearances and score 90 goals for Wednesday in a career that extended to 1965, and there were few more resilient players.

Goalkeeper was the position that caused the most trouble. Charlie Pllu began 1957–58 as first choice but damaged a finger early in the game at Tottenham in September when first Don Gibson and then Walter Bingley accepted the green jersey as the Owls fell to a 4–2 defeat. Brian Ryalls then had a short run, Pllu returned only to damage an ankle, and McIntosh was given a brief recall. Amateur international Mike Pinner was introduced for five games but conceded 21 goals,

so Ryalls came back. The problem was not solved until just before the transfer deadline when Wednesday paid £10,000 to bring Ron Springett from Queen's Park Rangers. It was often said that if Springett had been signed sooner Wednesday might not have been relegated. The consolation was that they had acquired one of the finest goalkeepers in the game, and he was destined not only to play a major part in the success of the early 1960s, but would become the club's most-capped England player. In fact, he was to hold the Owls' record for caps with 33 until Irishman Nigel Worthington claimed the distinction in the early 1990s.

The match for which the 1957–58 campaign is best remembered was Wednesday's FA Cup fifth-round tie with Manchester United on the evening of 19th February. It was United's first game after the Munich air disaster of thirteen days earlier, which had claimed 23 victims. They had been returning from a European Cup quarter-final game with Red Star in Belgrade when their chartered BEA Elizabethan aircraft had crashed on its third attempt to take off: those who failed to survive included eight of the famous Busby Babes, among them Duncan Edwards, Tommy Taylor and Roger Byrne. Busby himself was still fighting for his life in intensive care in a Munich hospital as a near-60,000 crowd packed Old Trafford to pay homage.

The tragedy had stunned the nation, and the atmosphere in the ground was like nothing ever experienced before at a football match. It was a night super-charged with emotion, the sense of sadness and sympathy quite overwhelming.

A Wednesday team of 1955 which features the famous trio of inside-forwards Froggatt, Quixall and Sewell shortly before record signing Sewell left to join Aston Villa.
Back row: Gibson, Staniforth, McIntosh, O'Donnell, Curtis, T. McAnearney.
Front row: Froggatt, Sewell, Shiner, Quixall, Broadbent.

Wednesday found themselves in the unenviable position of being almost incidental to proceedings. It was unreal, and there was no way there could be any other result but a Manchester victory; it was what not only the crowd but the country at large wanted as a symbol of a United rebirth.

The truth was that, even in normal circumstances, it was a game from which Wednesday could have expected little. They had won only one away game all season, a Cup-tie at Hereford, and 38 goals had been conceded in the last 13 matches. Such was the situation that manager Taylor dropped skipper Don McEvoy (he did not play again) and brought in Peter Swan, a centre-half destined for high honours. The biggest blow was the

enforced absence of Roy Shiner, and defender Peter Johnson was converted into an emergency leader. The captaincy passed to Quixall, which, in the light of later events, was an appointment not without irony. Jimmy Murphy, acting chief in the absence of Busby, was evidently impressed with the Owls' skipper's manner, and this may have made him an early candidate when United discussed men they might look to in the near future.

Poignantly, the match programme left eleven blank spaces for the names of the United team which, when announced, included two survivors of the crash: goalkeeper Harry Gregg and defender Bill Foulkes. Teenager Mark Pearson, a Sheffield lad who would join Wednesday in 1963, and

Shay Brennan, aged 20, were given their senior debuts; while Alex Dawson, 17, and reserves Ian Greaves, Freddie Goodwin, Ron Cope and Colin Webster were also promoted. It summed up the mood of the moment that the Football Association's reaction to the tragedy was to waive the normal Cup rules to permit United to play two new signings, Ernie Taylor and Stan Crowther, who were technically ineligible. Taylor, 32, was hurriedly bought from Blackpool for £8,000; Crowther, who cost £35,000, was a wing-half who had already played for Aston Villa in that season's competition—and he signed for United barely an hour before the kick off!

The tension was almost unbearable, and it got to Wednesday early in the game. On 27 minutes Ryalls conceded a needless corner, then helped Brennan's flag-kick into the net! Brennan made it 2–0 after 70 minutes when Ryalls blocked but did not hold a Pearson shot, and Dawson scored a third five minutes from the end. Wednesday would have many better days at Old Trafford.

The appointment of Harry Catterick prior to the start of the 1958–59 campaign was noted earlier. Here it is relevant to mention that he took up his duties on the first day in September, by which time Wednesday had launched their promotion bid with two wins in their first three games; and within barely two weeks of starting work he had made two of his most important decisions. He appointed a new coach, Tommy Eggleston, and sold Albert Quixall.

Eggleston's arrival provoked little comment. Jack Marshall, the previous trainer-coach, had left to succeed

Catterick as manager at Rochdale, and the new Owls boss chose Eggleston, an astute but friendly North Easterner, to fill the vacancy. He was a former Derby, Leicester and Watford player and had served his coaching apprenticeship at Brentford prior to a spell with Watford. He and Catterick established a formidable partnership and provided a brand of tough discipline and professionalism forming the basis of the success that followed in the next three years.

However, the sale of Quixall was sensational news, though in truth, it was not entirely unexpected. After the Owls had fallen into the Second Division yet again, Quixall felt the situation was unlikely to boost his hopes of further international recognition or improve prospects of collecting major club honours. Moreover, Catterick seemed to consider Quixall something of a luxury, and felt he could afford to let him go—though we shall never know whether there were other influences at work behind the scenes.

Many years later, Quixall insisted he would have been happy to remain at Hillsborough for the rest of his career, though he admitted he never had any regrets about the move. He was the first player whom Matt Busby signed personally after the Munich disaster, and knowledge that the Manchester United manager wanted him was common gossip for weeks before anything developed—Quixall was flattered by this. When it was clear that Catterick was not opposed to the sale, negotiations opened in earnest. Busby initially wanted to pay £35,000, thus equalling the fee the Owls had spent on Sewell, but Taylor refused to budge until the figure had grown to £45,000.

Wednesday were halfway through what proved to be an eleven-match unbeaten run when Quixall made his farewell appearance in his 260th League and Cup game in the Owls' colours against Sunderland at Hillsborough on the evening of 10th September 1958. Everyone knew this was likely to be his last game for the club: that morning the newspapers had revealed Quixall had submitted a formal transfer request—done to safeguard Wednesday from any criticism over the sale. A 33,000 crowd was not disappointed; the departing idol produced a memorable display and scored his 65th Wednesday goal, while Froggatt produced an outstanding performance topped by a hat-trick in a brilliant 6–0 victory.

Quixall's Manchester United debut came ten days later, and he went on to make 183 appearances and score 56 goals. In two of his first three seasons at Old Trafford, he was to finish on the losing side against

Wednesday in FA Cup ties (including a 7–2 triumph for the Owls in February 1961); and Busby's team were defeated by Spurs in a Hillsborough semi-final in 1962. However, in 1963 Quixall emerged with an FA Cup winner's medal. He concluded his career with Oldham and Stockport and later went into the scrap metal business in the Manchester area. He did not return to Sheffield and continued to reside on the other side of the Pennines, but at heart he remained the Meynell Road kid whose favourite team played in blue and white just down the hill from the family home at the Wadsley Bridge end of Parson Cross.

Those who followed Sheffield football in his time at Hillsborough would subscribe to the theory that he was very much a symbol of his era—much as those other blond heroes, Mick Jones, Alan Birchenall and Tony Currie were in later years across the city at Bramall Lane.

Quixall beats the goalkeeper but just misses the target at Tottenham in the 1950s.

Harry Catterick was Wednesday's manager from 1958 to 1961. After leading the Owls to the Second Division title in 1959, he took them to runners-up in the league championship race in 1961 before leaving to return to Everton.

Wednesday: On the Brink under Catterick

THE EARLY 1960s have passed into Hillsborough history as a time when opportunity knocked but the door remained closed. In particular, Harry's Catterick's short spell as Wednesday's manager is remembered as the period when the club stood on the brink of glory only for the promise to prove an illusion.

Catterick remained for only two years after guiding the Owls back from the Second Division in 1959. In their first term after returning to the top grade they climbed to fifth in the table and reached the FA Cup semi-final. Then, in 1960–61, they finished runners-up with a record which, in another season, might have clinched the Championship—but this was the year when a magnificent Tottenham side romped to the first League and Cup double achieved in English football since 1897.

It sums up Wednesday's form in those two seasons that they won 49 and lost only 21 of the 95 League and Cup games played, but sadly, just before they concluded that sequence, Catterick had walked out to rejoin Everton, the club where he had been a player. Having spent so little and achieved so much in Sheffield, Catterick could not resist the greater resources and bigger personal rewards available at Goodison. Catterick, who had rejected other offers, might have gone to Everton anyway, for it was the club that meant the most to him; but he often said he had become frustrated at Wednesday because he lacked the financial clout to push the club that one extra step that might have brought honours. Remarkably, his costliest acquisition was Bobby Craig, the inside-forward signed from Third Lanark in November 1959 for a mere £6,500.

Much was also made of his deteriorating working relationship with Eric Taylor. They were both strong personalities, and Catterick became increasingly resentful of the general manager's influence and authority. Catterick had arrived in Sheffield as a managerial unknown, his spell with Wednesday had considerably enhanced his reputation and fame, and he was no longer ready to play second fiddle to anyone. Moreover, he felt that some people at the club were more interested in developing the ground than the team!

Catterick succeeded largely with the players he had inherited, and it was in his time in charge that Ron Springett, Peter Swan and Tony Kay won international recognition, while John Fantham, Derek Wilkinson and Don Megson also gained representative honours.

Peter Swan

They were, of course, all players signed by Taylor, but there is not much doubt that they profited from Catterick's influence. Kay, the fiery locally-born half-back, made dramatic progress under the new manager. Significantly, Catterick subsequently paid £55,000 (then a British record for a wing-half) to take Kay to Goodison. Megson always credited Catterick with the decision that transformed his career.

Don Megson

Megson joined the Owls in 1952 as an amateur outside-left, and later went through a phase when he played in almost every position in the Central League side. At one stage he looked certain to settle at centre-half, but, after completing his National Service and becoming a full-time professional, Megson was encouraged to have a run at left-back in the reserves. He was quickly promoted to the senior side and went on to make over 440 appearances in the number 3 shirt and, of course, he later emerged as an outstanding captain.

In fact, the introduction of Megson, and the arrival of Craig, in November 1959 coincided with the start of a run in which Wednesday lost only one of 18 League and Cup games, which consolidated their place among the First Division's leading pack and prompted dreams of reaching Wembley for the first time since 1935.

They had their share of fortune on the Cup trail. A Tom McAnearney penalty set them on course for a 2–1 defeat of Middlesbrough in the third round, and after a Craig double had ousted Jimmy Hagan's Peterborough at the next stage, Wednesday profited from another spot-kick to seal a narrow fifth-round triumph at Manchester United. Many years later, Megson admitted that, at Old Trafford, the referee failed to notice an Albert Quixall shot that had beaten Springett and gone across the line before Swan cleared it; and the clearance led to Fantham bursting forward only to be brought down by Maurice Setters for the decisive penalty.

The manner in which Wednesday beat Sheffield United in the quarter-final at Bramall Lane served only to strengthen the feeling in the Owls' camp that their name was already on the Cup. This was a tie that attracted a 59,692 crowd (over 3,000 were seated on a temporary stand erected on the cricket side) and receipts of £8,530. How the Blades failed to win was one of the mysteries of the season. Ron Springett often recalled that it was one of those days when everything United threw at him stuck in his hands. Megson commented: 'We were only in the game for about fifteen minutes in the first half, but in that time Derek Wilkinson scored twice. United dominated most of the game, but our goal had a charmed life and they just couldn't score!'

Sadly, Wednesday's luck evaporated when they faced Blackburn in the semi-final at Maine Road. Irishman Derek Dougan put Rovers ahead after only eleven minutes, and the Owls knew it wasn't going to be their day when Alan Finney had an effort disallowed because Wilkinson was offside. Dougan notched a second on 71 minutes, and though Fantham pulled one back soon afterwards it proved only a consolation goal. Of the team that played in the semi-final, only three men survived to figure in the side that beat Blackburn on the way to Wembley six years later: Springett, Megson and Fantham. However, two others destined to be in the 1966 Cup final team had a few outings in that 1959–60 season: Gerry Young and Johnny Quinn. Young, in fact, had made his debut in early 1957, and this dependable Geordie was to tot up over 340 appearances. Quinn, a product of St Helen's, had made his bow in late 1959. They had in common a capacity to play in a variety of roles. Young played in attack before becoming a notable defensive wing-half; and Quinn began as an inside-forward but graduated into an outstanding utility man who ought to have enjoyed more than 195 outings in his nine years at Hillsborough.

John Fantham

Wednesday's second term back in the First Division was truly memorable as they attained their highest placing since winning the title in 1930. The previous year Burnley had won the Championship with 55 points, but this time round the Owls' haul of 58 was eight fewer than Spurs collected. The top of the table at the end of the season read:

Ron Springett

	P	W	D	L	F	A	Pts
1. Tottenham	42	31	4	7	115	55	66
2. Wednesday	42	23	12	7	78	47	58
3. Wolves	42	25	7	10	103	75	57

The only blight on the season was an accident that occurred when the team's coach crashed on the Great North Road at Alconbury Weston, near Huntingdon, on the way back from the 1–1 draw at Arsenal on Boxing Day. Duggie McMillan, who had travelled to Highbury as reserve, was trapped in the wreckage and had to have his right leg amputated before he could be freed. Peter Swan suffered a fractured shoulder and Tony Kay was taken to hospital with concussion.

Wednesday, whose strength was more in defence than attack, began the campaign with a twelve-match unbeaten run and then, between early December and April, enjoyed another sequence of nineteen games without defeat. The Owls actually had a better home record than Spurs, in that they lost one less game and conceded eleven fewer goals; but the North London side's sixteen away victories put them in a class of their own. However, they got nothing at Hillsborough on 12th November, when a 56,363 crowd witnessed a memorable match and a famous Owls' triumph. Wednesday went into this eagerly-awaited clash boasting 24 points (ten wins, four draws) from their fifteen games, while unbeaten Spurs had dropped just one point in sixteen matches—and scored 53 goals! The teams lined up as follows:

Wednesday: McLaren; Johnson, Megson; T. McAnearney, Swan, Kay; Griffin, Craig, Ellis, Fantham, Finney

Spurs: Brown; Baker, Henry; Blanchflower, Norman, Mackay; Jones, White, Smith, Allen, Dyson

Roy McLaren and Billy Griffin, neither of whom were regulars, emerged as two of the leading heroes in a splendid team performance which brought a 2–1 victory. Goalkeeper McLaren, signed from Bury in 1958 and limited to 29 League games in his time at Hillsborough, produced an outstanding display. One of three brilliant saves he made in the first half inspired the move which led to Wednesday's first goal, crashed home by Griffin after 40 minutes. Griffin had the distinction of scoring 20 goals in only 35 senior outings between 1958 and 1962, but none was more satisfying than this one. Unfortunately, within two minutes Maurice Norman had headed Spurs level. But Wednesday went back in front to stay after 68 minutes, when Fantham pounced on a rebound and shot past Brown.

Ironically, Wednesday's form took a sudden dip immediately after this triumph. They lost three games on the trot and won only one in seven—the solitary victory in this sequence being an unforgettable duel with

Blackburn in which the Owls scrambled to a 5–4 victory after leading 5–1 at half-time. Yet that success launched them on a nineteen-match unbeaten run in the League which was ended when they played the return with Spurs at White Hart Lane in April.

In the meantime, they enjoyed another notable Cup run, reaching the quarter-final before falling in a replay at Burnley. Wednesday's victims included Leeds and Leyton, but it was a famous 7–2 triumph at Manchester United that provided the highlight of the abortive trip along the road to Wembley. When the Owls only managed a 1–1 draw in their home fourth-round clash with Busby's side, few gave them much hope of success at Old Trafford. Big centre-forward Keith Ellis claimed a hat-trick and Fantham and Finney each emerged with doubles.

With the fifth round seeing Wednesday winning 2–0 at Leyton, and the Blades beating Blackburn 2–1 at Bramall Lane, Sheffield football supporters were grateful when the quarter-final draw kept the local clubs apart. However, while United enjoyed a famous triumph at Newcastle, Wednesday had to settle for a home draw with Burnley—and they lost in the replay at Turf Moor. It was to be another thirty years before Sheffield could savour a Wednesday–United semi-final!

Three weeks later, Wednesday returned to Manchester United and registered a 5–1 victory in which Gerry Young, turned into an emergency centre-forward, grabbed a hat-trick; and this success left the Owls only three points behind Spurs in the table. Sadly, they failed to stay in such close touch with the leaders, and by the time the clubs met in April the gap was six points. Spurs beat Wednesday 2–1, coming from behind after Megson had notched his first senior goal, and the Championship was bound for White Hart Lane.

Unfortunately, Wednesday had gone into the game without a manager. Catterick had resigned and gone to Everton. By coincidence, his first match in charge of the Merseysiders was at Hillsborough. Sitting in the directors' box, he was roundly booed, but many of those who were pained by his departure accepted that he couldn't be blamed for going where he would have a better chance of achieving long-term success . . . and there was to be irony in the way Everton won the FA Cup in 1966 by beating Wednesday in the final, and, when they had just clinched the League title in 1970, their first trip just happened to be to Hillsborough—and at the very moment when the Owls were fighting a losing battle to stay in the top grade! Perhaps it was no wonder that (and all the more so with hindsight) most Wednesdayites regretted Catterick's departure. Those were the days when big changes were coming in the game, with the removal of the maximum wage, but Wednesday were still of the school that believed success in top-class football went in cycles and was not related to the authority accorded a team-manager.

For the record, Wednesday's League appearances and scorers in this memorable season were:

Appearances: *Craig 37, Ellis 31, Fantham 39, Finney 42, Griffin 12, Hill 4, Johnson 42, Kay 42, Lodge 3, Tom McAnearney 39, McLaren 4, Martin 2, Megson 38, Meredith 1, O'Donnell 6, Quinn 13, Ron Springett 38, Swan 36, Derek Wilkinson 26, Young 7*

Goals: *Fantham 20, Ellis 14, Craig 12, Griffin 8, Finney 5, Young 4, Wilkinson 3, Quinn 3, T . McAnearney 3, Lodge 2, Megson 1   Own-goals 3*

(Blades' records for their 1960–61 promotion campaign are shown in the notes at the end of this book.)

The 1960–61 campaign had been one of the most intriguing in Sheffield football history, and there seemed to be every reason to look forward with optimism. United were back to the top grade and Wednesday had worn the look of title candidates for the first time in thirty years; moreover there was a hint that, at last, the top honours were within reach. Glory, surely, was only a corner-kick away!

Much, of course, would depend upon how the Sheffield clubs responded to the challenges waiting just round the corner. Yet, whatever, there was nothing more certain than that the remaining years of the 1960s would be eventful and exciting . . . and decisions taken in those years in response to some traumatic moments, would influence the course of Sheffield football history through-out the rest of the twentieth century!

A pre-1914 Sheffield and Hallamshire team which played Glasgow in an inter-city match.
Back row: Fox (secretary), Lloyd (reserve), Brittleton, Benson, Lievesley, Holbeim, Boyle, Sturgess, Proctor (linesman),
Parramore (trainer).
Fornt row: Walton, Chapman, Kitchen, Hardinge, Foxall.

Appendix and Notes

Sheffield FC's First Playing Rules 1857

1. The kick off from the middle must be a place kick.
2. Kick out must not be from more than 25 yards out of goal.
3. Fair catch is a catch from any player provided the ball has not touched the ground or has not been thrown from touch and is entitled to a free kick.
4. Charging is fair in case of a place kick (with the exception of a kick off as soon as the player offers to kick) but he may always draw back unless he has actually touched the ball with his foot.
5. Pushing with the hands is allowed but no hacking or tripping up is fair under any circumstances whatever.
6. No player may be held or pulled over.
7. It is not lawful to take the ball off the ground (except in touch) for any purpose whatever.
8. The ball may be pushed on or hit with the hand, but holding the ball except in the case of a fair kick is altogether disallowed.
9. A goal must be kicked but not from touch nor by a free kick from a catch.
10. A ball in touch is dead, consequently the side that touches it down must bring it to the edge of the touch and throw it straight out at least six yards from touch.
11. Each player must provide himself with a red and dark blue flannel cap, one colour to be worn by each side.

A Sheffield FC team of the early 1950s, almost 100 years after the clubs formation.

Sheffield v. London Matches

Sheffield FC team versus London, Battersea Park, 3rd March 1866

W. Chesterman (capt.), H.W. Chambers, F. Knowles, J. Knowles, J.K. Swift, J. Denton, A.A. Dixon, W. Baker, J.C. Shaw, J.D. Webster, A. Wightman

Sheffield v London, played at Bramall Lane, 4th December 1871. First inter-association match. Sheffield won 3–1.

Sheffield: J. Marsh (capt.), J.C. Clegg, W.E. Clegg, W. Lockwood Jnr, T.C. Willey, G.H. Sampson, A. Wood, W.H. Carr, C. Mills, J. Hollingworth, H. Ash London: C.W. Alcock (capt.), C.J. Chenery, P. Currey, P.B. Soden, P. Revitt-Carnae, R.C. Welch, C. Warner, C.W. Stevenson, P. Weston, E. Weston, J.C. Shaw

Note: J.C. Shaw of Sheffield played for London after the visitors arrived a man short. C.W. Alcock, who produced the London team, agreed to play the game under Sheffield rules, on the understanding that, when Sheffield went south, they would play under London rules. There was no referee in this game, just two umpires. Normal arrangement at this time was for both teams to supply an umpire and each umpire controlled one half of the field; though in fact, it was only a few months after this game, possibly due to the creation of the FA Cup, that the FA decided to introduce a referee to work with the umpires, and each umpire had to appeal to the referee on behalf of his own team. In 1891 umpires became linesmen and the referee was given charge.

Wharncliffe Charity Cup

The first final, in 1879, saw Wednesday defeat Heeley 3–1 at Bramall Lane. The teams were:

Wednesday: *F. Stacey, E. Buttery, W.H. Stacey, T. Buttery, C.L. Statford, A. Woodcock, G. Anthony, T. Bishop, J. Bingley, W.E. Clegg, J.C. Clegg*

Heeley: *H.N. Moss, J. Hunter, T.A. Tomlinson, H. Barber, R. Barrington, S. Scaife, T.A. Sorby, J. Wild, P. Andrews, J. Tomlinson, W. Moss*

Note: When Wednesday won the first Sheffield Challenge Cup final in 1877 their team included three pairs of brothers— the Staceys, Butlers and Cleggs; while in the above 1879 final there were also three pairs of brothers in their side—the Staceys and Cleggs again, plus the Butterys. The Heeley team in both games included the Tomlinson brothers, Joe and Tom. Joe Tomlinson was to emerge a key figure in Sheffield United's early history.

Sheffield Zulus, 1879–1882
(see 'The Early Professionals').
The first novelty match featuring these players was at Scarborough in August 1879, and in the following November they played a Sheffield XI at Bramall Lane, using the names of Zulu warriors and lining up as follows:

Ulmathoosi (H. Hinchcliffe), Vetewayo (Tom Buttery, capt.), Dabulamanzi (Jack Hunter), Sirayo (G. Herring), Methlagazulu (Arthur Malpass), Umcilyn (A. Ramsden), Ngobamabrosi (G. Butcher), Magnenda (S. Earnshaw), Jiggleumbeno (Tom Cawley), Muyamani (G. Ainley), Amatongoa (S. Lucas).

The Sheffield team was: *W. Turner, A. Woodcock, J. Slack, G. Harris, E. Lawton, G. Anthony, W. Mosforth, C. Elliott, W. Orton, J. Whittam, W. Lax. Referee: W. Littlehales. Umpires: G. Cropper, E. Bowling.*

Football Alliance v Football League
A unique representative match was staged at Olive Grove on Monday 20th April 1891 when the Football Alliance and the Football League met for the only time. A crowd of 5,000 saw the teams share a 1–1 draw, with Harry Davis (then of Birmingham St George's but later to join Wednesday) scoring for the Alliance, and Everton's Edgar Chadwick equalising. The only Wednesday man on duty in the

Alliance side was Harry Brandon, while Joe Tomlinson, a prominent figure in Sheffield United's early history, was the referee.

Football Alliance

Formed in 1889, when Sheffield Wednesday helped persuade other clubs refused admission to the Football League to get together to create a rival league competition. John Holmes, of the Wednesday club, was elected president, and the new organisation's founding members were: Wednesday, Nottingham Forest, Crewe, Walsall Town Swifts, Grimsby Town, Sunderland Albion, Newton Heath, Bootle, Darwen, Birmingham St George's, Small Heath and Long Eaton Rangers.

Floodlit Football

Teams in unique match staged at Bramall Lane on Monday 14th October 1878:

Reds: *F. Stacey, J. Housley, J. Hunter, E. Buttery, F. Hinde, J.C. Clegg, W. Mosforth, A. Woodcock, C. Stratford, H. Barber, G. Anthony*

Blues: *T. Lawson, W.E. Clegg, R. Gregory, T. Buttery, W.H. Stacey, G.B. Marples, A. Malpass, J. Tomlinson, E. Barber, T. Bishop, P. Paterson*
Referee: *W. Pierce-Dix*

Sheffield's first FA Cup semi final was staged at Bramall Lane on 16th March 1889. Preston beat West Brom 1–0. Teams:

Preston North End: *Mills-Roberts; R. Howarth, Holmes; Drummond, Russell, Graham; Gordon, Ross, Goodall, Dewhurst, Thomson*

West Brom: *Roberts; Green, Robinson; Timmins, C. Perry, Horton; Pearson, Wilson, Bayliss, W. Perry, Bassett*

Referee: *J.C. Clegg (Sheffield)*
Attendance: *22,688 (Rec. £700)*

Sheffield FC and Hallam

The first matches between Sheffield FC and Hallam were staged in December 1860 (when Hallam had the help of some Stumperlowe players) at Sandygate (Sheffield won 2–0), and in December 1861 at Hyde Park, as noted in Chapter Four.

When Hallam won their first trophy, the Youdan Cup, on 5th March 1867, they beat Norfolk in the final by two rouges after dismissing Heeley, Norton Oaks and Mackenzie in earlier rounds. The next trophy that Hallam won was the Hatchard Cup in 1903, when they beat Thorpe Hesley in the final.

The Sheffield FC team that won the FA Amateur Cup in 1904 (they beat Ealing 3–1 in the final at Bradford) was:

Bolsover, E. Chambers, F.H. Milnes, A. Frost, P. Green, Harry Potts (capt.), 'Tim' Forsdike, G. Hoyland, H. Bedford, E. Hoyland, W. Sylvester.

Hallam reached the last eight of the FA Amateur Cup in 1924–25, when they beat Sheffield FC, Rotherham Amateurs, Youlgreave, Whitehall (Leeds) and Attercliffe, but then, after defeating Bishop Auckland 2–1 at Sandygate, they lost in the fourth round proper at Forest Hills where Clapton won 1–0 with a penalty. In 1952–53, when they were elected to the Yorkshire League, Hallam reached the third round of the Amateur Cup before falling to Leytonstone; and in the previous round they had, thanks to a goal from Ernest Ward, defeated Dulwich Hamlet 1–0 at Hillsborough (Att: 13,855). They also reached the third round in 1953–54, 1958–59 and 1960–61. In 1953–55 they beat Corinthian Casuals before being knocked out by Bishop Auckland.

Sheffield FC's first match at Abbeydale Park was in the preliminary round of the FA Cup v Grassmoor Ivanhoe in September 1921.

Sheffield Clubs in the Football League

1892–93
First League matches: 3rd September 1892
Sheffield United 4 (Hammond 3, Wallace), Lincoln City 2
Team: J.W.Lilley; Whitham, Cain; Howell, Hendry, Needham; Wallace, Dobson, Hammond, Davies, Drummond

Notts County 0 Sheffield Wednesday 1 (T. Brandon*)
Team: Allan; T. Brandon, Mumford; H. Brandon, Betts, Hall; Dunlop, R.N. Brown, Davis, Brady, Spiksley
* Some records give Harry Davis as the scorer.

Test match: 22nd April 1893 at Nottingham
Sheffield United 1 (Drummond), Accrington FC 0
Team: Howlett; Whitham, Cain; Howell, Hendry, Needham; Hill, Gallacher, Hammond, Watson, Drummond

Sheffield United, League Champions 1897–98
Appearances: Almond 20, Bennett 26, Blair 1, Bradshaw 1, Cain 30, Cunningham 24, Foulke 29, French 1, Gaudie 6, Hedley 2, Howard 3, Howell 24, Jenkinson 2, Johnson 10, McKay 25, Logan 5, Morran 26, Morton 2, Needham 29, Priest 28, Thickett 29, White 6, Whitham 1
Goals: Bennett 12, Almond 9, Needham 8, Cunningham 7, McKay 6, Priest 4, Logan 4, Gaudie 2, Johnson 2, Cain 1, Morren 1

Sheffield Wednesday, League Champions 1902–1903
Appearances: Barron 1, Beech 3, H. Chapman 32, P. Crawshaw 1, Tom Crawshaw 33, H. Davis 26, Ferrier 33, Hounsfield 2, Langley 34, Layton 29, Lyall 33; Malloch 33, Marrison 1, Moralee 1, Ruddlesdin 34, Ryalls 1, G. Simpson 1, V.S. Simpson 3, Spiksley 32, Stewart 1,
Stubbs 1, Thackeray 5, Wilson 34
Goals: Davis 13, Chapman 12, Wilson 12, Spiksley 8, Langley 5, Ruddlesdin 2, Malloch 1, Marrison 1

Sheffield Wednesday, League Champions 1903–1904
Appearances: Bartlett 4, Beech 4, Burton 26, Chapman 34, Crawshaw 32, Davis 32, Eyre 1, Ferrier 31, Hemmingfield 6, Hoyland 1, Jarvis 1, Langley 8, Layton 34, Lyall 33, Malloch 25, Moralee 1, Ruddlesdin 30, Ryalls 1, G. Simpson 24, V.S. Simpson 7, Stewart 10, Wilson 29
Goals: Chapman 16, Wilson 10, G. Simpson 7, Davis 5, V.S. Simpson 2, Malloch 2, Hemmingfield 1, Langley 1, Stewart 1

Sheffield United 1923–28
In this period United reached the semi-final twice and the final once, and it will be of interest to compare their line-ups in these games.

Semi-final 1923 v Bolton	Final 1925 v Cardiff	Semi-final(3 games) 1928 v Huddersfield
Blackwell	Sutcliffe	Alderson
Cook	Cook	Chandler*
Milton	Milton	Birks
Pantling	Pantling	Sampy
Waugh	King	Matthews
Plant	Green	Green
Mercer	Mercer	Partridge
Sampy	Boyle	Blair
Johnson	Johnson	Johnson
Gillespie	Gillespie	Gillespie
Tunstall	Tunstall	Tunstall

* King replaced Chandler in second replay

Sheffield Derbies

Note that in 1925 and 1928 (See Chapter 27) United and Wednesday met in the FA Cup for the first time since the epic duels of 1900. The teams on these occasions were:

1925 (Round 2) United 3 Wednesday 2
Att: 40,266
United: *Sutcliffe; Cook, Birks; Pantling, King, Green; Mercer, Sampy, Johnson, Gillespie, Tunstall*

Wednesday: *Brown; Inglis, Felton; Toone, Wilson, Powell; Lowdell, Hill, Trotter, Taylor, Richardson*

1928 (Round 5) Wednesday 1 United 1
Att: 57,076
United 4 Wednesday 1 Att: 59,447
United: *Alderson; Chandler, Birks; Sampy, Matthews, Green; Partridge, Blair, Johnson, Gillespie, Tunstall*

Wednesday: *Brown; Walker, Blenkinsop; N. Smith, Kean, Marsden; Hooper, Strange, Harper, Seed, Rimmer*

Shefield Wednesday, League Champions 1928–29

Appearances: Allen 35, Blenkinsop 39, Brown 42, Burridge 2, Felton 3, Gregg 30, Hargreaves 2, Harper 6, Hatfield 1, Hill 1, Hooper 42, Kean 4, Leach 36, Marsden 42, Rimmer 34, Seed 39, Strange 42, Trotter 6, Walker 41, Whitehouse 6, Wilkinson 6, C. Wilson 3
Goals: Allen 33, Hooper 15, Seed 8, Rimmer 7, Gregg 7, Harper 5, Strange 5, Blenkinsop 1, Hargreaves 1, Marsden 1, Trotter 1, Whitehouse 1, C. Wilson 1

Sheffield Wednesday, League Champions 1929–30

Appearances: Allen 41, Beeson 2, Blenkinsop 39, Brown 41, Burgess 39, Burridge 2, Gregg 5, Hooper 42, Jones 1, Mackey 1, Marsden 37, Mellors 1, Millership 6, Rimmer 40, Seed 32, Smith 4, Strange 41, Walker 34, Whitehouse 4, Wilkinson 1, Wilson 9, Leach 40
Goals: Allen 33, Burgess 19, Hooper 18, Rimmer 15, Seed 9, Marsden 3, Strange 3, Leach 2, Millership 1

Sheffield United, Division Two Runners-up 1938–39

Appearances: Smith 42, Hooper 22, Cox 27, Carr 24, Jackson 23, Jessop 11, Johnson 30, Settle 42, Young 11, Eggleston 11, Barton 28, Hagan 28, Dodds 29, Hampson 40, Henson 10, Joyner 2, Leyfield 4, Pickering 23, Reid 13, Richardson 2, Sandford 5, Robinson 2, Toothill 12, Jones 21
Goals: Dodds 17, Hampson 13, Hagan 10, Barton 6, Henson 5, Jones 4, Reid 4, Pickering 4, Settle 2, Sandford 1, Jessop 1, Hooper 1

Sheffield Wednesday, Division Two Runners-up 1949–50

Appearances: Bannister 8, Dooley 1, Fletcher 1, Fox 9, Froggatt 30, Gannon 40, Henry 14, Jackson 1, Jordan 26, Kenny 40, Locherty 1, McIntosh 39, McJarrow 12, Marriott 30, Morton 3, Packard 42, Quigley 10, Rickett 30, Rogers 18, Swift 35, Tomlinson 22, Westlake 1, Witcomb 41, Woodhead 8
Goals: Froggatt 14, Jordan 12, Quigley 10, Rickett 5, McJarrow 5, Henry 4, Rogers 4, Fox 2, Tomlinson 2, Witcomb 2, Woodhead 2, Gannon 1, Packard 1

Sheffield Wednesday, Second Division Champions 1951–52

Appearances: Bannister 31, Curtis 21, Davies 19, Dooley 30, Edwards 2, Finney 26, Froggatt 23, Gannon 40, Henry 4, Jackson 10, Jordan 1, Kenny 22, McIntosh 42, McJarrow 3, Marriott 8, O'Donnell 13, Packard 4, Quixall 26, Rickett 30, Sewell 35, Thomas 9, Turton 25, Whitaker 1, Witcomb 21, Woodhead 16
Goals: Dooley 46, Sewell 23, Woodhead 9, Froggatt 7, Finney 4, Quixall 3, Rickett 3, McJarrow 2, Witcomb 2

**Sheffield United,
Second Division Champions 1952–53**

Appearances: Burgin 42, Furniss 42, Wood 5, G.Shaw 37, Hitchen 16, Brook 36, Toner 15, Latham 25, J. Shaw 42, Ringstead 42, F.A. Smith 3, Browning 39, Hagan 37, Bottom 6, McNab 5, Hawksworth 42, Denial 9, Johnson 15, Hutchinson 3, Wragg 1
Goals: Ringstead 22, Brook 17, Browning 17, Hagan 16, Hawksworth 10, Furniss 4, Bottom 3, G. Shaw 2, McNab 1

**Sheffield Wednesday,
Second Division Champions 1955–56**

Appearances: Bingley 21, Broadbent 41, Curtis 23, Finney 25, Froggatt 41, Gibson 27, Howells 2, Kay 8, Martin 2, Jim McAnearney 1, T. McAnearney 27, McEvoy 24, McIntosh 33, O'Donnell 32, Quixall 39, Sewell 16, Shiner 42, Staniforth 37, Swan 4, D. Wilkinson 3, Williams 9
Goals: Shiner 33, Quixall 17, Froggatt 14, Sewell 13, Broadbent 12, Finney 6, Staniforth 2, Gibson 1, Howells 1, O'Donnell 1, Wilkinson 1

**Sheffield Wedneday,
Second Division Champions 1958–59**

Appearances: Ballinger 3, Curtis 42, K. Ellis 3, Fantham 33, Finney 37, Froggatt 37, Gibson 23, Griffin 1, Johnson 7, Kay 27, Jim McAnearney 11, T, McAnearney 33, Mclaren 8, Martin 14, O'Donnell 3, Pinner 2, Quixall 4, Shiner 38, Springett 32, Staniforth 20, Swan 39, D. Wilkinson 39, E. Wilkinson 1, Whitham 2, Young 3
Goals: Shiner 28, Froggatt 26, Fantham 12, Wilkinson 12, Finney 11, Curtis 5, Kay 3, J. McAnearney 3, Quixall 2, Ellis 1, T. McAnearney 1, Young 1

**Sheffield United,
Second Division Runners-up, 1960–61**

Appearances: J. Shaw 42, Summers 42, Pace 42, Hodgkinson 41, Coldwell 41, Richardson 41, Russell 41, G. Shaw 31, Hodgson 23, Mason 18, Nibloe 16, Hamilton 14, Simpson 11, Kettleborough 9, Allchurch 8, Shiels 3, Hartle 3, Wilson 3, Thompson 1, Ridge 1, Hoyland 1, Docherty 1, T. Wagstaff 1
Goals: Pace 26, Russell 18, Simpson 11, Allchurch 6, Hodgson 5, Nibloe 4, Kettleborough 2, G. Shaw 2, Mason 2, Hamilton 1, Summers 1, Shiels 1, Coldwell 1, Own-goal 1

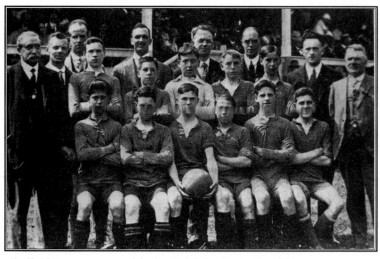

Sheffield Boys, winners of the English Schools Trophy 1925.

Wartime Representative Games in Sheffield

The following games, staged mainly for the purpose of fund-raising during the Second World War, are often forgotten when big matches in the city are discussed, yet they often prompt debate and queries from football fans, and, as they have not been placed on record since 1946, it seems appropriate to do so again now.

March 25th 1940 at Bramall Lane

Yorkshire XI 4 (Cochrane 2, Pickering, Stabb), FA XI 1 (Barton). Att: 14,814

Yorkshire: *Smith (Sheff. U.); Cox (Sheff. U.), Catlin (Sheff. W.); Stabb (Bradford), Harper (Barnsley), Buck (Leeds); Cochrane (Leeds), Barclay (Huddersfield), Bastow (Rotherham), Pickering (Sheff U.), Burbanks (Doncaster)*

FA XI: *Swinden (Arsenal); Cook (Everton), Hodgson (Grimsby); Mills (Rotherham), and Busby (Liverpool), Charlesworth (Grimsby), Graham (Nottm F.); Matthews (Stoke), Fagan (Liverpool), Dodds (Blackpool), Barton (Sheff. U.), H. O'Donnell (Preston).*

Note that Mills and Busby filled the right-half position in the FA side at different stages in the game. Eddie Burbanks was best known as a Sunderland winger who played in the 1937 FA Cup final.

January 18th 1941 at Hillsborough

Football League XI 5 (Worrall, Hanson, Stephenson, Butt 2), All-British XI 3 (Mutch, Doherty, Nieuwenhuys). Att: 4,409.

Football League: *Middleston (Chesterfield); Sproston (Man. City), Crook (Blackburn); Willingham (Huddersfield), Harper (Barnsley), Mercer (Everton); Worrall (Portsmouth), Butt (Blackburn), Westcott (Wolves), E. Stephenson (Leeds), Hanson (Chelsea)*

All-British XI: *Breedon (Man. U.); Cook (Everton), Hayes (Huddersfield); Russell (Sheff. W.), Millership (Sheff. W.), Livingstone (Bury); Nieuwenhuys (Liverpool), Mutch (Preston), Dougal (Preston), Doherty (Man. City), H. O'Donnell (Preston)*

Note that Ken Willingham was a well-known former Sheffield schoolboy star, while Breedon was a former Wednesday player.

May 10th 1941 at Hillsborough

Army XI 2 (Hunt, Regan), RAF XI 5 (Hullett 3, Doherty 2). Att: 4,836

Army XI: *Rutherford (Aston Villa); Shufflebottom (Ipswich), Gadsby (Leeds); Miller (Northampton), Glover (Barnsley), Connor (Sunderland); Hunt (West Brom), Regan (Dundee), Bramham (Rotherham), Padgett (Leicester), Gray (—)*

RAF XI: *Smith (Sheff. U.); Turner (Middlesbro'), Butler (Blackpool); Marsh (Bolton), Brown (Huddersfield), Moore (Stoke); Murphy (Man City), Dickie (Blackburn), Hullett (Man. U.), Doherty (Man. City), Meek (Spurs)*

April 4th 1942 at Hillsborough

England 4 (Lawton 3, Edelston), Scotland 1 (McKennan). Att: 28,567.

England: *Swift (Man. City); Bacuzzi (Fulham), Taylor (Wolves); Britton (Everton), Welsh (Charlton), Mercer (Everton); Birkett (Newcastle), Edelston (Reading), Lawton (Everton), Hagan (Sheff. U.), D. Compton (Arsenal)*

Scotland: *Lynch (Dundee); Carabine (Third Lanark), Beattie (Preston); Kirton (Stoke), Busby (Liverpool), Collier (Third Lanark); Thornton (Rangers), McKennan (Partick), Black (Portsmouth), Bremner (Arsenal), Strauss (Aberdeen).*

November 25th 1944 at Hillsborough

Scotland 7 (Liddell 2, Black 2, Fagan, Busby, Dodds), RAF 1 (Mortensen). Att: 40,172.

Scotland: *Brown (Queen's Park); Harley (Liverpool), Stephen (Bradford); Busby (Liverpool), Thyne (Darlington), Macaulay (West Ham); Delaney (Celtic), Fagan (Liverpool), Dodds (Blackpool), Black (Hearts), Liddell (Liverpool)*

RAF XI: *Williams (Walsall); Scott (Arsenal), Hughes (Birmingham); Soo (Stoke), Joy (Arsenal), Burgess (Spurs); Matthews (Stoke), Carter (Sunderland), Drake (Arsenal), Mortensen (Blackpool), Smith (Brentford)*

Sheffield United
League matches with Wednesday 1893–1959

1.	16.10.1893	(h)	1–1	Hill	Div. I
2.	13.11.1893	(a)	2–1	Drummond, Hammond	Div. I
3.	27.10.1894	(a)	3–2	Hill, Hammond, Howell	Div. I
4.	12.1.1895	(h)	1–0	Watson	Div. I
5.	7.9.1895	(a)	0–1		Div. I
6.	26.12.1895	(h)	1–1	Watson	Div. I
7.	26.12.1896	(h)	2–0	Priest, Howell	Div. I
8.	2.3.1897	(a)	1–1	Needham	Div. I
9.	16.10.1897	(a)	1–0	Bennett	Div. I
10.	27.12.1897	(h)	1–1	Earp (o.g.)	Div. I
11.	3.10.1898	(a)	1–1	Priest	Div. I
12.	26.12.1898	(h)	2–1	Beer, Morren	Div. I
13.	15.12.1900	(h)	1–0	Field	Div. I
14.	29.4.1901	(a)	0–1		Div. I
15.	2.11.1901	(a)	0–1		Div. I
16.	1.3.1902	(h)	3–0	Bennett (2), Priest (pen.)	Div. I
17.	1.9.1902	(h)	2–3	Priest, Lipsham	Div. I
18.	11.10.1902	(a)	1–0	Priest	Div. I
19.	12.12.1903	(h)	1–1	Lipsham	Div. I
20.	9.4.1904	(a)	0–3		Div. I
21.	10.12.1904	(a)	3–1	Brown (2), Donnelly	Div. I
22.	8.4.1905	(h)	4–2	Brown, Donnelly, Priest, Drake	Div. I
23.	21.10.1905	(h)	0–2		Div. I
24.	18.4.1906	(a)	0–1		Div. I
25.	3.11.1906	(a)	2–2	Brown, Needham	Div. I
26.	4.4.1907	(h)	2–1	Drake, Lipsham	Div. I
27.	9.11.1907	(h)	1–3	Levick	Div. I
28.	7.3.1908	(a)	0–2		Div. I
29.	25.12.1908	(a)	0–1		Div. I
30.	26.12.1908	(h)	2–1	Hardinge (pen.), Peart	Div. I
31.	6.11.1909	(h)	3–3	Brelsford, Simmons (2)	Div. I
32.	19.3.1910	(a)	3–1	Hardinge (2), Evans	Div. I
33.	22.10.1910	(a)	0–2		Div. I
34.	25.2.1911	(h)	0–1		Div. I
35.	4.11.1911	(h)	1–1	Kitchen	Div. I
36.	9. 3.1912	(a)	1–1	Wilkinson	Div. I
37.	10.10.1912	(a)	0–1		Div. I
38.	1.3.1913	(h)	0–2		Div. I
39.	25.10.1913	(h)	0–1		Div. I
40.	28. 2.1914	(a)	1–2	Kitchen	Div. I
41.	5.9.1914	(h)	0–1		Div. I
42.	2.1.1915	(a)	1–1	Davies	Div. I
43.	27.9.1919	(a)	1–2	Tummon	Div. I
44.	4.10.1919	(h)	3–0	Kitchen, Masterman, Tummon	Div. I
45.	28.8.1926	(a)	3–2	Johnson (2), Hoyland	Div. I
46.	15.1.1927	(h)	2–0	Tunstall, A. Mercer	Div. I
47.	24. 9.1927	(h)	1–1	Tunstall	Div. I

48.	4.2.1928	(a)	3–3	Blair (2), Partridge	Div. 1
49.	22.9.1928	(a)	2–5	Gibson, Tunstall	Div. 1
50.	2.2.1929	(h)	1–1	Phillipson	Div. 1
51.	28.9.1929	(h)	2–2	Tunstall (2)	Div. 1
52.	1.2.1930	(a)	1–1	Dunne	Div. 1
53.	6.9.1930	(h)	1–1	S. Gibson	Div. 1
54.	3.1.1931	(a)	3–1	Dunne, Oxley, Tunstall	Div. 1
55.	21.11.1931	(a)	1–2	Dunne	Div. 1
56.	2.4.1932	(h)	1–1	Barclay	Div. 1
57.	24.9.1932	(a)	3–3	Oswald, Barclay, Dunne	Div. 1
58.	4. 2.1933	(h)	2–3	Dunne (2)	Div. 1
59.	21.10.1933	(a)	1–0	Williams	Div. 1
60.	3.3.1934	(h)	5–1	Boyd (3), Pickering, Stacey	Div. 1
61.	16.10.1937	(a)	1–0	Eggleston	Div. 2
62.	26. 2.1938	(h)	2–1	Barton, Dodds	Div. 2
63.	29.10.1938	(h)	0–0		Div. 2
64.	4.3.1939	(a)	0–1		Div. 2
65.	17.9.1949	(a)	1–2	Hutchinson	Div. 2
66.	21.1.1950	(h)	2–0	Brook, Warhurst	Div. 2
67.	8.9.1951	(h)	7–3	Hawksworth (2), Brook (2), Ringstead (2), F.Smith	Div. 2
68.	5.1.1952	(a)	3–1	Ringstead (2), Hutchinson	Div. 2
69.	12.9.1953	(h)	2–0	Hagan, Hawksworth	Div. 1
70.	23.1.1954	(a)	2–3	Brook (2)	Div. 1
71.	18.9.1954	(h)	1–0	Waldock	Div. 1
72.	5 2.1955	(a)	2–1	Cross, Ringstead	Div. 1
73.	4.10.1958	(a)	0–2		Div. 2
74.	21.2.1959	(h)	1–0	Pace	Div. 2

Sheffield Wednesday
League Matches with United 1893–1959

1.	16.10.1893	(a) 1–1	Spiksley	Div. I
2.	13.11.1893	(h) 1–2	Miller	Div. I
3.	27.10.1894	(h) 2–3	Spiksley, Davis	Div. I
4.	12.1.1895	(a) 0–1		Div. I
5.	7.9.1895	(h) 1–0	Bell	Div. I
6.	26.12.1895	(a) 1–1	Brady	Div. I
7.	26.12.1896	(a) 0–2		Div. I
8.	2.3.1897	(h) 1–1	Brandon	Div. I
9.	16.10.1897	(h) 0–1		Div. I
10.	27.12.1897	(a) 1–1	Spiksley	Div. I
11.	3.10.1898	(h) 1–1	Hemmingfield	Div. I
12.	26.12.1898	(a) 1–2	Hemmingfield	Div. I
13.	15.12.1900	(a) 0–1		Div. I
14.	29.4.1901	(h) 1–0	Wilson	Div. I
15.	2.11.1901	(h) 1–0	Wilson	Div. I
16.	1.3.1902	(a) 0–3		Div. I
17.	1.9.1902	(a) 3–2	Spiksley, Wilson, Davis	Div. I
18.	11.10.1902	(h) 0–1		Div. I
19.	12.12.1903	(a) 1–1	Wilson	Div. I
20.	9.4.1904	(h) 3–0	Chapman (2), Simpson	Div. I
21.	10.12.1904	(h) 1–3	Wilson	Div. I
22.	8.4.1905	(a) 2–4	Stewart (2)	Div. I
23.	21.10.1905	(a) 2–0	Chapman, Stewart	Div. I
24.	18.4.1906	(h) 1–0	Davis (pen.)	Div. I
25.	3.11.1906	(h) 2–2	Wilson (2)	Div. I
26.	4.4.1907	(a) 1–2	Maxwell	Div. I
27.	9.11.1907	(a) 3–1	Brittleton, Chapman, Stewart	Div. I
28.	7.3.1908	(h) 2–0	Wilson, Maxwell	Div. I
29.	25.12.1908	(h) 1–0	Simpson	Div. I
30.	26.12.1908	(a) 1–2	Bradshaw	Div. I
31.	6.11.1909	(a) 3–3	Kirkman (2), Chapman	Div. I
32.	19.3.1910	(h) 1–3	Brittleton	Div. I
33.	22.10.1910	(h) 2–0	Chapman (2)	Div. I
34.	25.2.1911	(a) 1–0	McLean	Div. I
35.	4.11.1911	(a) 1–1	Wilson	Div. I
36.	9.3.1912	(h) 1–1	Glennon	Div. I
37.	26.10.1912	(h) 1–0	Glennon	Div. I
38.	1.3.1913	(a) 2–0	Robertson, McLean	Div. I
39.	25.10.1913	(a) 1–0	Glennon	Div. I
40.	18.2.1914	(h) 2–1	Glennon, McLean	Div. I
41.	5.9.1914	(a) 1–0	Wilson	Div. I
42.	2.1.1915	(h) 1–1	Wilson	Div. I
43.	27.9.1919	(h) 2–1	Campbell, Gill	Div. I
44.	4.10.1919	(a) 0–3		Div. I
45.	28.8.1926	(h) 2–3	Trotter (2)	Div. I
46.	15.1.1927	(a) 0–2		Div. I
47.	24.9.1927	(a) 1–1	Trotter	Div. I

48.	4.2.1928	(h)	3–3	Wilkinson (2), Harper	Div. 1
49.	22.9.1928	(h)	5–2	Hooper (2), Allen (2), Rimmer	Div. 1
50.	2.2.1929	(a)	1–1	Hooper	Div. 1
51.	28.9.1929	(a)	2–2	Seed, Allen	Div. 1
52.	1.2.1930	(h)	1–1	Burgess	Div. 1
53.	6.9.1930	(a)	1–1	Burgess	Div. 1
54.	3.1.1931	(h)	1–3	Ball	Div. 1
55.	21.11.1931	(h)	2–1	Ball, Stephenson	Div. 1
56.	2.4.1932	(a)	1–1	Ball	Div. 1
57.	24.9.1932	(h)	3–3	Ball, Rimmer, Hooper	Div. 1
58.	4.2.1933	(a)	3–2	Starling, Ball, Stephenson	Div. 1
59.	21.10.1933	(h)	0–1		Div. 1
60.	3.3.1934	(a)	1–5	Burrows	Div. 1
61.	16.10.1937	(h)	0–1		Div. 2
62.	26.2.1938	(a)	1–2	Drury	Div. 2
63.	29.10.1938	(a)	0–0		Div. 2
64.	4.3.1939	(h)	1–0	Fallon	Div. 2
65.	17.9.1949	(h)	2–1	Jordan, Quigley	Div. 2
66.	21.1.1950	(a)	0–2		Div. 2
67.	8.9.1951	(a)	3–7	Woodhead (2), Thomas	Div. 2
68.	5.1.1952	(h)	1–3	Dooley	Div. 2
69.	12.9.1953	(a)	0–2		Div. 1
70.	23.1.1954	(h)	3–2	J. Shaw (2), Sewell	Div. 1
71.	18.9.1954	(a)	0–1		Div. 1
72.	5.2.1955	(h)	1–2	Marriott	Div. 1
73.	4.10.1958	(h)	2–0	Froggatt, Shiner	Div. 2
74.	21.2.1959	(a)	0–1		Div. 2

A Wednesday team from the early 1950s

Big Matches at Bramall Lane

Internationals			Attendance	Reciepts
10 March 1883	England 2	Scotland 3	7,000	
5 Feb 1887	England 7	Ireland 0	6,000	
29 March 1897	England 4	Wales 0	4,900	£912
4 April 1903	England 1	Scotland 2	31,799	
20 Oct 1930	England 5	Ireland 1	39,064	£2,647

FA Cup Final replay

April 24 1912	Barnsley 1	West Brom 0	a.e.t. 38,555	£2,615.9s

FA Cup Semi-Finals

16 March 1889	Preston NE 1	West Brom 0	22,688	
28 Feb 1891	Sunderland 3	Notts County 3	22,000	
11 March 1891	Sunderland 0	Notts County 2	13,147	
27 Feb 1892	Aston Villa 4	Sunderland 1	25,000	
4 March 1893	Preston NE 2	Everton 2	26,000	
16 March 1893	Preston NE 0	Everton 0	15,000	
10 March 1894	Notts County 1	Blackburn 0	22,000	
20 March 1897	Aston Villa 3	Liverpool 0	30,000	
19 March 1898	Nottm F. 1	Southampton 1	30,000	
March 9 1900	Bury 3	Nottm F. 2	11.200	
March 27 1909	Man. United 1	Newcastle 0	40,118	
March 25 1911	Bradford C. 3	Blackburn 0	36,479	
March 29 1913	Sunderland 0	Burnley 0	33,655	
March 27 1920	Aston Villa 3	Chelsea 1	37,771	
March 19 1924	Aston Villa 3	Burnley 0	54,531	
March 27 1926	Man. City 3	Man. United 0	36,450	
March 26 1938	Preston NE 2	Aston Villa 1	55,129	

SHEFFIELD UNITED

Big Matches at Hillsborough

Internationals

			Attendance
10 April 1920	England 5	Scotland 4	25,536

'B' Internationals

18 Jan 1950	England B 5	Switzerland B 0
23 Mar 1955	England B 1	Germany B 1

Under 23 Internationals

8 Feb 1956	England U23 3	Scotland U23 1
24 Sep 1958	England U23 4	Poland U23 1
16 Mar 1960	England U23 5	Holland U23 2

Youth International

Nov 1957	England 2	Belgium 0

Inter-League

Oct 1951	Football League 2	Scottish League 1
Oct 1955	Football League 4	Scottish League 2

FA Cup Semi-Finals

1912	West Brom 1	Blackburn Rovers 0	20,050
1921	Tottenham 2	Preston NE 1	43,320
1922	Preston NE 2	Tottenham 1	49,282
1946	Derby County 1	Birmingham C. 1	65,000
1948	Man. United 3	Derby County 1	65,000
1949	Man. United 1	Wolves 1	62,250
1951	Wolves 0	Newcastle 0	65,000
1952	Blackburn 0	Newcastle 0	65,000
1955	York City 1	Newcastle 1	65,000
1956	Birmingham 3	Sunderland 0	65,000
1957	Birmingham 0	Man United 2	65,000
1959	Nottm F. 1	Aston Villa 0	65,000

Big matches listed at Bramall Lane and Hillsborough only include those before 1961. A full list will appear in the second volume.

Bibliography and Acknowledgements

Bibliography

Gordon Smailes, *The Breedon Book of Football League Records*

Denis Clarebrough, *The First 100 Years, the Official Centenary History of Sheffield United.*

R.A. Sparling, *Romance of the Wednesday.*

Keith Farnsworth, *Wednesday! Sheffield Wednesday, A Complete Record 1867–1987.*

Fred Walters, *Sheffield FC Centenary History.*

John A. Steele, *The Countrymen: The Story of Hallam FC.*

Newspapers:
Sheffield Telegraph, The Star, Green 'Un, Sheffield & Rotherham Independent, and *News of the World*.

Football Annuals:
Playfair Football Annuals, FA Year Books.

I have also referred to many of the volumes in the Breedon series of *Complete Records* of a wide range of clubs, and several autobiographies of old players, notably *The Jimmy Seed Story* and naturally, much of the material gathered in tackling earlier ventures has been drawn upon.

Acknowledgements

I wish to thank the many friends and colleagues who have helped by providing cuttings, loaning old match programmes, and generally assisting in aspects of research.

I particularly thank my wife Linda, who has helped with preparation and proof reading and given me great support in pursuing my career. Special thanks to those former players and officials who have contributed and thus made the task easier, and Pauline Shearstone for the use of her drawing of the Adelphi Hotel.

Finally, I would like to thank Pauline Climpson, Mark Glover and all the staff of The Hallamshire Press for the many hours they have spent producing this book.

VOLUME II

OF

SHEFFIELD FOOTBALL
A HISTORY

BY

KEITH FARNSWORTH

COVERING THE YEARS 1961–1995
WILL BE AVAILABLE IN LATE AUTUMN

QUICKSILVER

This was champion, Wednesday

By J. F. McDERMOTT

Bury .... 2 Sheffield W. 5

THIS was champion, Sheffield Wednesday. Main need now at Hillsborough is coaching in the essential def...

---

the lot

By ALAN THOMPSON

Sheffield Wednesday 0, Sheffield Unite. 2

★★★

A L A N
18-year
this 196th
"tickles
morning

Dooley talks of 'the ne Dooley'

By ROSS JENKINSON

Alan Birchenall, 19 - year - old forward smuggled into League football with Sheffield United by manager John Harris at Stoke last Wednesday and pitched immediately into the hot-pot of Sheffield's 196th derby clash with Wednesday three days later to emerge with two goals a rocketting reputation,

---

By

IN the ninth m
great roar swel
lane. In a sudden,
Sheffield Wednes
United defence. T

Feb 195